Mobilizing Teachers

The political participation of public school teachers in new democracies has generated heated debates. In some countries, teacher strikes shutter schools for months each year; in others, teachers' unions have become powerful political machines and have even formed new political parties. To explain these contrasts, *Mobilizing Teachers* delves into changes in education politics and the labor movement. Christopher Chambers-Ju argues that union organizations fundamentally shape teacher mobilization, with far-reaching implications for politics and policy. With detailed case studies of Argentina, Colombia, and Mexico, this book is the first comparative analysis of teacher politics in Latin America. Drawing on extensive field research and multiple sources of data, it enriches theoretical perspectives in political science and sociology on the interplay between protests, electoral mobilization, and party alliances. This title is part of the Flip it Open Programme and may also be available in Open Access. Check our website Cambridge Core for details.

Christopher Chambers-Ju is an assistant professor of political science at the University of Texas at Arlington. He has worked on education politics for nearly twenty years, in academic and policy circles, and has conducted field research throughout Latin America. He holds a Ph.D. in political science from the University of California, Berkeley, and was the recipient of the Spencer Dissertation Fellowship.

CAMBRIDGE STUDIES IN THE COMPARATIVE
POLITICS OF EDUCATION

Mobilizing Teachers

Editor

Terry M. Moe, *Stanford University*

Education and its reform are matters of great political salience throughout the world. Yet as Gift and Wibbels observed, "It is hard to identify a community of political scientists who are dedicated to the comparative study of education." This series is an effort to change that. The goal is to encourage a vigorous line of scholarship that focuses squarely on the politics of education across nations, advances theoretical thinking, includes a broad swath of educational terrain – from elementary and secondary education to vocational education to higher education – and explores the impacts of education on key aspects of society. The series welcomes books of very different types. Some may be grounded in sophisticated quantitative analysis, but qualitative work is welcome as well, as are big-think extended essays that develop agenda-setting ideas. Work is encouraged that takes on big, important, inherently messy topics, however difficult they may be to study. Work is also encouraged that shows how the politics of education is shaped by power, special interests, parties, bureaucracies, and other fundamentals of the political system. And finally, this series is not just about the developed nations, but encourages new work on developing nations and the special challenges that education faces in those contexts.

Books in the series

The Comparative Politics of Education: Teachers Unions and Education Systems around the World
Edited by Terry M. Moe and Susanne Wiborg

A Loud but Noisy Signal? Public Opinion and Education Reform in Western Europe
Marius R. Busemeyer, Julian L. Garritzmann and Erik Neimanns

The Politics of Comprehensive School Reforms: Cleavages and Coalitions
Katharina Sass

Making Bureaucracy Work: Norms, Education and Public Service Delivery in Rural India
Akshay Mangla

Education for All? Literature, Culture and Education Development in Britain and Denmark
Cathie Jo Martin

Mobilizing Teachers

Education Politics and the New Labor Movement in Latin America

CHRISTOPHER CHAMBERS-JU
University of Texas at Arlington

Shaftesbury Road, Cambridge CB2 8EA, United Kingdom

One Liberty Plaza, 20th Floor, New York, NY 10006, USA

477 Williamstown Road, Port Melbourne, VIC 3207, Australia

314–321, 3rd Floor, Plot 3, Splendor Forum, Jasola District Centre, New Delhi – 110025, India

103 Penang Road, #05–06/07, Visioncrest Commercial, Singapore 238467

Cambridge University Press is part of Cambridge University Press & Assessment, a department of the University of Cambridge.

We share the University's mission to contribute to society through the pursuit of education, learning and research at the highest international levels of excellence.

www.cambridge.org
Information on this title: www.cambridge.org/9781009368070

DOI: 10.1017/9781009368049

© Christopher Chambers-Ju 2024

This publication is in copyright. Subject to statutory exception and to the provisions of relevant collective licensing agreements, no reproduction of any part may take place without the written permission of Cambridge University Press & Assessment.

First published 2024
First paperback edition 2025

A catalogue record for this publication is available from the British Library

Library of Congress Cataloging-in-Publication data
NAMES: Chambers-Ju, Christopher, author.
TITLE: Mobilizing teachers : education politics and the new labor movement in Latin America / Christopher Chambers-Ju.
DESCRIPTION: Cambridge, United Kingdom ; New York, NY : Cambridge University Press, [2024]. | SERIES: The comparative politics of education | Includes bibliographical references.
IDENTIFIERS: LCCN 2023037460 | ISBN 9781009368056 (hardback) | ISBN 9781009368049 (ebook)
SUBJECTS: LCSH: Teachers' unions – Latin America. | Teachers – Political activity – Latin America. | Education – Political aspects – Latin America.
CLASSIFICATION: LCC LB2844.53.L29 C53 2024 | DDC 331.88/113711098–dc23/eng/20240122
LC record available at https://lccn.loc.gov/2023037460

ISBN   978-1-009-36805-6   Hardback
ISBN   978-1-009-36807-0   Paperback

Cambridge University Press & Assessment has no responsibility for the persistence or accuracy of URLs for external or third-party internet websites referred to in this publication and does not guarantee that any content on such websites is, or will remain, accurate or appropriate.

*Para Ángela,
el amor de mi vida.*

Contents

List of Figures	*page* ix
List of Tables	xi
Preface and Acknowledgments	xiii
List of Abbreviations	xix
1 Why Teachers?	1
2 How Union Organizations Shape Teacher Mobilization	13
3 The Origins of National Teacher Organizations	35
4 Organizational Consolidation in Mexico	70
5 Instrumentalism in Mexico	89
6 Organizational Weakening in Argentina	111
7 Movementism in Argentina	131
8 Factionalism in Colombia	153
9 Leftism in Colombia	171
10 Teacher Politics in Comparative Perspective	192
References	219
Index	235

Figures

4.1	Starting teacher salary in minimum wages, Mexico	*page* 78
6.1	Teacher salaries versus income per capita, Argentina	126
7.1	Individual workdays lost to teacher strikes, Argentina	148
9.1	Vote share of Colombian Senate candidates, linked to teachers, 1994–2010	178
9.2	Number of teacher protest events, Argentina versus Colombia	180

Tables

1.1	The size of teacher organizations	*page* 5
2.1	Types of political strategies	14
2.2	The organizational argument	25
5.1	Vote share *New Alliance*, lower house (proportional representation)	94
7.1	Former union leaders (CTERA) who became national deputies	141

Preface and Acknowledgments

This book marks the end of a long journey. In literal terms, writing this book involved traveling overseas for field research. Metaphorically, the book required me to trek into faraway intellectual and spiritual planes. The project began in a city, Bogotá, where I became interested in the Federation of Colombian Educators in 2006 as a Fulbright Scholar. Later, this research took me to Mexico City and Buenos Aires to locate Colombian teachers in comparative perspective. I spent countless hours on buses, in union halls, and at schools, talking informally with teachers and sipping tiny Dixie cups of coffee as I waited for interviews. This book was also marked by my journey through the academic job market. My search for a tenure-track job was twisting and winding, with many stops along the way. I zigzagged eastward and then westward across the continental United States, taking a postdoctoral position in New Orleans and then a position as a visiting assistant professor in Worcester before finally settling in Dallas. The consolation prize was that in each place I connected – and later reconnected – with kind, thoughtful, and dynamic people. The journey has been filled with joyful and sad moments. It makes sense here to pay tribute to the good company I kept along the way: guides, fellow travelers who plodded along the same path for a time, and travel companions who were with me the whole way.

This book took an unexpected turn into the spiritual realm, raising questions about life, love, and mystery. It is a cruel twist of fate that Luz Ángela Campos Vargas, my late wife, who was my main travel companion on this journey, did not live to see the completion of this project. Ángela attended a large public high school in Bogotá, Colegio Camilo Torres, and later a large public university for teachers, National Pedagogical

University. We initially became friends because of our shared interest in education politics. She worked in the Secretariat of Education of Bogotá (SED) and witnessed firsthand the forces shaping education policy. Her boss, William René, a former leader of the teachers' union, was by all accounts a good man with strong political commitments. Ángela helped me to identify teachers to interview, connected me with people in the SED, transcribed interviews, and talked with me late into the night about her experience. She was the love of my life. While I spent countless hours writing and rewriting this book, she took care of Luca, our son. We deferred too many dreams imagining a better future together. What follows, then, is a labor of love, and not my labor alone. The first part of her name, "Luz," means light and her memory continues to light up my life and show me the way. Her love, dedication, and memory have motivated me to keep working, especially on the several occasions when I started to flag. This book is dedicated to her.

My intellectual journey took place mostly on the seventh floor of the Social Sciences Building (formerly Barrows Hall) at the University of California, Berkeley. I was lucky to find two dedicated advisers who took me under their wings. I spent scores of afternoons listening to Ruth Berins Collier as she showed me how to map out my core argument. Down the hall, Jonah Levy was a crucial interlocutor who tirelessly read hundreds of pages of drafts and helped me to turn them into something better. Ruth taught me how this project connected to a research tradition rooted in labor, political parties, and the representation of the popular sectors. Jonah taught me to pay attention to big issues of political economy, especially broader tensions between economic liberalization and democracy. The tutelage of both Jonah and Ruth toughened my thinking and helped me to write with rigor, precision, and clarity.

I am grateful to other advisers and mentors as well who provided vital support and insights. David Collier, whose exercises solving Sherlock Holmes mysteries helped me to crack these three cases. I had the good fortune to work with him editing articles and book chapters on the concept of "critical junctures," and this opportunity helped me to think about the comparative-historical elements in this project. Kent Eaton, who taught my first graduate seminar on Latin American politics, reminded me to avoid methodological nationalism and not lose sight of subnational politics. Laura Stoker has helped me to think about many aspects of this project, including research design and methods, and she encouraged me to pursue a project with a small number of cases. She also challenged me to find joy, both in work and in my daily life. Kim

Voss pushed me to think about teachers as workers and to keep an eye on the labor movement in the United States. Leah Carroll gave incisive feedback on my framing of teachers and the left in Colombia. We shared a common bond of having married Colombians and having started intercultural families. I am also grateful to other faculty members – Leonardo Arriola, Alison Post, Steve Vogel, Chris Ansell, and Paul Pierson – for their advice and helpful comments. Finally, Dan Slater helped me to get this project off the ground when he supervised my master's thesis at the University of Chicago.

Thinking back, the journey really started earlier. Javier Corrales, my undergraduate advisor, initially got me interested in Latin American politics – he has been a first-class mentor and inspired me to pursue an academic career. I am also thankful for colleagues at the Inter-American Dialogue's Education Program, especially Jeff Puryear and Tamara Ortega-Goodspeed, for teaching me about education policy in Latin America. Before entering the Ph.D. program at the University of California, Berkeley, I had the opportunity to do field research in El Salvador, Guatemala, Honduras, Nicaragua, and Peru. I had the privilege of engaging in extensive conversations with union leaders, teachers, students, academics, policymakers, and journalists. These conversations furnished me with valuable raw material for this book.

The graduate student community at Berkeley was a vital source of intellectual energy. I am particularly grateful to Jessica Rich, Lindsay Mayka, Andres Schipani, Tomas Bril-Mascarenhas, Hernan Flom, Tara Buss, Lucas Novaes, Eugenia Giraudy, Brian Palmer-Rubin, Candelaria Garay, Mathias Poertner, and Ben Allen. Seminars played a crucial role in shaping me as a scholar, providing me with helpful (and often challenging) feedback. I was lucky to have other comrades in arms, including Chloe Thurston, Athmeya Jayaram, Dann Nasseemullah, Anne Meng, Fiona Shen-Bayh, and Suzanne Scoggins. Their support played a huge role in my success, especially in keeping me accountable. Finally, I had a foot in the sociology department, and I am grateful to Julia Chuang, Malgorzata Kurjanska, Freeden Oeur, Fidan Elcioglu, Abigail Andrews, Nick Wilson, and Maia Sieverding for shaping my thinking about deeper social structures and the common goals of the social sciences.

I am grateful to several individuals and institutions in Argentina, Colombia, and Mexico for helping me to get oriented in the field. In Bogotá, I am grateful to the Center for National Investigation and Popular Education, especially Mauricio Archila, Martha Cecilia García, María Clara Torres, and Álvaro Delgado for their steadfast support of this project. I also thank María Elvira Carvajal, Imelda Arana, María Rosario Saavedra, Ernesto Guarnizo, and Henry Bocanegra for orienting me on teachers in Colombia. Learning about Barrio Mariscal Sucre gave me a window into how schools are connected to vibrant communities. In Mexico City, Carlos Ornelas, Aldo Muñoz, Karla Fernández, Alberto Arnaut, and Aurora Loyo were generous in helping me to make contact with teachers and union leaders. I am grateful to CIDE (the Center for Investigation and Economic Teaching) and Gilles Serra and Joy Langston for providing me with an institutional home during fieldwork. In Buenos Aires, Carlos Freytes, Jimena Valdez, and Patricia Mascarenhas provided crucial support and solidarity.

A stop in New Orleans proved a lively place to revise this book. At Tulane University's Center for Inter-American Policy and Research (CIPR), I am grateful to Maria Akchurin, Hector Bahamonde, Katie Jensen, Jessica Price, and Xander Slaski for putting up with me as I wrestled with this project. Santiago Anria, a CIPR alumni, was a crucial mentor, friend, and guide. Ludovico Feoli, the director of CIPR, generously supported a book conference, and I am grateful to Wendy Hunter, Candelaria Garay, Jonah Levy, and Ruth Berins Collier – as well as faculty from the political science department and the Latin American group at Tulane, especially Mark Vail, Eduardo Silva, Martin Dimitrov, Virginia Oliveros, and David Smilde – for making this conference productive.

At the College of the Holy Cross, Maria Rodrigues and Danilo Contreras proved to be crucial travel companions. During my journey, I also had the good fortune of connecting with Alisha Holland, Sari Niedzwiecki, Ben Ross Schneider, Sebastián Etchemendy, Teri Caraway, Rebecca Tarlau, and Terry Moe, who have been mentors. Their incisive comments nudged this project along. At the University of Texas at Arlington, Rebecca Deen, Daniel Sledge, Christian Zlolniski, Mark Hand, and Xavier Medina Vidal, along with the political science department, supported me through grief.

I should also credit another key source of information: theses written by M.A. and Ph.D. students in universities in Latin America. Much of the social sciences is siloed and there is a tendency to write to a primarily U.S.-based audience. This book required me to delve into the interdisciplinary research of talented scholars in Latin America – some of them trained in U.S. institutions, others not – who have done excellent work on teacher politics but are virtually unheard of in the United States. In other words, this book is my attempt to follow the lead of scholars in the

Global South, reorient political science toward urgent policy questions, and foster a more inclusive research community.

These are some of the many people who have helped me to find my way to the end of this journey. I am grateful to the Spencer Foundation, which supported my dissertation research, and Amita Chugdar, for her mentorship and support. Aurelio Nuño's comments, based on his experience in government and his work as a scholar, have significantly improved sections of the book. Amanda Beatty, Shintia Revina, and Rezanti Putri Pramana helped me to understand the Indonesian case. The Chambers, Frame, Ju, Saavedra, Shoub, and Vargas clans all showed me love by feeding me. My editors, Rachel Blaifeder and Terry Moe, have offered support and incisive feedback. The two anonymous reviewers also provided helpful suggestions. Maya Corredor, an artist and one of Ángela's dear friends, illustrated the cover.

This book is my attempt to look at one key actor, teachers' unions, and to explain why teachers have participated in politics across countries in different ways. As the reader will discern, I have mixed feelings about teachers' unions. They lie at the heart of complex questions about education, social class, and power. I hope that this book serves to spark a broader debate among scholars and policymakers about the forces driving education and labor policy. By illuminating these forces, I hope this book contributes in some small way to help make public schools, such as Colegio Camilo Torres, better serve the needs of both the students who learn and the teachers who teach in them.

Abbreviations

AGECH	Chilean Educators' Association (Asociación Gremial de Educadores de Chile)
AMET	Argentine Association of Technical Teaching (Asociación del Magisterio de Enseñanza Técnica)
ARI	Affirmation for an Egalitarian Republic (Afirmación para una República Igualitaria), Argentina
ATE	Association of State Workers (Asociación Trabajadores del Estado), Argentina
CEA	Confederation of Argentine Educators (Confederación de Educadores Argentinos)
CEID	Center of Study and Research on Teaching (Centro de Estudios e Investigaciones Docente), Colombia
CGT	General Confederation of Labor of the Republic of Argentina (Confederación General del Trabajo de la República Argentina)
CINEP	Center for National Investigation and Popular Education (Centro de Investigación y Educación Popular), Colombia
CNOP	National Confederation of Popular Organizations (Confederación Nacional de Organizaciones Populares), Mexico
CNTE	National Coordinator of Education Workers (Coordinadora Nacional de Trabajadores de la Educación), Mexico
CODEMA	Cooperative of Teachers (Cooperativa del Magisterio), Colombia
CTA	Argentine Workers' Central (Central de Trabajadores de la Argentina)

CTERA	Confederation of Education Workers of the Republic of Argentina (Confederación de Trabajadores de la Educación de la República Argentina)
CTM	Confederation of Mexican Workers (Confederación de Trabajadores de México)
CUT	Unitary Workers' Central (La Central Unitaria de Trabajadores)
ELN	National Liberation Army (Ejército de Liberación Nacional), Colombia
FARC	Armed Revolutionary Forces of Colombia (Fuerzas Armadas Revolucionarias de Colombia)
FECODE	Federation of Colombian Educators (Federación Colombiana de Trabajadores de la Educación)
FER	Regional Education Funds (Fondos Educativos Regionales), Colombia
FONID	National Fund for Teacher Incentive (Fondo Nacional de Incentivo Docente), Argentina
FREPASO	Front for a Country in Solidarity (Frente País Solidario), Argentina
INEE	National Institute of Education Evaluation (Instituto Nacional para la Evaluación de la Educativa), Mexico
LFTSE	The Federal Law of Service Workers of the State (Ley Federal de los Trabajadores al Servicio del Estado), Mexico
M-19	19th of April Movement (Movimiento 19 de Abril), Colombia
MODAE	Movement of Education Action (Movimiento de Acción Educativa), Colombia
MOIR	Revolutionary Independent Labor Movement (Movimiento Obrero Independiente y Revolucionario), Colombia
MP	Pedagogical Movement (Movimiento Pedagógico), Colombia
OSPLAD	Teacher Social Welfare Fund (Obra Social de los Docentes), Argentina
PAN	National Action Party (Partido Acción Nacional), Mexico
PANAL	New Alliance Party (Partido Nueva Alianza), Mexico
PDA	Democratic Alternative Pole (Polo Democrático Alternativo), Colombia
PGRI	Teachers Association of the Republic of Indonesia (Persatuan Guru Republik Indonesia)
PISA	Program for International Student Assessment

PJ	Peronist Justicialist Party (Partido Justicialista), Argentina
PND	National Institution of Teacher Collective Bargaining (Paritaria Nacional Docente), Argentina
PRD	Revolutionary Democratic Party (Partido Revolucionario Democrático), Mexico
PRI	Institutional Revolutionary Party (Partido Revolucionario Institucional), Mexico
SADOP	Argentine Union of Private School Teachers (Sindicato Argentino de Docentes Privados)
SEP	Secretariat of Public Education (Secretaría de Educación Pública), Mexico
SNTE	National Union of Education Workers (Sindicato Nacional de Trabajadores de la Educación), Mexico
SUTE	Unitary Union of Education Workers (Sindicato Único de Trabajadores de la Educación), Chile
SUTEBA	Union of Education Workers, Province of Buenos Aires (Sindicato Unificado de Trabajadores de la Educación de Buenos Aires), Argentina
SUTEP	Unitary Union of Education Workers of Peru (Sindicato Unitario de Trabajadores en la Educación del Perú)
UCR	Radical Civic Union (Unión Cívica Radical), Argentina
UDA	United Teachers of Argentina (Unión Docentes Argentinos)
VIMA	Teacher Affordable Housing Fund (Fideicomiso de Vivienda Magisterial), Mexico

1

Why Teachers?

In 1998, Marta Maffei, secretary general of the Confederation of Education Workers of the Republic of Argentina (CTERA), staged a hunger strike in front of Congress with hundreds of teacher-activists, many of whom were women from faraway provinces. This protest, known as the "White Tent," became a national spectacle, with artists, athletes, and media figures joining in to show solidarity with poorly paid teachers (Corrales 2004, 342–4; Campo 2020). Since Argentina transitioned to democracy in 1982, teachers articulated demands through protests, road blockages, and other demonstrations. Because of the White Tent, the government enacted a new law in 1999, Law 25,053, which created a new fund that improved the salaries of the worst-paid teachers. Maffei's role in the protest bolstered her leadership credentials and, in 2003, she was elected to the Chamber of Deputies with the center-left party Affirmation for an Egalitarian Republic (ARI). But after taking her seat in Congress, her stature diminished. CTERA fostered autonomous movements and grassroots activism. Teachers mistrusted and rejected union leaders who became politicians; instead, they relied on protests and direct action to voice their interests.

Thousands of miles away in Mexico City, Elba Esther Gordillo, the head of the National Union of Education Workers (SNTE), emerged from a private meeting with President Vicente Fox. It was May 15, 2001, the National Teacher Day. Mexico had recently transitioned to democracy, with the Institutional Revolutionary Party (PRI), the hegemonic ruling party, peacefully conceding power for the first time in seventy years. While Gordillo held high-ranking positions in the PRI, she negotiated directly with President Fox, even though he was from the center-right

National Action Party (PAN) (Loyo 2008; Ornelas 2008). Fox lacked a congressional majority and turned to Gordillo for help with his legislative agenda (Muñoz Armenta and Castro Maravilla 2019). President Fox negotiated with Gordillo, and the government agreed to generous terms; in 2001, teachers' salaries increased by 10.5 percent and benefits were adjusted upwards by 2.5 percent.[1] While the smaller and regionally rooted dissident faction of the Mexican teachers' union, the National Coordinator of Education Workers (CNTE), regularly protested, SNTE, the mainstay of teacher organizing, rarely, if ever, protested. Instead, the union negotiated alliances with parties regardless of ideology, providing political support for material benefits.

Finally, also in 2001, Gloria Inés Ramírez, the President of the Federation of Colombian Educators (FECODE), organized a massive rally in the Plaza Bolivar, the main square in the capital. In an op-ed, she railed against neoliberalism, criticized the government for barring access to public schools, and condemned the education reforms proposed by President Andrés Pastrana.[2] Ultimately, Ramírez was unable to block Law 715, which froze teachers' salaries and held down education spending. However, she launched a campaign for election to the Senate. Ramírez, who was a member of the Communist Party, mobilized teachers across the country to vote for the left-coalition Democratic Alternative Pole (PDA). In 2022, when Colombia elected its first leftist president, Gustavo Petro, she was appointed Minister of Labor. Ramírez is not unique: Leaders of FECODE were regularly major candidates and leaders of left-leaning parties. As a result, FECODE had close ties to these parties, and left parties emphasized teacher and education issues.

These snapshots are remarkable because they demonstrate a new form of labor politics. In all three countries, powerful labor leaders emerged who were women. In the past, few women worked in the leading industrial sectors. Most teamsters, longshoremen, autoworkers, steelworkers, and miners were men. In the United States, when women did work in these industries, they were segregated in the workplace and paid less (Milkman 1987). While women have been active in organizing movements in "pink-collar" professions, notably garment workers, flight attendants, nurses, and clerical workers (Cobble 2003), none of these unions gained political power. By contrast, women were the majority in the teaching profession and female leaders, with the backing of strong labor organizations,

---

[1] SNTE–SEP Agreement 2001.
[2] Gloria Inés Ramírez, "Educación vs lógica de mercado," *Semana* June 29, 2002.

became national figures. These leaders shaped education and labor laws, negotiated new partisan alliances, and pursued public office. Although gender-based inequality persisted in many teachers' unions, with women underrepresented in top leadership positions, teacher organizations often framed demands in terms of gender equity, furnished a space for feminist activists, and provided a pathway for women leaders to enter politics.

The significance of these three cases lies in the different strategies that the unions developed. Political strategies are fundamentally connected to *how* teachers mobilize. They can be defined as the practices and repertoires used to articulate interests, specifically the balance between protests and electoral participation. Labor politics are often described as either cooperative or adversarial (Murillo 2001; Burgess 2004; Lee 2011). But teachers demonstrate that union strategies differed in whether they prioritized protest or electoral mobilization and also in the character of partisan alliances. The strategies of teachers point to some of the broader changes in how groups in society articulate interests. In the aftermath of monumental changes to political and economic life in Latin America, social movements, interest associations, and labor unions inserted themselves into politics in various ways, giving voice to new interests (Collier and Handlin 2009; Kapiszewski et al. 2021). Indeed, these vignettes of teachers highlight the divergent paths of labor unions and social movements.

For labor unions, economic restructuring in the direction of open market competition generated a steep decline in membership. Labor unions thrived for much of the twentieth century as a result of state subsidies and union-friendly labor laws. They were disrupted by globalization and the neoliberal economic model. In countries with party systems that mobilized labor, trade union density fell sharply between the peak level of union density in the mid-twentieth century and the 1990s; according to Roberts (2014, 100), it fell on average by nearly sixteen points. Labor-based parties faced pressure to hold down wages, impose fiscal discipline, and control inflation. In some countries, economic openings in the 1990s went hand in hand with labor repression (Dean 2022). Even when leftist governments were elected throughout Latin America in the early 2000s, responses to union demands were uneven at best (Cook and Bazler 2013). Few would dispute that organized labor is now weaker than it was before the adoption of the neoliberal model (Kurtz 2004; Roberts 2014; Posner et al. 2018). Labor-based parties turned away from workers and recruited new voters, often from the less organized informal sectors, into their coalitions (Levitsky 2003). The generic story of labor unions is one of decline.

However, teachers did not experience the same disruption that many trade unions in Latin America experienced. By the late twentieth century, public school teachers emerged in many (if not most) parts of the world as the largest and most politically active group of workers. Indeed, as economic restructuring in the 1990s resulted in mass layoffs for many industries, teachers saw continuous hiring as governments pushed to universalize primary school enrollment and achieve significant gains in secondary school enrollment. By the time democratization swept the world in the 1980s, teachers were an organized group that forcefully pressed demands. The rise of teachers' unions marked the ascendancy of white-collar public-sector workers and the decline of blue-collar industrial workers. Indeed, the ascendancy of teachers suggests that scholars should pay more attention to other public sector workers (e.g., health workers and public employees) and workers in nontradable sectors (e.g., teamsters) that have become prominent in some countries. The strategies of teachers seemed to deviate from those of industrial workers: Teachers exhibited relative autonomy from the state, contentious mobilization and protest, and novel partisan alliances.

For social movements, democratic transitions afforded opportunities to mobilize around new issues and identities. More inclusive regimes, an expansion of rights, and new participatory institutions created space for emerging groups to assert material interests, such as high school and university students (Donoso 2016), informal sector workers (Garay 2017), and AIDS activists (Rich 2019). In addition, new groups organized around social identities, demanding new rights and political recognition: indigenous and Afro-descendant communities (Van Cott 2005; Paschel 2018), feminists (Baldez 2002; Daby and Mosley 2022), and LBGT+ activists (Corrales 2021). Like teachers, new social movements organized protests, formed new alliances with parties, or engaged in both strategies. Democracy enabled many groups in society to shape policy and consider strategies that included routine and contentious politics (Rossi and von Bülow 2016).

This book uses the case of teachers to explore why ascendant labor unions and new social movements developed different strategies. Teachers fell somewhere in between labor unions and social movements. As for other labor organizations, "second-generation" reforms posed a challenge to teachers because these policies, which included reforms to improve efficiency and service quality in the public sector (after "first-generation" macroeconomic stabilization reforms), threatened labor rights (Navia and Velasco 2003). But, as social movements did, teachers

TABLE 1.1 *The size of teacher organizations*

Country	Total population (2021)	Largest teacher organization	Number of members	Teachers led national labor or popular sector organization?
Argentina	46 million	CTERA	320,000	Yes (CTA)
Brazil	214 million	CNTE	1 million	Yes (CUT)
Colombia	52 million	FECODE	270,000	Yes (CUT)
Chile	19 million	Colegio de Profesores	100,000	Yes (CUT)
Mexico	127 million	SNTE	1.2 million	Yes (CNOP)

Sources: World Bank; Chiappe 2012; FECODE "Quienes Somos," accessed November 30, 2022 via https://fecode.edu.co/quienes-somos/; Inter-American Development Bank 2019; Secretaría de Educación Pública 2020

engaged in energetic forms of mobilization; in some cases, teacher movements drew attention to issues of teaching and pedagogy (Pulido Chaves 2007), professionalization and training (Finger and Gindin 2015), and democratic reforms (Cook 1996). Teacher protest movements emerged in parallel with other protest movements that demanded material benefits as well as rights and recognition.

Comparative research on interest representation from the standpoint of teachers' unions, currently the most powerful labor organization in many (if not most) countries worldwide, is overdue. While in recent years growing interest in education politics has drawn attention to teachers' unions, few studies have undertaken a sweeping comparative and historical analysis of them. This research aims to do just this. Teachers' unions bring together public school teachers at the primary and secondary levels (and sometimes at the preschool, technical levels, and teacher college levels), but rarely organize workers in private schools and universities. Teachers usually have a single national organization or a large, dominant federation that is the primary vehicle for representing interests. When surveying Latin America, countries such as Argentina, Brazil, Chile, Colombia, and Mexico each have a teachers' union that brings together hundreds of thousands of dues-paying members, translating into substantial resources to finance campaigns and build a voting bloc (see Table 1.1). Because teacher organizations maintained robust member bases (while other trade unions lost members), teachers headed national labor federations. As political rights expanded, teachers gained power because parties wanted to benefit from their organizational clout (Nelson 2007, 85). Owing to their organizations' size and salience, teachers now play a prominent role in interest group politics and party systems.

THE MAIN ARGUMENT

Contemporary economic and political changes opened new strategic options for teachers, as they did for other social movements and public sector unions. This book conceptualizes three distinctive strategies of teachers' unions and then explains why they were adopted using a comparative-historical analysis of Argentina, Colombia, and Mexico. Why did national teacher organizations develop different strategies – with contrasting emphases on protest versus electoral mobilization and divergent relationships with political parties? As the introductory vignettes suggest, some teachers' unions exert pressure on politicians by subjecting them to the threat of disruptive protests. This pattern, which I call "movementism," is present in countries such as Argentina, Bolivia, and Peru, where teachers have been at the forefront of labor conflict. In Colombia and Chile, teachers also protested, but their main strategy of interest representation involved strong ties to left-leaning parties, or "leftism." Finally, some teachers constructed alliances with successive parties, a strategy that I call "instrumentalism." In Mexico, and also perhaps Indonesia, union leaders exchanged political support for common points of agreement with whatever party was in power.

My explanation for these outcomes depends on the answer to two organizational questions. First, do unions form political alliances, or do they avoid party politics and engage in strategies of protest? Second, if they make alliances, are these alliances ideologically consistent, or are they instrumental and shifting? For the former, I demonstrate that *hierarchical relations* within unions are necessary for negotiating partisan alliances since these relations give union leaders the capacity to deliver a bloc of votes in exchange for political representation. To this end, national union leaders need a chain of command in which local union leaders who can mobilize teachers' votes follow orders. Unions with weak hierarchies, by contrast, cannot dependably mobilize voters, and instead deploy strikes and other forms of labor militancy to press demands.

Second, I show that the dynamics of *factional competition* shape different kinds of partisan alliances. Competition among factions leads unions to align with the left because rival factions maneuver to outbid one another in appealing to the base. This dynamic makes alliances with left-wing parties likely. By contrast, when a single faction is hegemonic, union leaders establish instrumental alliances, throwing their support to the party that makes the best offer at a given time, even if such support is unpopular with the base. A hegemonic faction makes the union leadership autonomous from the rank and file because rival leaders and dissenting voices lack any real power to contest such opportunistic behavior.

The focus is on the ways that organizational structure has consequences for political behavior. But I go on to identify how teacher organizations developed in relation to the state, how union leaders accumulated resources, and what the distinguishing traits are that characterize unions across countries. The analysis uncovers the historical origins of organizations in the mid-twentieth century and their subsequent development. Important features of unions, especially the characteristics of union factions, were set during the 1950s, 1960s, and 1970s. But I also highlight the 1980s as a period when teachers in Argentina, Colombia, and Mexico took advantage of democratic openings to unleash robust movements and demand an end to the austerity measures set during the "Lost Decade" or debt crisis of the 1980s, when governments could not make payments on their sovereign debt. During the early 1990s, policymakers responded to teacher movements in different ways across countries, as economic conditions improved. These responses also shaped the organizational traits of unions. When policymakers distributed subsidies, improved teacher salaries, and offered resources to national union leaders, they inadvertently helped to centralize labor organizations and consolidate factions in unions. By contrast, policymakers could also respond by ignoring teacher demands and undermining union centralization by withholding subsidies and freezing education spending. This weakened national union leaders and dispersed power to an activist base. In other words, I approach labor organizations by examining how they are embedded in the state. Teachers' unions are situated in different policy frameworks and institutions, which has helped to define the character of union organizations.

THE NORMATIVE DEBATE: TEACHERS, EDUCATION REFORM, AND LABOR ACTIVISM

A focus on teachers' unions' strategies informs discussions of the forces behind labor and education policy. In policy circles, in the media, in the business community, among private foundations, and in universities, teachers' protests and electoral participation have generated debate – and sometimes outrage. Teachers' unions have played a leading role in shaping landmark education legislation. Union leaders drafted articles that were included in the General Law of Education in Colombia in 1994 and the National Law of Education in Argentina in 2006, among others. Such laws were important milestones for establishing national standards for the career ladders and pay scales of the teaching profession. Against the backdrop of these laws, scholars have criticized unions for focusing narrowly on labor issues and establishing standards that were too uniform and not oriented toward improving teacher professionalism or promoting effective pedagogies. Other scholars, however, have defended teachers' unions as playing a vital role in democratic engagement and education policymaking.

Indeed, there are sharp disagreements. Some economists and political scientists argue that teachers' unions are "vested interests" or entrenched interest groups that are a pernicious obstacle to education reform (Bruns and Luque 2014; Moe and Wiborg 2017). Teachers have been construed as labor market insiders that advocate for narrow economic interests (i.e., rent seeking). Even if teacher salaries in Latin America are often modest, teachers enjoy other benefits, such as job security and a work schedule that affords them the possibility of taking a second job, as well as health insurance and a guaranteed pension (Elacqua et al. 2018, 20). Although the profession has lost prestige, it affords teachers advantages that other workers do not have. In this account, distributional politics can be seen as zero-sum. Increasing teacher salaries increase pension liabilities, which squeezes budgets that could be otherwise used to address more pressing problems (Anzia 2022). In the Latin American context, where social policies are highly segmented (Arza et al. 2022), teacher demands for higher pay may exacerbate the segmentation between the formal and informal sectors.

Vested interests can be an impediment to better public schools. Citing Latin America's low rankings on international standardized tests such as the Program for International Student Assessment (PISA) in the subject areas of math, reading, and science, scholars and policy observers have argued that teachers' unions block reforms that would incentivize innovation in teaching and generate better learning outcomes and problem-solving skills (PREAL 2006). As Latin American countries strive to compete in the knowledge economy and escape the "middle-income trap," union opposition to new teacher career structures, performance-based pay, and more rigorous evaluations – policies to upgrade and professionalize teachers – indicate that teachers' unions defend the status quo (Doner and Schneider 2016). Indeed, Finger (2018), in her statistical analysis of states in the United States, shows that stronger teachers' unions are associated with a lower likelihood of performance pay policies. Some conclude that teachers' unions operate like labor organizations with economic interests rather than like professional associations that care whether students learn basic knowledge and skills (Moe 2011).

The political participation of teachers can have negative externalities. In developing democracies with weak institutions, teachers may mix their official capacity as public servants with work for political campaigns and inappropriately influence parents and students. Given widespread patronage politics in low- and middle-income countries, teachers' unions may become political machines, and they may contribute to problems such as clientelism in teacher transfers and promotion and the hiring of teachers in the run-up to elections (Duarte 2003; Pierskalla and Sacks 2020; Schneider 2022). Moreover, participation in protests exacerbates teacher absenteeism. In Argentina, students regularly miss weeks and sometimes months of instruction each year because teachers are on strike (Carnoy 2007, 113).

There are other perspectives in the literature, however. Teachers' unions may use their expertise to block misguided education policies that do not benefit students. Sociologists and education scholars have defended teachers' unions, arguing that they mobilized against policies that harm children, such as excessive standardized testing and poorly regulated charter schools (Ravitch 2013; Bascia 2016). Teachers have been critical of school choice and accountability policies that problematically use standardized test scores to measure teacher quality. They argue that these policies conceptualize learning in a mechanical and superficial way, ignoring other important dimensions of teaching such as encouraging student motivation, curiosity, and socioemotional growth. If teachers have been reluctant to embrace a narrowing of focus on skills and drills, they have advocated on behalf of more inclusive public schools and services that benefit students and communities (Lavery 2020).

Further, some evidence shows that teachers' unions do not exert influence on policy. Paglayan (2019) finds, using longitudinal data and rigorous econometric models, that in states in the United States where teachers have laws that legalize collective bargaining there is not a consistent effect on the increase in the size of government. In other words, teachers' unions may oppose policies that make schools worse, and they may have little influence on policy.

The political action of teachers may also generate positive externalities. With a diminished labor movement and rising socioeconomic inequality, teachers can articulate demands that benefit other workers. In Argentina, the labor central that was founded by leaders of the teachers' union, the Argentine Workers' Central (CTA), was crucial for the formation of an "insider–outsider coalition" that brought together organized labor and informal sector workers (Garay 2023). In the United States, teacher mobilizations engender broad public support for teacher actions and also for labor mobilization more generally (Hertel-Fernandez et al. 2021), and teachers may serve as a linchpin for progressive coalitions (Lyon 2023). Barnes et al. (2023) have shown that more working-class representation in national legislatures in Latin America improves perceptions of democratic legitimacy through descriptive representation and policy responsiveness. If teachers are, indeed, lower- and middle-class workers, then teacher representation in the legislature may bolster the articulation of nonelite interests.

For scholars who prioritize equity and inclusion, teacher organizations advocate for a model of education that is centered on promoting the holistic development and well-being of children – beyond learning as measured by PISA scores. Teachers, as ordinary citizens with expertise in pedagogy, have a right and even a duty to participate in debates about public education. This is particularly true in new democracies, where authoritarian regimes have excluded them from politics and violently repressed demands for basic labor rights. Indeed, the teaching profession has faced violations of human rights in Argentina, Colombia, and Mexico. Colombia stands out as a troubling case. Between 1977 and 2015, over 1,000 teachers have been confirmed killed and more than 10,000 have faced death threats.[3]

Debates about whether teachers' unions are good or bad for democracy and whether they help or harm public schools are ongoing and unresolved. Indeed, my conclusion is that teachers, like other sectors of labor, are akin to the "contingent democrats" described by Bellin (2000), and that the answers to these questions should be analyzed in relation to material interests and the state, which vary across countries and time. I add nuance to such debates by illuminating how the answer may also depend on the strategies of teacher organizations. In some instances, teachers are reformist outsiders who draw attention to fundamental

---

[3] Ángel Pérez, "Las amenazas a los profes y la perpetuación de la violencia en Colombia," *Semana* July 15, 2018.

problems of neglect in the public school system, as in Argentina in the 1980s and 1990s. In others, teachers are privileged insiders whose political strategies are the root cause of corruption and mismanagement in public school systems, as in Mexico in the 2000s and 2010s. Teachers can play various roles in politics and policy, and more comparative analysis is needed to deepen understandings of these differences. The bottom line is this: Teachers are political actors who have certain interests, and they should be studied as such. This book is an initial step in shedding light on these questions.

PLAN OF THE BOOK

Chapter 2 provides an overview of the literature on labor politics, social movements, and political parties, and locates the main argument in this literature. It operationalizes the two organizational traits, hierarchical relations and factionalism, to show how they produce three strategies. It concludes by laying out the research methods used to carry out the analysis and reach these conclusions.

Chapter 3 analyzes historical legacies of union-founding to establish whether these legacies had enduring consequences for subsequent patterns of teacher mobilization. It examines the development trajectories of teacher organizations from 1900 to 1979. The chapter analyzes several themes: church–state conflict over mass public schooling in the early twentieth century; contrasts between the political incorporation of industrial workers versus teachers; patronage politics in public schools and the education bureaucracy; teacher struggles for labor codes and professional autonomy; and restrictions on political rights under nondemocratic regimes. I demonstrate how corporatist legacies set unions on different paths.

Chapters 4 and 5 argue that a hierarchical and consolidated leadership explains "instrumentalism" in Mexico. The Mexican teachers' union was involved in electoral politics, and it crafted flexible partisan alliances. Notwithstanding a few enduring enclaves of militant teachers, protests are a secondary mode of political representation. The primary strategy involves negotiating alliances with presidents and governors, no matter their ideology. A major reform in 1992, purportedly to decentralize education to the state level, ultimately strengthened national leaders. The strengthening of the national leadership enabled the union to respond to growing electoral competition and partisan turnover by launching a new teacher-based party, which gave the union strategic flexibility. With power over the union locals, national union leaders faced few constraints on seeking diversified political alliances.

Chapters 6 and 7 argue that a weak organizational hierarchy explains "movementism" in Argentina, where there were recurring teachers' protests and limited involvement in electoral politics. The fragmentation among teachers in Argentina is the product of the education decentralization reforms of 1978 and 1993, which reduced the federal government's role in financing public education. As a result, national union leaders were weakened relative to provincial leaders and grassroots activists. National leaders had a limited capacity to mobilize protests and they depended on the energy of provincial leaders and grassroots activists. The regionalized structure of the union prevented national leaders from endorsing parties or mobilizing teachers as voters.

Chapters 8 and 9 show that a hierarchical and factionalized leadership is the explanation for "leftism" in Colombia. The union leadership developed strong ties to the left. Education decentralization was modest, and the power structure of the union was centered on the national executive committee. Some factions affiliated to left parties took root in the 1970s when a fragmented teacher movement consolidated. Still, the Constitution of 1991 and a new set of electoral rules institutionalized multiple factional currents in the union leadership, since factions became viable electoral vehicles that could secure legislative representation. Union leaders politicized teachers and encouraged their affiliation with left parties. The presence of rival factions, however, created a tendency for ideological rigidity and limited the possibilities for negotiation with nonleft parties.

Chapter 10 considers insights from the argument that extend to a broader set of cases, given the remarkable global scope of teacher mobilization. It analyzes the shadow cases of teachers in Chile (leftism), Peru (movementism), and Indonesia (instrumentalism). Finally, it considers avenues for future research on education policymaking, interest representation, and labor politics. A more comparative approach to the study of education is needed in political science to get a handle on the different dynamics unfolding in public school systems in countries around the world.

2

How Union Organizations Shape Teacher Mobilization

The strategies that trade unions adopt are an abiding question in comparative politics. Around the world, labor unions are crucial vehicles for working-class representation and shed light on democratic governance in unequal societies. The scholarship is rich. Union strategies are studied in relation to regime change, economic restructuring, the welfare state, and the party system. This literature covers many world regions and time periods. The unit of analysis can be scaled up to labor as a macropolitical actor (Collier and Collier 1991; Rueschemeyer et al. 1992) or it can be scaled down to specific union locals (Murillo and Ronconi 2004; Tarlau 2022). Strategies entail dilemmas concerning how labor movements emerge, develop, and are incorporated into mass parties. In the early twentieth century, as the labor movement became more militant, workers in Western Europe and Latin America faced the anarcho-syndical dilemma: whether to abstain from elections and forego the benefits of political power or participate but dilute their party program to broaden their appeal (Przeworski and Sprague 1986, 13–18). A subsequent question was whether parties maintain ties to workers during periods of political and economic stress. In the late twentieth century, in the context of economic restructuring, union leaders faced dilemmas regarding maintaining their allegiance to party leaders (even when labor-based parties supported unpopular reforms) or embracing militant opposition to those reforms (Murillo 2001; Burgess 2004; Teitelbaum 2011).

This chapter presents the main argument of this book against the backdrop of this body of scholarship. The first section conceptualizes the "thick" strategies of teachers' unions involving protest and various roles in electoral politics. It then surveys existing explanations from research on labor politics, social movements, and left parties to assess how well each explains these strategies. I present my argument, which is situated in an analytic tradition that centers on organization, to show how the specific traits of teachers' organizations offer the best explanation for political strategies. It ends with a discussion of the research methods used to carry out this analysis.

CONCEPTUALIZING POLITICAL STRATEGIES

Political strategies are the outcome of interest. I use this concept to move up Sartori's (1970) ladder of abstraction and focus on various patterns of mobilization and political action. Strategies are the ways in which social movements and labor unions orchestrate contentious and electoral forms of collective action to make claims on the state. This concept opens a dialogue with social movement and labor scholars writing on contentious mobilization as well as scholars working on partisan voting.

The task of conceptualizing political strategies is challenging because they have layers. In large, federal countries, such as Mexico and Argentina, many labor unions have encompassing, federated structures. In these unions, there are some differences in strategy across union locals. Moreover, strategies also evolve over time, in response to institutional openings, labor grievances, or new governments. There may be periods when different factions in the same union simultaneously experiment with protests and some electoral participation while exploring negotiations with new parties.

The goal is to develop analytic categories that accurately capture cross-national differences. These categories should match with the actions taken by union leaders in the national executive committee and in most union locals. I will show that teachers settled on relatively well-defined strategies across countries. I label these "instrumentalism," "movementism," and "leftism"; they are defined by their mode of mobilization and partisan alliances, as outlined in Table 2.1.

TABLE 2.1 *Types of political strategies*

	Instrumentalism	Movementism	Leftism
	Mexico	Argentina	Colombia
Primary Mode of Mobilization	Electoral	Contentious	Electoral
Partisan Alliances	Shifting alliances with different parties	No party alliance	Stable alliance with left parties

Instrumentalism. Unions shape policy by delivering votes to the party that makes the best offer at a given time or seems most likely to win the next election. In this pattern, unions vow to cooperate with the government (at least in public). Protests may occur at the subnational level, but they are not the primary way in which these unions articulate interests. Rather, with instrumentalism, union leaders voice support for the priorities of the government and seek to discourage and distance themselves from the sporadic protests that arise in a few territorial enclaves. The primary strategy has been to express interests by forming a coordinated voting bloc. The vote share of parties with strong ties to the union is a good way to measure the level of electoral mobilization.

In addition to high levels of electoral mobilization and low levels of protest, instrumentalism is characterized by shifting alliances and ongoing negotiations with multiple parties. Unions maneuver to become a viable coalition partner and to align with the party in power. They behave strategically and offer only short-term support. These shifting alliances spark public debate about the union's role in politics and speculation about the exchanges that take place behind closed doors. In negotiations, unions seem to prioritize a narrow set of economic interests, often centered on particularistic demands for political patronage and side payments, which parties from across the ideological spectrum can accommodate. By downplaying programmatic principles, unions prioritize ongoing access to policymakers, which creates opportunities for policy negotiation; the union is unlikely to be completely excluded from the policy process. However, access does not always guarantee influence over policy decisions.

The Mexican teachers' union nicely illustrates instrumentalism. In 2006, the contested presidential election in Mexico drew national attention to the mobilization of teachers. After Felipe Calderón won the presidency by a margin of 0.58 percent, the leader of SNTE, Elba Esther Gordillo, claimed credit for delivering pivotal votes. She directed teachers to cast a split ballot, voting for Calderón for president and her newly formed teacher-based party, New Alliance, for congress. New Alliance outperformed expectations, surpassing the 2 percent vote threshold needed to maintain a party registry and win seats in the legislature (Muñoz Armenta 2011). President Calderón acted as if teachers were pivotal in his victory. He appointed Gordillo loyalists to cabinet positions and awarded contracts to SNTE, even though such actions generated outrage in the media and in his own party (Raphael 2007; Ornelas 2012). Thus, the teachers' union redirected support to a new party, even to one that was ideologically opposed to labor, in exchange for patronage and government contracts.

Movementism. Teacher organizations have used protests to bring policymakers to the negotiating table. Protests are frequent, often spontaneous, and scale up across territory. They are mobilized against both the national and subnational governments. Movementism makes teacher protests the main political problem in the education sector. Teacher militancy sparks national debates about the legitimacy of grievances and the economic and social costs associated with the disruptive actions, which periodically shut down public schools and shorten the academic calendar. Policymakers respond to protests with sticks (i.e., penalties for participating in strikes) and carrots (i.e., salary increases to address grievances) to achieve labor peace, but to little avail. Teacher protests that garner a high level of participation and are sustained over time can pose a threat to governability, as politicians worry that they will spiral out of control.

Unions that embraced movementism kept their distance from parties and have refused to engage in electoral brokerage. This pattern is like the one described by Teitelbaum (2011) in which unions are independent of political parties. Rather than using teacher votes as the basis of negotiations, unions instead promise to scale back protests, although union leaders do not always deliver on these promises. Unions avoid entangling themselves in electoral politics and therefore largely avoid demands for side payments and political patronage. However, strikes are costly and an overreliance on them may result in only intermittent access to policymakers. Their demands can be one-dimensional, focusing narrowly on teacher pay, potentially generating a public relations problem when schools remain shuttered for long periods of time.

Argentina's CTERA is a paradigmatic case of movementism. Since the democratic transition in 1982, protests have routinely challenged governability and are widely expected. Teachers initially mobilized around labor grievances, demanding an end to irregular practices in public administration, such as the late payment of salaries. By the late 1990s, these protests generated public sympathy because of the real hardship that teachers faced. Protests, however, persisted even after 2006 when policymakers adopted new labor laws that instituted collective bargaining and improved teacher salaries. Teachers remained dissatisfied, calling for even higher salaries. These insatiable demands generated frustration among parents, who were unable to send children to school during strikes. CTERA remained combative, even when parties sought to nudge the union toward a more institutionalized role in politics.

Leftism. Enduring alliances with left parties represent a third way in which teachers have mobilized. Under this pattern, teachers have allied with ideologically compatible parties whose programs are closely aligned with teachers' interests. Thus, in contrast to instrumentalism, negotiation and exchange were restricted to the subset of left parties that supported labor rights and more resources for public schools. This pattern is like the one described by Teitelbaum (2011) in which unions are affiliated with small parties or a "narrow interest union."

Typically, leftism has meant that teachers' unions mobilize electoral support for a specific set of parties. As such, mainstream, governing parties that were nonleftist viewed the teachers' union as an adversary with an incompatible policy agenda. The union's alignment with the left limited its ability to negotiate. Leftism was more oppositional and reactive than instrumentalism. With this strategy, the union supports programmatic policies that are strongly associated with certain parties, but this support can prevent it from gaining access to policymakers. Unlike movementism, the union avoids an overreliance on costly strikes but may also expose itself to patronage politics.

Although leftist unions encouraged teachers to voice discontent with ruling parties through protests, this was not the primary means for articulating interests. Compared with unions that embraced movementism, teacher protests were not on the same scale nor were they as recurrent. Therefore, policymakers were more likely to ignore them. Rather, leftist unions mobilized members as voters, forming a key part of the opposition. To appeal to teachers, left parties developed pro-teacher programs. Teachers became a bastion of support, and union leaders became candidates and brokers for these parties. Teachers' unions then articulated a set of partisan interests, with union demands closely aligned with left-party programs.

In Colombia, FECODE embraced leftism. The union's partisan identity became salient in the wake of the country's Constitution of 1991, when left parties recruited FECODE leaders as political candidates. In the 2000s, leftist political groupings in Colombia (i.e., Democratic Pole, Progressives, and Green Alliance) established close alliances with FECODE and developed education programs to appeal to teachers. Electoral returns show that former union leaders who targeted teachers as voters won a large vote share.

EXPLANATIONS FROM THE LITERATURE

To explain these strategies, there are several helpful starting points. First, I provide a broad overview of the literature on labor politics in new democracies from different regions of the world. This research highlights the roles of corporatist legacies, political opportunities, and the exchanges between unions and political parties. A second body of work, which has a regional focus on Latin America, examines the evolution of social movements and left parties. These literatures provide insights into the mechanisms that generate different forms of mobilization. They help to orient the argument in this book, although they do not fully account for the three patterns identified here.

Labor Politics

The labor politics literature traces the origins of union strategies to historical legacies. Corporatism, consisting of labor law, rights to unionize and bargain collectively, subsidies, and other union regulations, is the key concept. It highlights a pattern of state-labor relations characterized by a substantial degree of cooptation and labor peace (Schmitter 1974; Collier and Collier 1991). The focus is on the political elites that established corporatist structures and the parties that "incorporated" workers into parties and, thereby, gained control over them. Legacies of corporatism were often established during authoritarian rule in the twentieth century and endured – they remained in place even after countries democratized (Caraway et al. 2015). Corporatism explains contemporary patterns of labor mobilization because they endowed unions with resources and shaped organizations.

Historical legacies are central for interpreting whether unions revolted against authoritarian regimes as protest movements (Hartshorn 2019; Bishara 2020; Evans 2022) and whether they became supporters of political parties in new democracies (Lee 2011; Caraway and Ford 2020). The ways teachers' unions were founded and recognized by the state shed light on the strategies that were adopted. Tarlau (2022), focusing on teachers' unions in the Mexican state of Oaxaca and the Brazilian state of São Paulo, argues that legacies of labor incorporation under authoritarian rule (how the state sanctions and regulates the labor movement) shaped contemporary strategies (support for left parties versus autonomy from parties).

When analyzing teachers' political strategies in Argentina, Colombia, and Mexico, corporatist legacies are part of the explanation. But there is some evolution in how teachers' unions developed after authoritarianism. Authoritarian legacies are fixed and rooted firmly in the past (Hite and Cesarini 2004). By contrast, the development of teacher organizations is more of a moving target, as institutional and policy changes in the 1990s reshaped organizations and reinforced differences across cases. I draw attention to how organizational traits become more pronounced during or after democratization. Moreover, while the corporatism literature highlights a relatively uniform working-class identity, this book seeks to account for segmented patterns among teachers and industrial workers.[1] During labor incorporation, teachers were not at the forefront of the labor movement (as they are now) and attention should be paid to the diverse pathways of incorporation and the distinctive time periods when different groups of workers entered politics.

A second factor in the labor literature is opportunity structures, namely the possibilities, constraints, and threats afforded by the political environment. Some scholars focus on the party system and electoral rules that accompany democratic transitions to explain the strategies of unions. Electoral systems, and the incentives they generate, might induce some union leaders to pursue electoral strategies, while pushing others into the streets, in line with findings from South Korea and Taiwan (Lee 2011). In Indonesia, electoral rules were unfavorable to workers because they set high barriers to forming new political parties and barred independent candidates (Caraway and Ford 2020, 13). Institutional rules could be more permissive or restrictive, amplifying or reducing the political representation of workers, depending on how the geographic density of union members (and their votes) mapped onto the rules of the game. Therefore, it is important to examine the institutional landscape and consider whether political openings set unions down different paths.

Undoubtedly, teachers responded to institutional opportunities, and my analysis attends to these factors and demonstrates their effects. However, the concept of opportunity structures is conceptually difficult to wield. It is hard to pinpoint a consistent set of factors that make up an opportunity structure, especially in a multicountry analysis, where possibilities, constraints, and threats have different meanings. In Mexico, there

---

[1] To foreshadow Chapter 3, I will show that labor-based parties have different social bases across countries, and teachers sometimes are not part of these bases. For instance, in the 1940s, Argentine teachers thought of themselves as middle-class professionals and rejected the Peronist political project, including the curriculum (vom Hau 2009). Unlike other workers, many Argentine teachers were supporters of the Radical party, which positioned itself against Peronism.

was a "protracted" process of democratic transition (Eisenstadt 2000). The hegemonic ruling party, facing an emboldened opposition, clung to power by strengthening the teachers' union, which purported to be loyal to the ruling party. Ironically, the powerful union proved disloyal to the PRI and eventually broke away since union leaders had the resources and organization to make strategic alliances. The opportunity came in 2000, when a dominant party system turned into a competitive three-party system, increasing the number of political allies that were available to teachers. In Argentina, by contrast, a military junta stepped down in 1982, handing power over to elected civilians, but elected leaders were unresponsive to teachers because they faced more pressing economic and political problems (Munck 1998). Teacher grievances festered and teachers developed an adversarial relationship to the state. The opportunity came much later, in 2003, when a prolabor president was elected. In Colombia, there was a political opening in the 1990s, and various societal and political groups that had been excluded, including teachers, were encouraged to participate in a new constitutional convention (Wilson and Carroll 2007). Moreover, the new Constitution established a new electoral system that facilitated the formation of small teacher-based electoral vehicles. These three countries experienced different kinds of regime openings; the institutional changes are multidimensional and difficult to compare.

Moreover, in all three cases, there were some institutional openings that induced union leaders to enter politics, as union leaders in all three countries did become politicians. However, some unions, like the one in Argentina, were more resistant. Even though the electoral rules in Argentina did not foreclose opportunities for leaders of CTERA to participate in politics, those leaders did not take full advantage of the opportunities that were available. External features of the political environment undoubtedly mattered, but they did so in idiosyncratic ways for each case. It is difficult to pin down a common set of elements that make an opportunity structure.[2] Therefore, this analysis is not centrally focused on opportunities as the main cause of political strategies.

Scholars who work on labor during the implementation of economic reforms in the 1990s have zoomed in on intraorganizational dynamics. There are complex exchanges between political parties, union leaders,

---

[2] The challenge is compounded when opportunity structures are defined as an interaction between an objective condition and a frame, and are partially interpreted or constructed by the movement itself (McAdam et al. 1996, 8).

and rank-and-file workers (Silva 2009). Murillo (2001) focuses on competition between unions as they relate to problems in coordinating strikes as well as competition within them and the threats of replacement by rival union leaders. Burgess (2004) focuses on the capacity of the party to punish union leaders, the legal framework for industrial relations, and the structure of the labor movement. These frameworks, which center on dynamics among rival leaders in labor organizations and the capacity of the base to punish union leaders, influenced union militancy and restraint in many contexts (Levitsky and Mainwaring 2006; Caraway 2012; Bishara 2018). They take a soft rational choice approach, and the key mechanism is the incentives of union leaders to remain loyal. My analysis also focuses on intraorganizational dynamics, but I focus less on individual incentives and more on organizational resources and capabilities. Moreover, my analysis also identifies teachers' unions as key actors that make autonomous choices vis-à-vis party alliances, rather than as second movers responding to party decisions to move ahead with economic reforms.

Social Movements and Political Parties

Teacher mobilization could also fit with a social movement framework. Political changes such as democratization, more inclusive regimes, an expansion of rights, left governments, and participatory institutions created a fertile ground for social movements to flourish (Wampler and Avritzer 2004; Rossi and Della Porta 2015; Abers and Tatagiba 2016). To explain the outburst of new social movement activities, scholars focus on framings (Daby and Moseley 2022), strategic actions by activists (Paschel 2018), political opportunities (Rosaldo 2016), allies in the state who furnish activists with resources (Rich 2019), or grievances (Simmons 2016). These factors may be relevant for teacher strategies because they shaped movements that mobilized contemporaneously with teachers and made similar demands for rights, recognition, and material benefits. As noted in Chapter 1, teachers' unions resemble new social movements in several important ways. They gained momentum from democratization and a more open political environment. They frequently used street protest tactics to demand inclusion in the policy process. Prodemocracy teacher movements emerged in Mexico (as well as Brazil and Chile) in the 1970s and 1980s (Foweraker 1993; Cook 1996).

Still, there are important differences between teachers' unions and social movements. In many countries, teachers' unions have close ties to the state and a bureaucratic leadership that restrained protests. In Mexico, for example, by the early 1990s SNTE succeeded in demobilizing, restraining, and gaining control over the dissident teachers that constituted CNTE, a more autonomous teacher movement. Even the movement-like teachers' union in Argentina, CTERA, had a permanent organization with multiple locals and branches across territory and, as public employees, it depended on the state for resources. By contrast, new social movements such as the Brazilian environmental movement have weaker organizations and pose more of an outsider challenge to the state (Hochstetler and Keck 2007). They come together around social networks, shared identities, and culturally resonant frames. Grassroots activists organize collective action through diffuse, decentralized networks, especially those that are organized virtually (Tarrow 2011, 119–39).[3] While activists identify with social movements, there is no formal relationship; by contrast teachers' unions have dues-paying members who derive material benefits from union membership. In other words, teachers more strongly resemble organized interests.

The mechanisms that account for episodes of contentious politics must also explain the short life cycle of protest movements (Snow and Soule 2010, 172–5; Tarrow 2011, 131–5). By contrast, teacher mobilization tends to become a recurrent feature of politics – whether it takes the form of protest or party politics. In the tripartite framework of the social movement canon – resource mobilization, political opportunities, and frames – the resource mobilization component seems especially relevant to teachers' unions (McAdam et al. 1996). While social movements have varied structures, teachers tend to have denser and more bureaucratic organizations with more mechanisms to control the base. Opportunities and frames do not seem to fit teachers as well, at least not to explain strategies that persist over time.

A final literature to consider is on political parties. Scholars uncovered the internal operation of political parties, especially as they confront political and economic change, build new coalitions, and change their programmatic profile (Duverger 1954; Panebianco 1988; Kitschelt 1994). This literature has made contributions to understanding the internal organization of left parties and the roles of labor unions and social movements in those parties (Hunter 2010; LeBas 2011; Anria 2018; Schipani

---

[3] Indeed, much of the emphasis on new social movements is on the ways that diffuse networks of activists form virtually, through social media platforms (Castells 2012).

2022) as well as programmatic profiles (Handlin 2017; Lupu 2016). Teacher mobilization and partisan identification can be interpreted from the standpoint of the political behavior and voting literature (Calvo and Murillo 2019). For instance, Baker and Greene (2011) look at the profiles of left voters and find they are skeptical of neoliberal reforms. When considering the class identity and policy preferences of teachers, it is easy to understand why they might have left-leaning identities. Teachers are a group of lower- and middle-class voters who generally have low salaries, even if they enjoy the privilege of employment stability and relatively generous fringe benefits (Elacqua et al. 2018). As public employees, teachers favor more state spending and less marketization, issues that are aligned with the left. Moreover, socialization in normal schools or teacher colleges that have curriculums that emphasize social justice and have university student movements should all contribute to a tendency of leftism (Ginsburg and Tidwell 1995).[4] Indeed, Brown and Hunter (2004, 845) note the special affinity of teachers and left parties.

Teacher alliances with left-wing parties are a recurring pattern in Latin America. However, there are different kinds of left parties – new versus old, populist versus technocratic, radical versus centrist, and so on (Levitsky and Roberts 2011). Teachers can be more supportive of mainstream left parties (e.g., the Workers Party in Brazil), or smaller, protest parties (e.g., the Maoist party, the Revolutionary Independent Labor Movement, in Colombia). Moreover, an alliance between teachers and a left party is not a foregone conclusion. Teachers' individual preferences do not necessarily translate into support for left parties at the ballot box. Rather, unions are crucial intermediary organizations that aggregate and shape teachers' voting behavior. For instance, in Mexico rank-and-file teachers have leftist political attitudes, with surveys showing strong support for left parties such as the Revolutionary Democratic Party (PRD) and the National Regeneration Movement; the union pressured its members to vote for a teacher-based party, New Alliance, that adopted a more catch-all strategy (Raphael 2007, 281). Indeed, SNTE – and other unions – have influence over the voting behavior of teachers. Union leaders might decide that an

---

[4] Quinto de la Cruz (2007, 19) notes that in Peru, "the genesis of the partisan identity of teachers was in centers of teacher training, that is universities and pedagogical institutes.... In the 1970s [these institutions] were influenced by APRA [Popular Revolutionary Alliance]. During the 1980s left parties gained a presence and influenced the student leadership, and many teachers began to identify with the left."

alliance with a left-wing party limits the opportunities to advance their interests and instead call on teachers to vote for other parties.

To summarize, research on labor politics, social movements, and left parties provides a promising point of departure. All of these literatures indicate that organizations are crucial for understanding strategies. An analysis of teachers must consider the authoritarian legacies and policies that shaped the resources and organizations of unions. It also makes sense to focus on the inner workings of unions and their exchanges with political parties. The social movement literature provides insights into the parallels between teachers versus other activists who protested, but teachers' unions fit awkwardly with social movements because of close ties to the state, a bureaucratic leadership, and a dues-paying membership. The political parties literature suggests an affinity between teachers and left parties, but does not specify the character of this relationship. In the next section, I delve into the inner workings of union organizations: how they differ in their operations and the logics behind the ways they mobilize resources and members.

THE ORGANIZATIONAL ARGUMENT

The main argument is that teachers' strategies are rooted in the internal organization of the unions themselves. Many scholars have already developed sophisticated arguments based on the organizational characteristics of unions (i.e., union democracy and mechanisms of control) and the internal dynamics among union leaders (Cook 1996; Murillo 2001; Caraway 2012; Schneider 2022; Tarlau 2022). My innovation is to drill down into the specific traits of unions and to show how they contribute to different forms of collective action. I weave together insights from the labor politics, social movements, and political parties literatures into an analytic framework that helps to explain a range of strategies. My argument focuses on identifying the main actors in labor unions and analyzing where de facto power resides.

As a heuristic device, union organizations can be visualized as an organizational flowchart that identifies the relationships among national union leaders, their local counterparts, and rank-and-file workers. First, unions need the requisite hierarchical characteristics to form political alliances or, lacking those characteristics, instead engage in strategies of protest. Second, if unions do make alliances, those alliances are ideologically consistent or instrumental and shifting, depending on the factional rivalries in the national executive committee (see Table 2.2).

TABLE 2.2 *The organizational argument*

		Factionalism	
		Competition	Dominant Faction
Hierarchical Relations	Strong	Leftism	Instrumentalism
	Weak	Movementism	

Hierarchical relations in unions are the main variable. Such relations are necessary for negotiating partisan alliances since they give national union leaders the capacity to deliver a bloc of votes in exchange for political representation. Strong hierarchical relations indicate a robust chain of command linking national and local union leaders. Since Robert Michels (1962), a central issue for social movements, labor unions, and political parties has been the tendency to move toward a more top-down organizational model. Drawing on this idea of hierarchy, I examine the balance of power between the national executive committee, the union locals, and rank-and-file teachers. Whether teachers are organized into cohesive, national organizations or looser, more decentralized confederations has consequences for political strategies.

When power is located at the national level, and national union leaders are the primary actors, electoral mobilization becomes more salient than protest. This is because to build an electoral operation, national union leaders need local union leaders to follow orders. In Mexico and Colombia, the national leaders of teachers' unions had the backing of a robust union bureaucracy. They had discretionary control over union resources and policymaking authority to establish their political credibility. They persuaded local union leaders to follow orders by helping them rise through the ranks of the union or by threatening to punish them for disloyalty. Having a robust chain of command enabled the national leaders to scale up electoral participation. Electoral mobilization is a large-scale endeavor that requires resources, planning, and coordination. To influence election outcomes, national union leaders need a reliable network of local union leaders to mobilize the base.

By contrast, unions with weak hierarchies arrange strikes to press demands. Protests take place when mobilization is smaller scale and organized at the local level. In Argentina, the de facto power structure of CTERA was an archipelago of local union leaders and activists. The national executive committee lacked a sprawling bureaucratic structure to exert control. Moreover, it had few discretionary resources and a more limited policymaking authority; therefore, it lacked the capacity to mobilize teachers to vote. The key actors that organized collective action were local union leaders and activists in provincial organizations. Even if leaders in the national executive committee officially negotiated on behalf of teachers, local union leaders and activists were the real sources of power. Recurrent protests are observed when union locals and networks of activists act independently from the national leadership. With a restive base, unions reject electoral mobilization. Union members are unresponsive to the directives of national union leaders, who cannot mobilize voters. Therefore, party politics threaten union cohesion; union leaders set them aside to avoid conflict. Unions with bottom-up organizations assert political neutrality and refuse to negotiate alliances with political parties.

Hierarchical relations can be operationalized by examining the interactions between national and local union leaders. Relations are more hierarchical when the preponderance of union resources, staff, and organizational capacity resides in the national executive committee. Establishing whether national or local union leaders control union resources, hire their own agents, and have the means to reward and punish are crucial for assessing these relations. Such factors can be measured by looking at union statutes and de facto practices. Examining labor law, collective bargaining, and policymaking authority may also reveal whether national union leaders have an elevated status. In other words, it is necessary to follow the money and trace power relations. Who mobilizes resources, what resources are at their disposal, and what they do with those resources are central components of hierarchical relations.

If hierarchical relations are weak, then factionalism is not a centrally important feature because power resides in an activist base. However, if hierarchical relations are strong, then it is relevant to look at the character of relations in the national executive committee. Factionalism shapes the type of partisan alliances that unions pursue. Looking inside the national executive committee there may be factional divisions, which are closely related to the concept of "leadership competition," or multiple groupings of union leaders that compete to lead the union (Lipset et al. 1956; Voss and Sherman 2000; Murillo 2001; Burgess 2004; Caraway 2012; Bishara 2020). Power may also be concentrated in a single group of leaders – a dominant faction – that stifles dissent and emphasizes internal unity.

The presence of rival factions aligns unions with the left. Factional competition takes place in the context of union democracy. Within more democratic and pluralistic unions, rival factions maneuver to outbid one another to make inroads with the base. For FECODE in Colombia, competitive internal elections in the national executive committee created incentives for union leaders to criticize rivals for selling out the union by negotiating self-serving agreements with governments that generated few benefits for rank-and-file teachers. This dynamic activates opposition and makes alliances with left-wing parties a central component of the union's strategy. With factional rivalries, union leaders cannot act unilaterally, and pressure from opposing groups constrains strategic choices because rival factions articulate rank-and-file discontent. Factional competition pulls the whole union toward more ideological (and sometimes radical) positions and reduces the possibility for strategic negotiations, as union leaders want to avoid being outflanked.

When a single faction is hegemonic and crowds out rivals, union leaders establish instrumental alliances. The union leadership is more authoritarian since dissenting voices lack any real power, leaving leaders autonomous from the rank and file. Dominant factions can make political decisions that are unpopular with the rank and file and engender internal resistance such as alliances with new parties. No rival groups can channel resistance against such opportunistic behavior. In Mexico, power was concentrated in the figure of the union president or secretary-general. This national union leader has been surrounded by loyal lieutenants. With this unified structure, the union has overcome internal conflict and engaged in strategic negotiations with new political parties.

Factionalism can be operationalized by looking at the union statutes and procedures used to select union leaders. Some unions have established relatively open internal elections to select union leaders. Drilling down into the ways these elections are carried out and the results of internal union elections shed light on the character of factional competition. In other unions, the procedure for selecting union leaders is a labor congress, in which a convention of delegates selects the union leaders; this practice is less democratic since there is no direct input from the rank and file. Whether rival factions are present or not, the relative vote share of rival candidates, and what groups are represented in the union can all be assessed in this way.

Overall, whether the main divisions in unions are between local and national leaders or within the national executive committee itself has implications for the character of political action. The building blocks of the argument are the resources and strategic capabilities of union leaders. Unions have different capacities to direct political action, depending on who is really in charge, how strong their following is, and how far they can go in convincing followers to abide by their directives.

THE ORIGINS OF UNION ORGANIZATIONS

Union organizations do not exist in a vacuum. This raises the question of where they come from and when these structures were founded. I advocate an embedded, contextualized analysis of organizations, focusing on teacher–state relations. Teachers' unions were forged by a series of changes to political institutions as well as education and labor policies. The analysis searches for the major policy initiatives and institutional innovations that transformed teacher–state relations, in line with the proposal by Jacob Hacker and Paul Pierson (2014) for a more "policy-focused political science." It is necessary to analyze the full arc of the historical development of unions; specifically, how teachers' unions evolved alongside education policy, labor law, and state institutions. In other words, union organizations are nested in different policy and institutional matrices. For each case, it is crucial to identify the labor and education policies that give union organizations shape and substance.

Building on the labor literature, corporatist legacies are a crucial starting point. Following Collier and Collier (1991) there was a "project from above," in which teachers negotiated with, gained recognition, and were structured by the state. But there was also a "project from below," or the process of union organizing itself and the ways in which union leaders established more internally democratic institutions for the national executive committee. While focusing on the state structuring side is only half of what happened, it is helpful for identifying the policy and institutional changes that shaped organizations. A key finding in the labor literature is that corporatist institutions established by authoritarian regimes of the mid-twentieth century structured the subsequent development of labor organizations (Lee 2011; Caraway et al. 2015). Indeed, for teachers in Latin America, part of my story focuses on the ways in which authoritarian or semi-democratic regimes forged teacher organizations, noting the contrasts between teachers and industrial workers.

By the 1970s, labor policies cementing corporatist structures were in place in most countries. There were distinct patterns of state recognition of teachers' unions, national labor laws, and official roles for union leaders in the policy process. There was variation in the degree to which nation-states structured teacher organizations. Distinct organizational models were emerging across countries with discernible differences in union hierarchies and factional dynamics. When the state favored an official teachers' union, it concentrated power in a single, progovernment faction; when the state ignored teachers, multiple factions worked to consolidate national organizations. The encompassing populist regime in Mexico helped union leaders to build a centralized union, in which power was concentrated in a dominant faction. By contrast, in Argentina, military regimes set back union-building efforts, and, in Colombia, political elites largely ignored teachers; in both countries, teachers' unions developed an adversarial relationship with the state. The question was what, if any, resources and institutional privileges the state afforded to union leaders.

These arrangements were partially disrupted by the "Lost Decade" of the 1980s, when the region experienced hardship from the debt crisis and economic restructuring. In this period, political elites struggled to manage the debt crisis and imposed austerity measures that reduced education spending. But contemporaneously, military regimes handed over power to civilians and democratic regimes were established; these regimes had the potential to be more responsive to teacher demands. The economic shocks and political disruptions weakened and destabilized teacher organizations; they signaled a broader transformation in teacher–state relations. The grievances of teachers, in addition to the weakening of repressive regimes, generated widespread protests that challenged established union leaders. Dissident teacher movements emerged in Mexico (Cook 1996) and other countries as well, where there was growing discontent. Dissident groups denounced official union leaders for being disconnected from the rank and file and demanded changes to strengthen union democracy. My comparative analysis is grounded in a common point of departure in the 1980s, when teachers in Argentina, Colombia, and Mexico contested austerity measures and labor unions faced pressure to democratize their leadership.

The 1990s was a moment when various issues were on the education agenda, namely decentralizing education and addressing labor grievances. How policymakers responded to these dual challenges and how decentralization policies were designed and implemented reinforced different organizational models that endured. Differences in the ways that unions were organized can be traced back to the ways in which these policies were negotiated and implemented. Indeed, other scholars have shown how decentralization could be used to structure teachers' unions. Decentralization could be more rhetorical and less substantive, preserving the core features of teachers' unions, as in Mexico (Grindle 2004a), or decentralization could be used as a political weapon to weaken teachers' unions, as in El Salvador (Vargas 2022).

There were different responses to teacher movements across countries by policymakers in the 1990s as economic conditions improved.

Etchemendy (2011) argues that some labor unions were compensated to go along with neoliberal economic reforms. This insight is helpful for thinking about teachers since, when education finally was put on the political agenda, multiple issues came to the fore. Teachers had experienced erosion in salaries throughout the 1980s, which triggered demands for dramatic salary improvements. At the same time, there was an impulse to decentralize education, led by technocrats and policy experts who sought to improve the efficiency of highly centralized bureaucracies by handing over administrative, fiscal, and political functions to regional and local governments (Eaton 2004; Montero and Samuels 2004; Falleti 2010). This decentralization agenda was orthogonal to the labor grievances of teachers. This coincidence of an impulse to decentralize with an impulse to address labor grievances created mounting pressures on elected leaders to push forward ambitious education reforms.

In this context, broader education reform packages in the 1990s that contained proposals for decentralization either strengthened or undermined teacher organizations. These were major political reforms that involved multisided negotiations among union leaders, ministers of education, ministers of finance, governors, mayors, and presidents. These policies fundamentally altered unions' organizational trajectories because teachers' unions were positioned to gain access to new resources and negotiate the terms of decentralization. Union leaders could consolidate power in the national executive committee if they negotiated compensation in the form of better salaries for teachers and subsidies for the union. Policymakers granted compensation to union leaders in exchange for union leaders agreeing to a degree of decentralization. However, teacher organizations could be weakened if decentralization was imposed on them and used to undermine union leaders (Vargas 2022). This kind of decentralization effectively dispersed power in union locals and the activist base. Tiramonti (2001, 17) observes that "a decentralized [school] system forces [teachers'] unions to redistribute power within their organization, and the local unions become protagonists in processes of negotiation and the main references of the base and the government." Building on the literature on decentralization, which focused on the political *causes* that shaped policy design and implementation (Murillo 2001; Grindle 2004b; Falleti 2010), I analyze the *effects* of these policy decisions on union organizational hierarchies and factional dynamics.

The organizational structures of unions evolved in the aftermath of the debt crisis and with the onset of regime openings; historical legacies do matter, and so too did major shifts in teacher–state relations in the 1980s and 1990s. Indeed, this analysis highlights the institutional and policy changes that took place in the aftermath of the debt crisis, and how a new set of policies restructured teacher organizations. To analyze labor organizations, it is crucial to see how they are embedded within a broader set of institutions and policies.

RESEARCH DESIGN AND METHODS

This book presents a comparative-historical analysis of Argentina, Colombia, and Mexico to analyze the ways that the organizational development of teachers' unions produced distinctive political strategies. Even though teachers' unions in these three countries purported to represent the same underlying set of interests (i.e., teachers' professional and economic interests), they participated in politics in different ways. This book closely attends to political and policy factors that contribute to major differences in the observed outcomes. It compares three teacher organizations over a long period, exploiting the analytic advantages of a "controlled comparison" in a small-N analysis (Slater and Ziblatt 2013). This historical approach shows the causal weight attributable to policy decisions, examining the enduring consequences of sequence, timing, and contingency while taking contextualized comparisons seriously (Skocpol and Somers 1980, 178; Locke and Thelen 1995). My goal is to extend research on labor relations into a new policy domain and engage with a broader literature on macrohistorical change in labor relations in Latin America.

I selected the cases of Argentina, Colombia, and Mexico for two main reasons. First, these are three major countries in Latin America, and there has been much commentary about teachers in each, making it feasible to systematically collect data on them and study them over a long period. While there has been a revolution in the accessibility of quantitative data on various aspects of politics, there remain data limitations when looking at labor politics. Countries collect this data in idiosyncratic ways, and it is not always readily available. Small-N research designs are appropriate in contexts where large-N, cross-national data simply do not exist. Second, these cases demonstrate the wide range of variation among countries regarding how teachers mobilize in politics. Variation in the outcome variable facilitates theory building. Given the range of outcomes included in this analysis – movementism, instrumentalism, and leftism – the findings are likely to illuminate other Latin American countries and specific causal processes that define education politics.

To identify causal mechanisms, I rely on cross-case comparisons alongside within-case analysis. Although not without its limitations, this approach enables the identification of causal relations, the leveraging of multiple pieces of evidence, and the consideration of counterfactuals. The principal aim is to build theory by inductively using a small number of cases to generate broad claims that can be tested more widely in future research. I conducted within-case analysis by collecting all available single-country monographs of teachers' unions by various authors. I identified several historians, political scientists, sociologists, economists, think tanks, private foundations, and international organizations that had published extensively about Latin American teachers. My task was to build on this work by putting this research into a comparative frame and drilling down into political processes. This scholarship tended to be historical, with a focus on labor laws and education policy shifts. Latin American scholars – who lived in and were trained in the region – produced much of this work. I examine the political side of teacher labor relations by developing conceptual categories for distinct political mobilization types.

I collected available data on teacher protests. Event databases that use newspaper archives have been compiled by political scientists, think tanks, and government agencies. Bringing together data on teacher protests from three different countries and across different periods was challenging, owing to different measurement procedures and data limitations, especially for Mexico. The lack of a standardized set of measures for teacher protests posed a challenge to comparative analysis. Still, these data are helpful for capturing broad patterns over time and for identifying the extent to which teacher mobilization occurred across territory.

To analyze electoral mobilization, I collected data on the vote share of teacher-based political parties and the recruitment of union leaders as political candidates across the three countries. I mined databases of legislative CVs, searching for keywords that indicated past roles in the teachers' unions. I then conducted interviews with union leaders to confirm that the politicians I had identified had close ties to the teachers' union or whether these ties existed only on paper. In interviews, I identified other politicians who were not found in keyword searches of legislative CVs, and I eliminated politicians whose CVs were inaccurate and had tenuous ties to the union. This analysis sheds light on the partisan identities and types of electoral districts in which union leaders were most frequently elected to public office. It also provides an indicator of the overall level of electoral mobilization by teachers' unions. The voting behavior of teachers, as a group, is difficult to observe, because teachers are dispersed across territory. Surveys typically lump occupational groups together and rarely look explicitly at the political attitudes and behaviors of teachers. Thus, looking at the pathways that union leaders follow into politics sheds light on whether teachers are organized into a voting bloc.

I then conducted interviews with union leaders and other observers. This book relies on 129 interviews (57 for Colombia; 46 for Mexico; 26 for Argentina) conducted over 18 months. I recruited various participants, including teachers, union leaders, politicians, journalists, academics, and policy experts. Across Latin America, teacher protests, the participation of teachers in elections, and teachers' alliances with political parties are much discussed. I gained unprecedented access to union leaders by cultivating relationships and understanding the factional divisions in unions. Union leaders from dissident factions were eager to discuss sensitive topics, such as the partisanship and electoral mobilization of teachers, because they wanted to disclose conflicts of interest and malfeasance involving rival union leaders. A central contribution of this research is the original interview data that I collected, which illuminates these unions' internal operations. While much of the existing research on education politics analyze teachers' organizations from the outside, taking political elites' perspectives as the point of departure, my research provides insights into union leaders' and teachers' perspectives.

The quantitative data was used to structure interviews. I generated lists of union leaders who had run as candidates or were elected to the legislature, the number of votes they received, and the results of internal union elections. I presented these data to interviewees and asked them to help me to interpret them. Respondents were eager to give me the qualitative backstory of what these results meant for the balance of power in the union and the organizational practices that were used to produce them. In addition, I also asked politicians who were former union leaders to describe how the union helped them to enter politics. I attempted a similar exercise with data on teacher protests, but I found it harder to establish consistency across cases with the protest data and the answers were less clear. Overall, the interviews were grounded in empirical data, both quantitative and historical, to analyze the underlying factors that generated these outcomes.

In sum, this book triangulates among multiple pieces of evidence. The core analysis is a small-N comparison, with various sources of data used to analyze each case. Moving between qualitative case narratives and interviews, on the one hand, and quantitative indicators of protest, candidate recruitment, and indicators of education policy, on the other, provides new insights into education politics and policy process. Given that comparative research on teachers and education is relatively new in political science, the rich description of these three cases is another contribution of this analysis.

3

The Origins of National Teacher Organizations

This chapter explores the founding of teachers' unions and the characteristics of union organizations that were in place by the mid-twentieth century. It goes on to examine how teachers mobilized in the context of a closed political environment. It also analyzes the tensions and contrasts between teachers and other groups of workers, in terms of how they were incorporated into politics, with particular attention to the labor laws and partisan affiliations of teachers in Mexico, Argentina, and Colombia. The analysis here sets up the main empirical chapters (Chapters 4–9), highlighting the different ways in which teachers participated in politics before and after regimes opened in the direction of democracy and greater political inclusion.

Comparative research on labor politics has shown that labor unions inherited resources from the state, often when new political regimes were founded, which put them on different paths. Indeed, research on "legacy unions" argues that the corporatist arrangements established under authoritarian regimes have shaped labor politics in the aftermath of democratization (Caraway et al. 2015). I show that while this argument mostly fits the teachers' union in Mexico, where labor incorporation spanned multiple sectors and brought in public sector workers, there were some important differences between labor and teacher incorporation for Colombia and Argentina: teachers formed unions later than other workers, they fell under different labor laws, and they established distinct relationships with the state and political parties. For Colombia, unions were weak and coopted by the traditional political parties, but teachers were strong and began to move decisively toward small opposition parties (Hartlyn 1984). For Argentina, workers had robust labor unions that were incorporated into the Peronist Justicialist Party (PJ), but teachers had a more heterogeneous set of partisan identities. Legacies of union founding in each case did foreclose certain possibilities and set unions on distinct paths. But these legacies were not fully locked in; in the 1980s, they would be disrupted by the debt crisis and the political opening that took place with democratic transitions. To understand the contemporary characteristics of teacher organizations and political strategies, historical legacies are important, although they are not the only storyline.

Before the 1980s, teacher mobilization was constrained by a closed political environment (i.e., fully authoritarian or semidemocratic regimes) and teachers' unions that were organizationally weak or dependent on political parties. Mobilization took the form of either protests that were repressed or ignored, or electoral mobilization in which union leaders mobilized at the behest of party leaders, and union interests were subordinated to those of political parties. This chapter analyzes how the organizational structures in place in the 1960s and 1970s generated these patterns of constrained mobilization.

Teacher movements from the 1900s to the 1940s in all three countries consisted of a fragmented field of mutual aid societies and professional associations. They were largely an urban phenomenon, with almost no presence outside large cities. Public school systems were initially rudimentary, with low levels of school enrollment, and so too were teacher organizations, which had a relatively small member base. However, labor grievances began to engender union organizing; over time, divided teacher movements coalesced, forming national organizations, albeit in different ways. After grueling struggles for labor rights, teachers secured important victories in all three countries, namely teacher labor codes that set rules for teacher hiring, promotion, and tenure. By the 1970s, national teacher associations had a degree of political power and they established distinct relationships with the state and political parties. In Mexico, the teachers' union had close ties to the party-state apparatus of the PRI, and SNTE developed a centralized organization. By contrast, in Argentina and Colombia, unions had weak ties to the state, more internal divisions, and were mobilized from the opposition.

This chapter sets up the main argument – that union organizations shape teacher mobilization – by analyzing the evolution of teacher organizations over several decades. The aim is to highlight the inflection points that changed union organizations fundamentally; this is not meant to be an exhaustive summary of the labor history of teachers in these countries. The first section describes the similarities among early teacher movements, which were born to address similar problems and labor grievances. At the onset, teacher organizations were highly fragmented. The second section examines the political projects of consolidating national organizations, and it demonstrates that these organizations developed distinct characteristics. The third section analyzes how national organizations shaped mobilization in the context of political constraints, in the form of limited political rights and weak or dependent union organizations.

THE EMERGENCE OF FRACTURED MOVEMENTS

Early teacher movements had a common starting point. At the dawn of the twentieth century, teacher organizations, like organizations for industrial workers, were fragmented and weak. There was an impulse for governments around the world to establish mass school systems. But in the early stages of the expansion of public education, teachers were mostly quiescent and only occasionally protested when labor grievances became unbearable. These grievances included low teacher salaries compared with other workers, salary disparities between different categories of teachers, especially urban versus rural, and the late payment of salaries stemming from governments hiring more teachers than they could afford to pay. Teachers – especially those who worked in rural primary schools – belonged to a proletarian class with precarious livelihoods. Over time, labor conflicts increased across Latin America. State responses ranged from efforts to improve teacher compensation and promote unions as legitimate organizations to efforts to ignore teacher demands, repress protests, and crack down on unions.

Mexico: The Revolution, Cultural Missionaries, and the Impulse to Consolidate

Although the Mexican teachers' union would become a behemoth by the twenty-first century, in the 1910s and 1920s, Mexican teachers were fragmented into many rival organizations. The dictator Porfirio Díaz (1876–1911) made some progress in expanding education institutions under the broader banner of modernization. However, he did so in mostly limited ways, with a restricted role of the federal government in expanding education and the tendency to neglect the rural sector and indigenous communities. Indeed, rates of illiteracy remained quite high in Mexico, even compared with other countries in Latin America, and they remained high well into the twentieth century.

When the Mexican Revolution (1910–20) broke out, the ensuing civil war among regional caudillos claimed about 1.5 million lives. This conflict grouped teachers into leagues with ties to the revolutionary leaders' personalistic factions (Peláez 1984, 17). As a key part of their social programs, revolutionary leaders such as Pancho Villa emphasized expanding public schools and ending illiteracy in his home state of Chihuahua (Hellman 1988, 11). During this period, the proliferation of regional school systems, competing alongside left parties and personalistic union leaders, produced a fragmented teachers' movement (Cook 1996, 62). By the 1930s, there were more than 700 teachers' unions, including two national organizations. Many of these organizations existed only in Mexico City – with no presence in the countryside (Peláez 1984, 19). Unions organized different categories of education workers. In the 1930s, school principals and inspectors formed one union, teachers who worked at technical schools formed another, and rural teachers formed yet another (Peláez 1984, 20–1). Other unions had strong partisan identities, such as those affiliated with the communist and socialist parties.

As a new political order emerged in the aftermath of the revolutionary violence, political elites made concerted efforts to centralize the school system – and the teachers who worked in it. The project aimed to construct a new, revolutionary nationalist identity for Mexican citizens. The secular, nationalist, and populist values of the revolution fitted hand in glove with a centralized educational system (Vaughan 1997). In 1921, President Álvaro Obregón (1920–4) created the federal Secretariat of Public Education (SEP), which launched a center-led expansion of education into the countryside. The first Secretary of Education, José Vasconcelos, had an ambitious vision of revolutionary education that included expanding rural schools to politicize peasants and construct a new national identity (Peláez 1984, 18). Vasconcelos encouraged state governments to expand public education and sent "cultural missions" by officials of the SEP to recruit, train, and hire teachers to work in distant rural communities. Until the 1940s, the federal and state governments ran separate, parallel school systems. State and municipal governments mostly operated schools in cities, and the federal government expanded rural schools (Cabal 2021, 52–3).

The center-led expansion of secular public education posed a challenge to the church and regional caudillos. Many of the revolutionaries were anticlerical, in part because the church had supported the dictatorship of Porfirio Diaz. The Constitution of 1917 declared the separation of church and state, but it also established a federalist system that protected state rights against the federal overreach that had taken place during the dictatorship (Cabal 2021, 15). President Plutarco Elías Calles (1924–8) set education policies that reinforced anticlerical laws involving harsh regulation of private schools, including federal supervision of private education (Cabal 2021, 57). The church in Mexico came under siege and "was subject to the most extensive anti-clerical movement anywhere in the region" (Collier and Collier 1991, 114). Calles' stance against the church sparked regional rebellions, known as the Cristero War (1926–9), in which 4,000 priests were killed or expelled from the country (Collier and Collier 1991, 222–3). After putting down these rebellions, President Calles called on regional allies to harass church leaders and replace parochial schools with secular public institutions.[1]

The federal government's expansion of public education also challenged regional elites. During the presidency of Álvaro Obregon (1920–4), the federal government offered subsidies to governors to take over public schools from municipal authorities (Loyo 1998). President Calles (1924–8) took a more hands-on approach; in 1924, he challenged the school systems run by regional caudillos, ending subsidies to state governments (Cabal 2021, 55). While the Constitution of 1917 had enshrined federalism and delegated authority to state and municipal governments, there was a de facto expansion of federal power in the education sector. The number of federally employed primary school teachers increased from 22,939 in 1921 to 104,718 in 1959 (INEE 2015, 21, Table 1.1). The more economically developed states, such as the State of México, Chihuahua, Puebla, and Nuevo León, maintained their own public schools. Yet the federal government played a greater role in the poorer states in the south, such as Oaxaca and Michoacán, which had rudimentary rural public school systems (Vaughan 1982). In 1934, a constitutional amendment made public education compulsory and free (INEE 2015, 20), which set the stage for the federal government to absorb some of the state-level school systems and to become the primary provider of education twenty years after the revolution.

During this early period, when public education was expanding, most teachers were poorly paid and had little training. They were often referred to as secular "missionaries" who brought literacy,

---

[1] Education policies in Mexico restricted the scope of the private school system. By 2006, Mexico had the largest public primary and secondary school system in Latin America; 88 percent of students were enrolled in public schools, while only 12 percent were in private schools (Pereyra 2008).

culture, and modernity to peasants in the most traditional and least developed parts of the country (Vazquez de Knaugh 1970). The Secretariat of Public Education maintained programs such as the "cultural missions" in which federal teachers were sent to the countryside to recruit and train rural teachers.[2] The reaction of communities to teachers varied; in some cases, teachers developed close ties to communities by promoting the national development agenda, while also reducing the strong anticlerical stance of the socialist curriculum. In others, especially those of indigenous people, teachers viewed themselves as modernizers who were culturally superior, which prompted community resistance (Vaughan 1997; vom Hau 2009, 142). The state was eager to expand the coverage of education, as few rural teachers had formal training. Officials simply could not wait for teachers to graduate from normal schools (i.e., secondary teacher colleges), and there were only a handful of rural normal schools (Vaughan 1982, 1997; Arnaut 1996). At that time, most rural teachers had only a few years of elementary education and so expanding opportunities for teacher training was an urgent priority. Overall, the massive expansion of public schools in Mexico created a relatively homogeneous teaching profession, with labor grievances that were notably similar across states: low salaries, salary disparities between rural versus urban teachers, and salaries that were often paid late because of limited budgets.

Owing to the revolutionary fervor for labor reform, political elites were largely responsive to teachers' demands for labor rights, and political elites adopted teacher labor laws relatively early. In 1929 and 1930, teachers secured federal laws for hiring and tenure. The expansion of labor law followed the logic of inducements and constraints, which were used to build corporatist labor unions loyal to the regime (Collier and Collier 1979). In 1929, federal teachers secured the Law of Employment Stability for Teachers and, in 1930, the Regulation of the Pay Scale of the SEP. These laws created tenure and a pay scale for employees of the SEP. In 1938, the Juridical Statute for Service Workers of the Union created a new category of public employee, with a special designation for education workers that carried its own system of hiring, promotion, and tenure. The special designation was part of a constitutional amendment that created section "B" of Article 123 of the Constitution.

---

[2] Literacy rates in Mexico lagged behind Argentina and also Colombia. By 1900, the literacy rate stood at only 22 percent, increasing to 36 percent in 1925, and 48 percent by 1946 (Engerman and Sokoloff 2002; Engerman, Mariscal and Sokoloff 2012).

Still, early labor laws did not consolidate a national teacher organization – at least not initially. Although the consolidation of teachers' unions began in the 1930s, it required decades of negotiation to establish a single national teacher organization with a mass-member base. Teachers proved harder to unionize than industrial workers and peasants. President Lázaro Cárdenas, who implemented major agrarian reforms and incorporated peasants, workers, and the military into a single party organization, had less success bringing teachers into his party as a result of factional splits and political divisions among them. A strong group of leftist teachers resisted incorporation into a new political party.

To demonstrate the elite efforts to organize teachers in the 1930s and 1940s, there were government-sponsored unity congresses, in which leaders of the teacher movement were invited to meet and begin to negotiate union consolidation. President Lázaro Cárdenas (1934–40), who launched a six-year plan to create a "socialist" curriculum that excluded religious doctrine, sponsored unity congresses to negotiate the consolidation of a single union. Yet these congresses failed to reach that goal (Cook 1996, 62).[3] Although the Sindicato de Trabajadores de la Enseñanza de la República Mexicana (STERM) emerged in 1938, and although this union covered most teachers, it was riven by factionalism, with tensions between the communists and union leaders from other parties (Peláez 1984, 24). Teachers lacked a stable, permanent organization, with ongoing jockeying for power by union leaders from left parties and factions organized around personalistic leaders (Espinosa 1982; Ornelas 2008).

Overall, the emerging hegemonic party in Mexico sought to overcome the divisions in the teacher movement. The party wanted encompassing sectoral organizations for each category of worker to connect workers directly to the party apparatus. Nonetheless, the teacher movement was highly fragmented, and during the heyday of labor incorporation under President Lázaro Cárdenas, the push to consolidate the teacher movement stalled.

Argentina: Uneven Modernization and a Segmented Teacher Movement

In Argentina, the teacher movement developed quite differently from Mexico. This difference stemmed from the fact that by the early twentieth

---

[3] On Cárdenas' education policies, see Collier and Collier (1991, 235) and Vaughan (1997) for the states of Sonora and Puebla.

century, Argentina had one of the most advanced economies in Latin America, and because of its national wealth, Argentina established an extensive public school system before other countries in the region. President Domingo Sarmiento (1868–74) promoted public education, quadrupling education subsidies from the national government to the provinces and increasing enrollment by 100,000 children, and as a result Argentina boasted one of the highest rates of literacy in Latin America (Falleti 2010, 87).[4] In 1884, President Julio Argentino Roca (1880–6) passed Law 1420, which enacted compulsory secular education and created the National Council of Education. Thus, while Colombia and Mexico had more rudimentary school systems by 1900, Argentina had made strides forward in literacy and primary school enrollment.

Several factors contributed to the early expansion of education in Argentina. First, Argentina embraced liberal reforms earlier than Mexico or Colombia, and the separation of church and state accelerated the expansion of public schools.[5] Second, in the late nineteenth century, Argentina experienced sustained economic growth from agricultural exports, which provided the revenue to pay for the construction of new schools and the hiring of more teachers. Third, because of the scarcity of labor and large swaths of uncultivated land, large numbers of immigrants, mostly from Spain and Italy, were drawn to Argentina. Many of these immigrants were already literate when they arrived, and they expected the state to educate their children. Moreover, the influx of immigrants created a social and political need to expand school enrollment to incorporate the newly arrived into the Argentine nation.

While Argentina boosted impressive early results in literacy and school enrollment, a highly segmented school system was emerging, characterized by a stark urban–rural divide (Galeano 2004; Mazzuca 2017). The Buenos Aires metropolitan area saw rapid economic growth attributable to an export boom and a growing middle class, but the interior provinces remained underdeveloped rural backwaters. The 1853 Constitution made the provinces responsible for providing primary education. This federalist arrangement enabled the rapid development of urban schooling. However, it also engendered inequality as rural communities lagged behind in building schools and hiring teachers.

---

[4] In 1890, 52 percent of Argentine citizens who were ten and older were literate; this number increased to 73 percent by 1925 (Engerman and Sokoloff 2002, 77).
[5] Church–state conflict erupted in the late nineteenth century, with liberal elites challenging the church and ultimately triumphing. Weak linkages between the church and the political elite limited the scope of the parochial school system (Tedesco 2003).

To mitigate this inequality and expand education to rural areas, the federal government stepped in to subsidize provincial governments. In 1905, the national government constructed its own nationally run "Láinez" schools in the provinces, which aimed to replace the need for federal subsidies (Falleti 2010, 85). Láinez schools offered teachers higher salaries and better working conditions than schools managed by the provinces (Nardacchione 2012, 27). In other words, the federal and provincial governments had parallel school systems, and teachers in these systems fell under different labor codes (Gindin 2011, 104).

The urban public schools, especially in Buenos Aires, and Láinez schools were relatively high performing. The teachers that staffed these schools were well trained, having received secondary or higher education. They earned middle-class salaries. However, these characteristics made them harder to unionize because the teachers thought of themselves as middle-class professionals who were fundamentally different from teachers who worked in elementary schools and rural areas and had less education and training (Vazquez and Balduzzi 2000, 22). Indeed, rural teachers in the interior provinces were seen as "apostles" who did not have labor rights, a term that was also used for teachers in Colombia. They were less like middle-class professionals than urban teachers. Rather, rural teachers were more like blue-collar industrial workers, and they were often incorporated into the patronage networks of regional party bosses. There was a separation between more professional urban teachers, who joined professional associations, tended to be more male, taught secondary school, had more training and subject matter expertise, and earned higher salaries than their rural counterparts. This cleavage between urban and rural teachers would endure. Teachers were divided by whether they had professional credentials and whether they taught at the primary, secondary, or technical level (Nardacchione 2014, 2). Patronage politics, rural–urban, and professional divisions made it difficult to build solidarity within the teaching profession. This made it hard to establish encompassing union organizations that brought together all teachers.

In addition to divisions among teachers, a hostile stance of regional political elites toward teachers' unions in the first half of the twentieth century further slowed unionization. Labor relations during this period were contentious since provincial governments often paid teachers late. For instance, in 1918 and 1919, teachers' organizations in the provinces of Santa Fe and Mendoza organized strikes after salaries were not paid for sixteen months (Ascolani 2019). These protests prompted a repressive state response and crackdown – teachers who participated were fired or transferred to undesirable, rural schools. Regional elites supported the creation of teacher federations with ties to the governing party, while they denied legal recognition of teacher associations that were in the opposition (Nardacchione 2014, 8). Facing the threat of teacher unrest in the 1930s, governors in the provinces of Buenos Aires, San Juan, and Santa Fe created parallel teacher organizations to coopt teachers (Gindin 2011, 101). Political elites sought to deter labor unrest by repressing teacher protests and undermining teachers' efforts to organize autonomous unions.

The presidency of Juan Domingo Perón (1945–55) further divided teachers. Perón coopted industrial unions and aligned them with his populist movement while marginalizing unions that resisted him. In speeches, Perón distinguished manual laborers from intellectual laborers, creating separate organizations for each. The blue-collar workers were larger and more loyal to Peron. He decided which unions were granted state recognition (i.e., a *personeria gremial*) and denied recognition to opposition unions. Labor laws in this period made union affiliation automatic and obligatory for industrial workers. A provincially divided industrial labor movement became centralized, as the General Confederation of Labor (CGT) aligned itself with the Peronist movement (Gindin 2011, 103).

Peron's populism generated a mixed reaction among teachers. To be sure, a fraction of teachers did align with Peron, especially those in the rural interior who thought of themselves as blue-collar workers (Vazquez and Balduzzi 2000, 26). In addition, the Peronists coopted the traditional leaders of the teacher movement, including unions aligned with Catholic teachers.[6] In 1953, the PJ sponsored a national organization, the United Teachers of Argentina (UDA) (Gindin 2011, 107). Instead of having a *personeria gremial*, a legal category that gave organizations the right to require universal and compulsory union membership and to engage in collective bargaining, UDA was awarded a *personeria professional*, making it a professional association for teachers and administrators that lacked the legal rights of labor unions.

But the UDA failed to incorporate teachers en masse because there were pockets of resistance to Peronism among them. Not only did teachers vigorously resist a 1947 teacher statute that Perón attempted to impose on them, which encroached on their professional autonomy by establishing

---

[6] In 1936, the church reestablished its role in providing education, and it sponsored the staunchly anticommunist Federation of Catholic Teachers and Professors, which teachers in parochial schools were obliged to join (Gindin 2011, 100).

religious instruction in public schools, but they also demanded political autonomy, invoking Law 1420 to protect themselves from political interference (Nardacchione 2014, 8; Gindin 2011, 102–5). The urban, professional teachers were particularly skeptical of Peronism. In part, their opposition stemmed from the alliance that Perón had formed with the church. In 1946, Perón imposed a curriculum that emphasized moral, religious, and civic education (Gindin 2011, 104; Aisenstein et al. 2017). He adopted textbooks that reimagined Argentine history around the Peronist personality cult, which was an affront to the professionalism and subject knowledge of many teachers (vom Hau 2009, 137). Urban teachers, who were more closely aligned with the middle sectors and the Radical Civic Union (UCR) resisted this curricular turn, and they developed various strategies of resistance to undermine the official doctrine (vom Hau 2009, 143–5).

Whereas industrial workers rallied around Peron, many teachers – especially those in large cities – aligned with the middle-class opposition. In the 1940s, socialists led the largest teacher associations, alongside radicals (UCR) and communists (Vazquez 2005, 9). In the 1940s, the Peronists repressed unions aligned with the political opposition, declaring them illegal and suspending their *personeria gremial* (Gindin 2011, 104). State repression of these non-Peronist unions had a profound impact on Argentina's teachers. For instance, teachers who did not affiliate with the PJ could be fired arbitrarily (Vazquez 2005, 9). This repressive approach sharpened the political divisions among teachers and reinforced organizational divisions in the teacher movement.

Colombia: The Conservative Hegemony and Political Apostles

If the school system in Mexico bore the legacy of the Mexican Revolution, the school system in Colombia was shaped by the period known as the "Conservative Hegemony" (1884–1930), when the Conservative Party continuously controlled the presidency. In contrast to Mexico, the national government of Colombia played a limited role in expanding public schools, and labor relations remained irregular and informal for a longer period. The teachers' labor movement was initially weak. Teachers' associations were apolitical. In the 1920s and 1930s, they existed only as professional associations or mutual aid societies with only a few members and no meaningful political influence (Bocanegra Acosta 2013, 163).

Whereas the Mexican Revolution set in motion the birth of a centralized public school system that expanded through the federal government and challenged the church, in Colombia, the Conservative Party's pact with the church restricted the scope of public schools and limited the opportunities for teachers to unionize. From 1903 to 1930, Conservative rule and the Organic Law of Education restricted the government's role in public education. The church, as a coalition partner of the Conservatives, operated a large network of parochial schools. Furthermore, even in the 1930s, when the Liberal Party finally came to power and adopted important education reforms, the public school system remained limited in scope.

During the "Conservative Hegemony" (1884–1930), the Conservative Party continuously held the presidency and the church, its coalition partner, operated a massive number of parochial schools. The Constitution of 1886 (which remained the highest law of the land until 1991) set the stage for an anemic public school system because it enshrined Catholicism as the official religion, with no separation of church and state. Disagreements over education and church–state relations triggered armed conflict between the Liberal and Conservative parties. Liberals wanted a secular state that made policy based on rational, scientific principles; Conservatives defended the privileges of the church and traditional notions of morality. Conflict came to a head in the Thousand Day War (1899–1902), which claimed between 100,000 and 150,000 lives – about 2.5 percent of the population. In the peace treaty of Neerlandia, the Liberal forces surrendered to the Conservatives. In the wake of this devastating war, roads, government offices, schools, and teaching materials were destroyed, and many students were forced to abandon their studies. The Conservative government promised to rebuild schools and modernize the education sector, but its main priority was to protect the church's role in providing education.

The Conservative government enacted the Organic Law of Education in 1903, which made primary education free but not compulsory (Bocanegra Acosta 2013, 106–7). It was not until Law 56 of 1927 was passed that primary education became compulsory, but even then, many children never attended school (Ramírez and Patricia Téllez 2006). Moreover, there were not enough teachers, resulting in high student–teacher ratios, especially in rural areas. The Organic Law of Education also strengthened the church's role in providing secondary and university education. The church profited handsomely since parochial schools received subsidies from the state and tuition payments from parents (Bocanegra Acosta 2013, 123). By 1920, half of all secondary schools were parochial; the state managed only 40 percent, and the remaining 10 percent were nonreligious private schools. Moreover, the public school curriculum contained religious instruction in the Catholic tradition, while scientific and political books were banned altogether. The Organic Law of Education reflected the interests of Conservative elites in their curricula and in the restriction of access to public education.[7] When considering Mexico and Colombia in comparative perspective, public and private school systems moved in opposite directions in the wake of horrific violence.

The national government's role in education remained limited in the 1920s.[8] In 1928, the national Ministry of Education was founded after the passage of Law 56 of 1927, but its aim was restricted to providing pedagogical materials to schools and setting curricular guidelines (Bocanegra Acosta 2013, 106–7, 125).[9] The departmental (regional) governments had the greatest authority over education policy since they were in charge of hiring and paying teachers, while municipal governments were in charge of building schools. There was confusion among national, departmental, and municipal governments about the roles each had in providing education since officials in each of these government tiers had overlapping policy authority (Ramírez and Patricia Téllez 2006).

In 1929, the Great Depression helped to bring an end to Conservative rule. During the "Liberal Republic" (1934–46) that ensued, the Liberal Party expanded public education, but the public school system remained limited in scope. President Alfonso López Pumarejo (1934–8), a Liberal, adopted a confrontational posture vis-à-vis the Conservative Party (Collier and Collier 1991, 292). To fund new social programs, he raised taxes on income, property, and tobacco. He also mobilized workers and peasants to support his policy agenda, although labor laws and land reforms were much more modest than those of revolutionary Mexico. In other words, addressing social needs was on the political agenda and labor unions were incorporated into the Liberal Party, but the policy changes were far more modest in comparison to countries such as Mexico that experienced full-blown populism.

---

[7] In this period, the lower classes demanded an expansion in public education. In the 1920s, worker organizations demanded *los tres ochos* (the three eights): an eight-hour work day, eight hours of rest, and eight hours of daily education for their children (Collier and Collier 1991, 295–6).
[8] Literacy rates in Colombia remained low well into the twentieth century. For Colombians aged fifteen and older, the literacy rate was 32 percent in 1918, 56 percent in 1938, and only 62 percent in 1951 (Engerman and Sokoloff 2002, 77).
[9] The national government invested little in teacher training and slashed funding during periods of economic downturn. The government developed teacher colleges late; in 1927, it founded the National Pedagogical Institute for Young Women (which became the National Pedagogical University in 1951).

Despite López's efforts, including a constitutional reform in 1936, the education policies adopted by the Conservative Party remained largely in place.[10] To be sure, López expanded the state's role in education. He scaled back religious instruction in public schools, promoted a secular curriculum, and bolstered teacher training (Collier and Collier 1991, 293).[11] Schools could no longer discriminate against students based on religion, race, or family origin. However, in reaction, the church pursued legal actions against the expansion of state-financed public schools and priests condemned public education in sermons. Countermobilization by the church was effective. For example, in the department of Antioquia, church pressure contributed to the closure of several public schools and their replacement with parochial schools.

Even with these reforms, the public school system was rudimentary, and teachers endured precarious working conditions. Teachers in rural schools often possessed only an elementary education. In 1916, 79 percent of teachers did not have teaching degrees, a percentage that decreased only modestly to 72 percent by 1928 (Ramírez and Patricia Téllez 2006). Teacher pay remained low, and the Labor Code of 1939 denied teachers the right to strike. There were informal arrangements to manage teachers. In rural areas, municipal councils made up of the parish priest, mayor, and municipal treasurer supervised teachers, evaluated their moral characters, and disciplined them for offenses such as not attending church services. Low pay for teachers resulted in high turnover, as teachers left the profession to pursue more lucrative careers. Moreover, departmental governments lacked the resources necessary to cover the cost of the teacher payroll. In hard times, governments issued IOUs to teachers or compensated them with bottles of *aguardiente* or cigars, which teachers had to sell in their own time as street vendors. Irregular payments meant that teachers had to survive on credit or other income sources when their salaries were withheld, sometimes for months. Teacher work in Colombia was seen more as a vocation or a calling – a

---

[10] This Constitutional reform guaranteed universal male suffrage and it guaranteed the freedom of religion by excluding all references of Catholicism as the official religion (Bocanegra Acosta 2013, 135).

[11] In his inaugural address, López said: "We don't have elementary and high school teachers because they have to train themselves, and they do so in only a few cases. There is no sustained state effort to train teachers, and there is no initiative to get teachers posted throughout the Republic who know what they teach and how to teach. Our universities are not academic; they are disconnected from the problems and reality of Colombia" (Bocanegra Acosta 2013, 131).

sort of volunteer work that was best suited for women who wanted to bring literacy and religion to poor peasants. It was not recognized as a serious profession.

Despite the weakness of the early teacher movement in Colombia, the refusal to pay teachers on time generated early episodes of labor conflict. For example, in the department of Nariño in 1923, teachers went on strike because salaries were not paid for eight months (Pinilla Diaz 2012, 262). However, labor conflict during the early decades of the twentieth century was low. Between 1930 and 1945, rising inflation eroded teacher salaries, which remained frozen (Bocanegra Acosta 2013, 148). The dearth of national education laws and the weaknesses of teacher organizations, which at this point were only mutual aid societies and professional associations, abetted a school system in which informal, patronage relations flourished. Teachers in Colombia – and elsewhere in Latin America – were referred to as "political apostles" since they were supposed to be motivated by the moral conviction of abolishing illiteracy rather than by a decent salary. Moreover, they owed their position to a political godfather (*padrino politico*) who distributed teaching positions as an act of political largesse.

As new teaching jobs were created, regional political bosses hired teachers based on political connections, especially in rural areas (Duarte 2003; Bocanegra Acosta 2013, 119). Teachers from opposition parties could be transferred to far-flung rural schools, suspended, or laid off, especially after elections brought new parties to power. They faced the vicissitudes of the political business cycle: "[T]eachers were hired en masse at election time, with little or no regard to the availability of funding (far less actual need)" (Lowden 2004, 353). Colombian teachers had no supportive labor regulations to protect them from political interference in personnel decisions.

THE CONSOLIDATION OF NATIONAL ORGANIZATIONS

As mass school systems continued to expand with rising levels of student enrollment, the construction of new schools, and the hiring of more teachers, national teacher organizations began to take shape. They demanded national labor laws for the teaching profession. In the 1940s, national teacher organizations were consolidated in Mexico, Argentina, and Colombia but they developed different organizational structures. These structures can be interpreted in terms of different types of corporatism or different teacher–state relations. In Mexico, the teachers' union followed a state corporatist model and became an extension of the party-state apparatus, with subsidies to the union and labor laws used to control teachers. In other words, the relationship that teachers developed with the state was quite similar to that of peasants and industrial workers. However, in Argentina and Colombia, the political incorporation of teachers did not follow the same pattern as industrial workers. Indeed, whereas industrial workers in both Argentina and Colombia formed alliances with populist or traditional parties, teachers posed an outsider challenge, and they formed labor unions that were oppositional and organized against the state. This section analyzes how these patterns were established.

Mexico: State Corporatism

In Mexico, the ruling party helped to consolidate a single teachers' union, which closely resembled Schmitter's (1974, 105) concept of "state corporatism." The pattern of political incorporation for teachers and industrial workers was quite similar. Official unions were supported by the state, and they developed hierarchical organizations. Middlebrook (1995, 72) notes that labor's alliance with the government hinged on "governments' provision of legal, financial, and political support to an 'official' (state-subsidized) labor movement." In 1936, the Confederation of Mexican Workers (CTM) was founded and became the dominant organization representing workers, although these unions were also a means to control workers and limit demand-making. Teachers, as public sector workers, were not affiliated to the CTM; they were instead affiliated to the National Confederation of Popular Organizations (CNOP).

For teachers, building a corporatist union began in the 1940s. While President Lázaro Cárdenas (1934–40) was the first to sponsor unity congresses, infighting among rival groups of teachers prevented consolidation (Cook 1996, 62). However, the teachers' union established an encompassing organization, and the PRI strengthened a progovernment leadership that purged leftist factions (Cook 1996, 61). Union consolidation finally took place under the more conservative President Manuel Ávila Camacho (1940–46), who brought together the fractious teacher movement.[12] Ávila Camacho marked a sharp break from the Cárdenas period's bold and far-reaching reforms; he took a conciliatory

---

[12] Ávila Camacho is significant in Mexican politics because he institutionalized the PRI as a hegemonic party and shifted policy to the right (Collier and Collier 1991, 407–20).

stance toward the church, reached an agreement with the United States on the expropriation of oil, ended the push for a socialist curriculum, and focused on developmental policies to increase productivity. Both Cárdenas and Camacho wanted to organize workers into national, sectoral organizations – including a single, dominant union that controlled teachers (Arnaut 1998, 233). Ávila Camacho picked up where Cárdenas had left off and finished the job. By creating a strong union, the PRI could delegate responsibilities for governing the education sector to this labor organization and use the education system as a means of political control. The teachers' union was designed to restrain rebellious teachers and enable the PRI to exercise power over society itself.

After negotiations related to the consolidation of a centralized union faltered in the 1930s, Ávila Camacho sponsored new unity congresses and made certain that his education minister, Jaime Torres Bodet, brokered union consolidation. Indeed, on December 30, 1943, rival union leaders announced that they had agreed on a unity pact (Cook 1996, 63). The executive committees of three unions – *Sindicato de Trabajadores de la Educación de la República Mexicana* (STERM), the *Sindicato Único de Trabajadores de la Educación* (SUNTE), and the *Sindicato Mexicano de Maestros y Trabajadores de la Educación* (SMMTE) – formed a single organization comprising all education workers.[13] On January 13, 1944, SNTE received legal recognition (i.e., *personalidad jurídica*), which granted union leaders legal powers. The union consolidated around a national executive committee and two sections per state, one for teachers on the federal payroll and the other for teachers on the state payroll. This consolidation was a landmark step in the union's development.

SNTE became the only officially recognized and legally sanctioned union for education workers. The Secretary of Finance transferred 1 percent of the salary of every teacher directly into the union's coffers (Ornelas 2008, 451). The 1946 Regulations of the General Work Conditions centralized power in SNTE.[14] Although union statutes did not formally affiliate teachers to the PRI, the informal practice known as "uses and customs" (*usos y costumbres*), in which the union was designed as the main authority that decided what teachers would get administrative positions in schools, was used to do just that (Muñoz Armenta 2008). Union leaders had an organic link to this party, and they pressured the rank and

---

[13] SNTE, "Quienes somos," accessed October 6, 2023 via https://snte.org.mx/razon-ser/.
[14] Gilberto Guevara Niebla, "Leyes que sustentan el poder del SNTE," *Nexos* June 1, 2012.

file to follow suit. Union consolidation then served the ruling party by homogenizing the teaching profession and establishing an encompassing organization that exercised strong political control.

The organizational link that connected the union to the ruling party was the dominant faction that controlled SNTE's leadership. As the PRI developed into a hegemonic and highly institutionalized political party, a clique of union leaders seized power and created a new national faction (Cook 1996, 62–4).[15] The secretary general of SNTE, Jesús Robles Martínez (1949–73), was the first leader to build a personalistic following. Like union leaders of other major labor organizations such as that of railroad workers and miners, Robles Martínez became the de facto power broker of the union (i.e., *cacique*) because of his loyalty to the PRI and his support for the party's presidential candidates. In 1952, he supported Adolfo Ruiz Cortines in what would be an especially competitive election within a one-party state. There was relatively more vigorous competition among candidates, and the losing side disputed the election result with protests. While Robles Martínez supported the PRI and its presidential candidates, he also restrained teachers' demands for higher pay. The national union leadership promoted loyal cadres and prevented the infiltration of outside groups. When Robles Martínez stepped down as the Secretary General, he remained the power behind the throne (Cook 1996, 71). Union leaders obtained political positions through his connections. He was widely regarded as the union *cacique*.

In exchange for the union's political support, the PRI gave Robles Martínez resources to purge rivals. In the 1960s, the union changed its statutes, setting strict seniority requirements that restricted access to senior leadership positions (Gindin 2011, 202). Owing to the PRI's support, dissident groups, such as the Revolutionary Teachers' Movement that supported the Communist Party, were relegated to regional strongholds such as Mexico City and Nayarit. Dissidents were excluded from the leadership since union elections took place through closed labor congresses, in which union cadres effectively handpicked their successors.

---

[15] According to Cook (1996, 64): "Robles Martínez blamed the poor conditions for teachers and problems in the union on the ideological conflicts that had been raging within the SNTE. He called for greater central control over union local governments in the states and put an end to the decision-making autonomy of locals and delegations, a holdover from the days when regional organizations were stronger than the center. The new leadership was also much more integrated into national politics and did not question its union's affiliation with or support for the government; involvement in the SNTE leadership came to be seen as a steppingstone on the way to political office."

Thus, SNTE went from an organization of rival factions to one controlled by a personalistic faction that benefited from the political favoritism of the PRI.

Argentina: Resistance to Corporatism

In Argentina, efforts by political elites to build a centralized organization to control teachers failed. Of the three cases, the Argentine teacher movement remained the most fragmented and divided. President Juan Perón was unable to organize teachers because urban teachers had a different profile from industrial workers, in terms of their identity as middle-class professionals, and they rejected his populist movement. Moreover, Argentine union leaders who tried to build a single teacher organization were unable to bring together the fractious movement. Union leaders were further hindered by interludes of military rule, in which the harsh repression of labor organizations forced union activities underground.

After a military coup removed Perón from the presidency in 1955, a divided teachers' movement demanded a teachers' statute and a pay raise (Vazquez 2005, 10). Teachers in many provinces began to protest. In Santa Fe, teachers organized a thirty-seven-day protest in 1957. Teachers won this strike, getting the pay raise they sought, the reimbursement of salaries that had been withheld from them, and the reinstatement of teachers who had been suspended from work because of their role in organizing the strike (Vazquez and Balduzzi 2000, 28). In 1958, teachers in Buenos Aires protested for almost a month and a half (Vazquez and Balduzzi 2000). Teachers demanded a labor code and equal pay for provincial and nationally hired teachers. These protests resulted in a 60 percent pay raise for provincial teachers.

After the coup against Perón in 1955, the opposition party, the UCR, split over whether to ban the PJ or form an alliance with it. President Arturo Frondizi (1958–62) adopted the strategy of seeking to align himself with the Peronist unions by embracing prolabor policies. However, this strategy ultimately failed because the unions remained loyal to Perón. Frondizi also faced pressure from ongoing teacher protests in the provinces to adopt a federal labor code.

In response to regional teacher protests, Frondizi passed the Teacher Statute on September 11, 1958. This labor code granted labor rights to teachers hired by the federal government. There were rules for teacher hiring, a pay scale, cost of living adjustments, guaranteed vacation days, and representation on councils for teacher evaluation and discipline (Perazza 2016, 67–8). Teachers won the right to associate (rather than unionize) and to be referred to as professionals (rather than as workers), marking a different set of labor laws for industrial workers and teachers (Vazquez and Balduzzi 2000). This statute gave teachers the freedom to join any union they wished, which provided the legal basis for multiple unions to represent teachers (Nardacchione 2014, 10). This law protected teachers hired by the federal government from political interference, thereby producing professional autonomy but planting the seeds for a divided teacher movement.[16]

Hence, in contrast to Mexico and Colombia, a sharply divided field of teacher organizations emerged in Argentina. Whereas teachers in Mexico coalesced in SNTE and teachers in Colombia coalesced in FECODE, teachers in Argentina were divided among several autonomous unions.[17] The professional associations of teachers began to operate as de facto labor unions, as teachers sought to draw attention to labor issues. In 1960, various teacher organizations coordinated a national teacher strike. This strike did not sway policymakers, but it did articulate new demands for salary and pension adjustments in line with the Teacher Statute. Even after teachers had won a landmark labor law, governments were often not in compliance with the statutes of this law.

Political developments during the tumultuous 1960s, which was marked by a military junta (1966–73) that had an agenda of economic modernization and social control, contributed to the teacher movement's organizational weakness and oppositional character. During this period, the left made inroads into the teacher movement. There were two main teacher confederations, one resembling a professional association

---

[16] This law also prompted provincial governments to establish labor codes for teachers, which helped to reduce patronage. The struggle for provincial teacher statutes was not easy, especially in traditional rural areas, such as Tucumán. There was considerable variation in the timing of provincial-level labor codes for teachers; in Buenos Aires, a provincial labor code was adopted in 1957, but in Chaco, Tierra del Fuego, and Salta, provincial labor codes for teachers were not adopted until 1990, 1991, and 1995, respectively (Perazza 2016, 129). However, even conservative provinces ultimately adopted teacher statutes. Still, in less-developed provinces, the public sector exhibited patronage politics throughout the 1980s. See "Letter from Menemland," *The Economist* October 6, 1990.

[17] These unions were Confederación Argentina de Maestros y Profesores, Federación Asociación Gremial de la Educación, Comité de Coordinación Intersindical Docente, and Unión Nacional de Educadores (Vazquez and Balduzi 2000; Nardacchione 2014, 10–11).

and the other a labor union.[18] One had more influence in Buenos Aires and the other in the interior provinces. During the Labor Congress of Córdoba (November 1971), a new commission was created to promote a unity congress (Nardacchione 2014, 13). However, there was tension and conflict regarding the timetable and degree of unity among teachers' organizations.

In sum, the development of teacher organizations differed markedly from the more familiar narrative of the Peronist unions in Argentina. Teachers organized multiple labor organizations, and most of these were autonomous from the PJ. There was partisan pluralism and fragmentation among these unions; by the early 1970s, there was no dominant teacher organization. Moreover, interludes of military rule set back efforts to build a strong, consolidated union. In the wake of harsh military rule and labor repression, teachers had to recover lost ground in terms of union organizing. As a result, Argentine teacher organizations were quite weak, especially at the national level, and there was a strong tendency for oppositional behavior.

Colombia: Oppositional Corporatism

In contrast to Mexico, the consolidation of a national teachers' organization in Colombia was more similar to "societal corporatism," in which groups in society organize themselves autonomously with little state control (Schmitter 1974). In Colombia, leftist parties brought the teachers' movement together from below, without state structuring and subsidies. During the 1950s and 1960s, the traditional parties promoted weak and politically dependent unions while ignoring teacher grievances.[19] This neglect enabled left parties to insert themselves into the union movement, establish enduring ties to teachers, and construct a centralized teacher organization through their own organizing initiatives.

In Mexico, the founding of SNTE coincided with the establishment of a one-party state. There was a parallel development in Colombia; the founding of FECODE coincided with that of the National Front regime

---

[18] These two labor organizations were Consejo de Unificación Docente de Acción Gremial and Confederación General de Educadores de la República Argentina.

[19] In the 1950s, the traditional parties sponsored organizations for primary school teachers. Primary and secondary school teachers had different associations (Interview, Bogotá, June 20, 2012). Each department had a union affiliated to the Liberal Party and another affiliated to the Conservative Party. The divisions in the teacher movement made it difficult to achieve unity (Pulido Chaves 2007).

(1958–74). FECODE was established on March 24, 1959. It received its legal registry on August 6, 1962, during the presidency of Alberto Lleras Camargo of the Liberal Party, who sought to support union leaders of the Liberal Party who were in FECODE's leadership. Initially, the union only organized primary school teachers. After a decade of *La Violencia*, a period of open partisan warfare between the Liberal and Conservative parties that left 200,000 dead, the traditional elites negotiated a power-sharing pact, the National Front. The Liberals and Conservatives alternated control over the presidency and divided cabinet positions and gubernatorial appointments to end bloodshed and ease partisan tensions. While partisan violence declined, the primary beneficiaries of this political arrangement were traditional elites; the lower classes – and teachers in particular – had little political representation. The traditional parties remained in power through restrictions on political competition and clientelism, which resulted in broader societal discontent from groups who were effectively excluded from politics (Hartlyn 1988; Buitrago and Dávila 1990).

Teachers mobilized against this exclusionary regime. Initially, FECODE's demands centered on the timely payment of salaries. In 1966, FECODE organized the Hunger March, the first major national mobilization by teachers, with a 600-mile march from the coastal city of Santa Marta to the capital city of Bogotá. These teachers arrived in Bogotá to demand that the president pay the teachers' salaries that were owed (Bocanegra Acosta 2013, 185–7). This protest turned the national political spotlight to the issue of teacher labor relations by demonstrating the abject nature of teachers' working conditions and the neglect thereof by regional authorities. President Carlos Lleras Restrepo (1966–70), from the Liberal Party, was forced to acknowledge the problems of clientelism in teacher hiring and the failure of departmental governments in managing the teachers' payroll. In 1968, President Lleras Restrepo created national transfers, or "regional educational funds" (FER), which guaranteed that departments could cover the costs of the teacher payroll (Gomez Buendia and Losada-Lora 1984, 63, 211).

However, the FER represented only a partial response to teacher grievances, since even with more funding for education, teachers still lacked a national labor code; there were teachers on the national, departmental, and municipal payrolls. Moreover, elementary school teachers were paid less than secondary school teachers. The exclusionary regime refused to fully address teacher demands, with presidents balking at the idea of establishing a national teacher labor code. This refusal set the stage for

FECODE to align with left parties. Initially, Adalberto Carvajal, who was the second president of FECODE (1962–70) and a member of the more progressive wing of the Liberal Party, aimed to become the strongman, or *cacique*, who controlled the union. He was a militant leader who had been imprisoned on multiple occasions for organizing strikes against the wishes of departmental authorities. Carvajal's militancy won him respect among teachers. He developed a cult of personality and began to consolidate power (Gomez Buendia and Losada Lora 1984, 201–2). FECODE seemed poised to tilt in the direction of a national union that mobilized departmental affiliates from the top down.

Yet Carvajal was unable to institutionalize control over the union because he lacked the support of his party. In Colombia, political elites in the Liberal Party refused to support union leaders in FECODE. In 1970, the Liberal Party denied Carvajal a political candidacy. Frustrated by this rejection, he launched his own electoral vehicle, the Movement of Education Action (MODAE), which ran lists of candidates in several departments. However, MODAE was a dramatic failure, electing only one departmental deputy and two city council members; Carvajal's bid for the lower house fell short by eighty-three votes (Bocanegra 2009, 76–7). This defeat weakened Carvajal. In the next Labor Congress of FECODE, he lost his position as president of the teachers' union, and he resigned.

An invigorated group of leftist union leaders replaced Carvajal. The union transitioned to a powersharing arrangement among multiple opposition parties (Gomez Buendia and Losada Lora 1984, 211). In 1970, the eighth National Congress in Santa Marta brought in a new cohort of leaders who radicalized the union (Gomez Buendia and Losada Lora 1984, 104, 212). Barred from participating in elections for public office under the National Front, some leftist partisans took up arms as guerrilla movements; others joined the university student movement and the labor movement. University student leaders and activists found refuge in FECODE (Gomez Buendia and Losada Lora 1984, 197). In 1968, the ten-member national executive committee was made up of seven liberals, two conservatives, and one independent. By 1973, it had two communists, two Maoists, two independent liberals, two Marxist-Leninists, one socialist, and one independent (Gomez Buendia and Losada Lora 1984, 212–13). Partisan pluralism in the national executive committee has remained in place to this day.

There are sharp contrasts between the Colombian and the Mexican experiences with union consolidation. Whereas the Mexican union was structured from above by the ruling party, the Colombian union organized itself from below via opposition parties. Whereas the Mexican union became organized around a dominant faction, the Colombian union became organized around several leftist factions that carved out enclaves of support among teachers. These different processes of union foundation would shape union organizations for decades to come.

TEACHER STRATEGIES IN A CLOSED POLITICAL ENVIRONMENT

During the 1960s and 1970s, when national teachers' organizations were still relatively young, semidemocratic or authoritarian regimes prevented teachers from exercising political rights. The lack of political rights limited the opportunities for teachers to fully participate in politics and develop political strategies. To be sure, the push for mass public education, and the ensuing expansion in school enrollment and teacher hiring, increased the size and political clout of the teaching profession. Teachers were a sector of labor that attracted growing political attention from politicians. Nevertheless, strategies of interest representation during this period involved either subordination to populist parties or outsider mobilization.

Mexico: Partisan Subordination

In Mexico, the teachers' union had considerable resources and a set of favorable labor laws, but the union was dependent on the hegemonic ruling party, the PRI. SNTE was a miniature replica of the regime it supported, both in terms of the procedures it used for selecting union leaders (which were decidedly undemocratic) and in the ways that it operated as an instrument of political control. Union leaders mobilized teachers on behalf of the goals of the one-party state. The union structure was vertical and hierarchical. The PRI delegated authority to SNTE, which was responsible for disciplining teachers and managing labor conflict. A handful of dissident groups remained, but they were constrained by the resources of the official union and they operated only on the margins. As such, teachers had a hard time mobilizing independently and making demands that challenged the regime.

Teacher mobilization during the 1960s and 1970s involved partisan subordination, as it did for other workers in Mexico. Workers – and teachers – were expected to mobilize electoral support for the PRI, regardless of whether the party enacted policies in line with their interests.

Moreover, teachers were particularly important to the PRI because they were dispersed across territory. Teachers had a presence in nearly every far-flung rural community, and they mobilized votes in the communities where they worked. SNTE was a vital cog for the regime because the union was well positioned to help turn out political support through its member base.

In the 1960s, teachers' political clout grew with the expansion of school enrollment. A favorable economic climate from 1959 to 1970 enabled the government to launch the "Eleven Year Plan to Expand and Improve Education." This helped to ensure that the enrollment rate for children aged six to fourteen reached 90 percent; the number of students in public schools increased from 4.9 million in 1959 to 9.3 million in 1970 (INEE 2015, 23). At the same time, SNTE membership increased from 70,000 in 1949 to 180,000 in 1964 and 270,000 in 1971 (Gindin 2011, 202). With a growing member base, SNTE gained political leverage within the ruling party.

But the growth in the teaching profession also posed a threat to governability since governments could not always control teachers. Because of this threat, the ruling party enacted new laws to ensure that union leaders had mechanisms to control the base, especially as the number of public school teachers grew. Federal Law of Service Workers of the State (LFTSE) of 1963 enhanced the power of union leaders over the rank and file by granting union leaders discretionary control over the assignment of teaching positions (Rodríguez 2014, 38–9). The law created Mixed Commissions of the Teacher Salary Scale, in which the union and the SEP each had 50 percent representation. In January of 1980, article 62 of the LFTSE was modified, which enabled the union to decide half of all teacher promotions. Labor law made SNTE leaders partners in governing the education system to prevent labor conflict. However, these laws produced clientelistic relations, as union leaders were responsible for many personnel decisions.

The political control over teachers originated with the influence of union leaders over the education bureaucracy, and thereby over the daily lives of teachers. Teachers remained loyal to SNTE because the union distributed social benefits, resolved labor problems, and advanced careers. For example, the LFTSE generated a parallel and informal marketplace for teaching positions organized through the union. The union assigned half of all teaching positions, and because of this authority over personnel decisions, teachers could buy, sell, and bequeath their salaried teaching positions to next of kin (Rodríguez 2014, 39). As teaching positions were a guaranteed source of income, this system provided an informal system of social protection, an alternative to giving teachers a pension. Aging teachers could ensure that their children continued to earn their salaries, or they could sell their position and retire with the proceeds of the sale. This law made union leaders brokers between buyers and sellers of teaching positions (Gindin 2011, 204). This informal system was rife with corruption, since selling teaching positions created ample opportunities for union leaders to receive bribes, and it was also a powerful way for union leaders to maintain control over teachers.

The linkage between the PRI and SNTE was present in the dominant factions that controlled the union. The union leadership accumulated resources to guarantee labor peace, discipline dissidents, and mobilize teachers as a voting bloc. When union leaders lost support, they were replaced. In 1972, President Luis Echeverría (1970–6) ended the reign of Robles Martínez as the *cacique* of the union. Members of the national executive committee accused the secretary general of SNTE, Carlos Olmos Sánchez – a close ally of Robles Martínez – of signing an agreement with the government without their consent. This accusation was interpreted as a pretext for a new group of leaders to seize power, and President Echeverría replaced Olmos Sánchez with Eloy Benavides Salinas, who was the handpicked successor of the power broker of SNTE Carlos Jonguitud (Cook 1996, 70–3). Jonguitud, who controlled the union from 1972 to 1989, became the "moral leader" of SNTE. He embraced new authoritarian practices that were even harsher than those of his predecessor, Jesús Robles Martínez. He also created his own faction, which he named the Revolutionary Vanguard, in which he concentrated power. This faction gave Jonguitud the capacity to exert influence in the party and to tighten his grip on the union. With this new leadership installed, the ruling party more overtly promoted SNTE for electoral purposes and posted union leaders in the education bureaucracy.[20]

By the 1970s, there were some early signs that the union had the capacity to pursue instrumental alliances. With a dominant faction that controlled most of the union, conflict shifted from ideological differences to personal loyalties to different factions in the PRI (Cook 1996, 66). Union leaders jockeyed for access to state resources, political positions, and other benefits, following different *camarillas* or political factions

---

[20] According to Loyo (2008, 37–8): "Since the seventies and perhaps before, the union leadership used the resources and accumulated experience of the organization as a bargaining chip during elections to get different types of benefits, some of which were personal, others of which were for the whole union."

in the party. SNTE leaders learned how to maneuver within the party, against the backdrop of the shifting fortunes of party factions. In Mexico, strict term limits for the presidency (and all other elected offices as well) meant that union leaders had to prepare to negotiate with new presidents every six years. Hence, SNTE leaders needed to be strategic and develop instrumental alliances within the ruling party, because political careers depended on the ability of union leaders to work with presidents from various PRI factions. However, these instrumental negotiations took place in the constrained environment of a one-party regime. Thus, in Mexico, teacher mobilization could only be directed toward one goal: delivering political support for the PRI.

Argentina: Protest and Political Autonomy

In Argentina, the teachers' movement remained highly fractious, and, unlike in Colombia, it had weak linkages to political parties. Within the teacher movement, there were multiple groups competing for influence. However, the union asserted its autonomy from party politics and refused to align itself with any politician. In the early 1970s, union leaders from opposition parties organized unity congresses without any assistance from the state. The first congress took place in Huerta Grande, Córdoba, in August 1973. The union's declaration of principles emphasized secular, state-provided public education (Nardacchione 2014, 14). In addition, the union "would not admit any type of political activity by parties" in order to "guarantee the absolute separation of union activities from political activities" (Nardacchione 2014, 14). Because of the experience with the PJ's failed efforts to gain control over teachers' organizations, teacher organizations staunchly defended their political autonomy.

The second congress took place in the capital, Buenos Aires, in September 1973. One hundred and forty teachers' organizations from across the country came together. Alfredo Bravo, a militant from the socialist party, played a major part in facilitating the negotiations among rival leaders that resulted in the founding of CTERA. This congress was significant because a national teachers' confederation was established with a degree of teacher unity and because it demonstrated that teachers in Argentina were becoming a larger, more organized political force. In fact, after the return to democracy in 1983, CTERA would become the primary labor organization that represented teachers because it had the largest member base.

In Argentina, since at least the 1950s, protests had been the main way for teachers to articulate their interests. However, before democratization, teacher protesters and union leaders were subject to harsh repression during interludes of military rule. Indeed, periodic coups that brought in military juntas stunted the political development of the teachers' union. The 1973 victory of union consolidation was short-lived. In 1977, the military seized power and began a violent crackdown on labor organizers and leftists. CTERA suffered severe repression. Union leaders faced state terrorism, with more than 600 teachers killed or missing. Others were summarily fired, unlawfully imprisoned, forced into exile, kidnapped, or tortured. The military denied CTERA a legal registry (*personeria gremial*) that would give it a monopoly on the representation of teachers, the right to engage in collective bargaining, and access to state subsidies. During military rule, teachers were banned from assembling and union publications were censored. The union could not collect dues, manage social programs, engage in economic activities, or negotiate with the government (Gindin 2006, 96). As such, the union was forced to operate clandestinely and in a diminished fashion.

Moreover, in 1978, the generals who led the junta forcibly decentralized primary school education. All primary schools were devolved to the provincial governments, with the aim of shrinking the education bureaucracy and controlling national expenditures, in line with the junta's neoliberal policy priorities (Falleti 2010, 79). This decentralization reform was imposed on teachers from above, and there was no increase in federal transfers to the provinces to help cover the added cost to the provincial teacher payroll. This policy went into effect immediately: "[M]ore than 6,500 primary schools, 64,000 teaching and administrative appointments, and almost 900,000 students (about one-third of the total system of primary public education) were transferred to the provinces" (Falleti 2010, 81). This policy was part of a broader austerity package that aimed to shrink the national deficit. Because decentralization was unfunded, meaning that schools were handed off to provincial governments without any additional federal revenues, between 1975 and 1980, 14 percent of public primary schools shut their doors (Falleti 2010, 101). Owing to the authoritarian practices of the military regime, teachers had no effective channels to voice opposition. The teacher movement in Argentina was only beginning to consolidate when it confronted violent repression, imposed decentralization, and steep cuts in education spending.

Colombia: Protest and Opposition Organizing

In Colombia, teachers were subject to repression, and most demands were made reactively, since official channels were unavailable or unresponsive to teachers. In contrast to Mexico, the political environment was more repressive for labor organizations. There was also a dearth of opportunities for left parties to participate in politics. As a result, teachers and left parties had a sort of elective affinity, with both excluded from participating in politics. In the 1970s, leftist groups within FECODE organized protests and engaged in party-organizing activities through the union. They took over the union's national executive committee, which served as a political refuge for political parties that were barred from elections and excluded from state institutions. In addition, the union harbored the political wings of guerrilla groups, which were part of the field of different political expressions of the left. These guerrilla groups, although they were a small minority, also sought to use the union to organize a political base.

Recall that in Mexico in the 1930s and 1940s, Presidents Cárdenas and Ávila Camacho had played a key role in sponsoring unity congresses to help consolidate teachers in SNTE. By contrast, in Colombia, presidents during and after the 1940s largely ignored teachers; it was up to left parties to consolidate a national teacher organization through their own initiatives. While FECODE emerged as the largest teachers' union in Colombia, organizing primary school teachers, other unions that organized teachers at other levels emerged as rivals. However, leftist groups led a major effort to bring together the divided teachers' movement, since these parties had cadres in multiple teacher organizations. Before this unification, left parties had performed poorly in the 1974 election (the year the National Front ended). They then banded together and built broad fronts (Gomez Buendia and Losada Lora 1984, 214). Left parties, relying on hierarchical and centralized party organizations, worked to disband parallel teachers' unions and affiliate all teachers to FECODE. The Pro-China Communist Party, which was known as MOIR, was a central protagonist. Maoist partisans held leadership positions in multiple teacher organizations. A shared partisan identity helped these cadres to negotiate the dissolution of old, redundant unions and the elimination of unnecessary leadership positions (Interview, Bogotá, July 22, 2009). By 1974, leftist organizing contributed to the affiliation of middle, secondary, technical-school teachers, and university instructors (for a time at least) to FECODE, and the elimination of the unions that had formerly represented these levels of instruction (Gomez Buendia and Losada Lora 1984, 202; 214–15).

In a repressive political environment, teachers had few opportunities to participate in politics. When teachers endured labor grievances, protests were the only means to express discontent. During the 1960s and

1970s, these protests often enjoyed widespread support from parents and the broader public. Protests targeted the late payment of salaries, the lack of a national labor code, and the abusive forms of clientelism by traditional politicians. During teacher strikes, parents expressed solidarity with teachers. One union leader described how the parents of students supported teachers:

> We worked with the parents [of the students]. We had the task of connecting the students to the school and organizing them. One task was to mobilize parents when the teachers went on strike. The parents were our collaborators. They participated in the marches, and they helped us to finance the strikes. When we went two or three months without pay, the parents would give us rice, sugar, and potatoes: this was great. Or they would invite us to eat at their homes. (Interview, Bogotá, June 14, 2012)

Protests publicized precarious working conditions and articulated demands for labor laws. However, labor laws prohibited teacher protests, and governments declared them illegal. They cracked down by suspending FECODE's legal registry, which froze union assets and shut down negotiations with the government while withholding salaries for the days spent on strike (Pulido Chaves 2007, 32). Still, government repression provided a short-term solution to the teacher problem, as teacher strikes continued.

By the 1970s, the National Front regime was under stress as candidates from the traditional parties resorted to fraud to win elections. The breakdown of this regime created an opportunity for teachers to assert their demands. In response to a teacher protest in 1971, governments declared the strike illegal and fired dozens of teachers (Bocanegra Acosta 2013). Still, this protest prompted the government to open negotiations on a national teacher labor code in response to growing, large-scale teacher unrest. From 1972 to 1975, FECODE and other teacher organizations mobilized major strikes and demanded that the national government take over the teacher payroll and adopt uniform labor standards for all public school teachers. Between 1968 and 1978, there were 98 teacher strikes, out of a total of 287 strikes by all sectors of labor, indicating a high level of teacher militancy (Gomez Buendia and Losada Lora 1984, 9). President Alfonso López Michelsen (1974–8), who showed some willingness to work with the left, helped FECODE secure a major legislative victory in 1975, when Law 43 made all teachers employees of the national government (Bocanegra Acosta 2013, 204). With this law, the national government took responsibility for financing secondary education (Duarte 1998, 134). This law was the product of recurrent teacher protests throughout the 1970s.

Negotiating a national labor code was a protracted process. While negotiations had started under President López Michelsen, ironically it was President Julio César Turbay (1978–82), who generally took a repressive stance toward labor and protest, who ultimately signed the Teacher Statute in 1979. The Teacher Statute was a landmark labor law that set national standards for teacher hiring (i.e., having a teaching degree), promotion (i.e., a pay scale with clear criteria for professional ascension), and tenure (i.e., a disciplinary code that laid out when teachers could be fired, but also included guarantees of employment stability). In addition, it extended pension benefits and social insurance to all Colombian teachers (Rodríguez 2002, 234–5; Bocanegra Acosta 2013, 203). Like teacher statutes in other countries, this law protected teachers from clientelism and professionalized teachers by prohibiting hiring based on political discretion. It also established well-defined rules for teacher pay and promotion, with incentives for teachers to pursue more training. FECODE has claimed that the government only adopted this law because of pressure from protests and strikes that the union organized. Union leaders argued that the pay scale helped teachers to improve not only their salaries but also their status as professional educators.

This 1979 legislative victory strengthened the union as an organization and protected teachers' political rights. Newly hired teachers were affiliated to FECODE, union dues were deducted, and FECODE became the only union that represented public school teachers. The Teacher Statute allowed teachers to exercise political rights and vote for whatever party they chose, since it protected against political patronage – before this labor code was enacted, incoming governments would fire teachers who were from opposing parties. Still, even with this labor law, teachers could vote only for a restricted set of political options because of the National Front. Many teachers had begun to identify with left parties because of the exclusionary, conservative regime. The teacher's oppositional, left-leaning orientation would carry over into the contemporary period.

CONCLUSION

The origins of teachers' unions are important in understanding why distinct political strategies developed for teachers in these three countries. This chapter has argued that the founding moment of teachers' unions helped to set the stage for the transformation of teacher politics that would subsequently take shape in the aftermath of the debt crisis and regime openings in the 1980s and 1990s. There are important continuities.

The corporatist legacy in Mexico and the persistence of national teacher organizations in Argentina and Colombia demonstrate the significance of legacies of union founding. It would be a mistake to overlook the divergence that was already in place by the 1960s and 1970s.

And yet historical legacies are not the only storyline of this book. The following chapters will show that institutional and policy changes in the 1980s and 1990s led to transformations in the organizational structures and political strategies of teachers' organizations in all three countries. The shock of the debt crisis and tumult from regime openings created a moment of uncertainty when teachers' unions seemed poised to transform their organizations and shift paths.

In analyzing the development trajectories of teacher organizations, this chapter debunks myths about the relationship between mass public education and teachers' unions. First, church–state conflict did not determine the trajectory of union development. To be sure, in Mexico the anticlerical position of the revolutionary regime helped to push for the mass expansion of public education and the creation of a powerful teachers' union. The political challenge posed by the church prompted revolutionary leaders to adopt a socialist curriculum, rapidly expand public education, and create a strong, corporatist teacher organization to control the expanding teaching profession. But in Argentina and Colombia, church–state relations had a less discernible effect on the development of teachers' unions. In Argentina, the church faced liberal reforms earliest, in the late nineteenth century, and Argentine reformist presidents expanded public education the fastest in the region. And yet, despite this early expansion of schooling and mass hiring of teachers, teachers' unions were weak and fragmented in that country. In Colombia, the church maintained a vast network of parochial schools for a long time; the Conservative Party's hold on power for much of the twentieth century slowed or even blocked liberal reforms that would open the door to secular public education. And yet the power of the church did not ultimately prevent the state from expanding mass public education, nor did it prevent a strong teachers' organization from being established. Robust teachers' unions were born in both inclusive, revolutionary regimes and exclusionary, conservative regimes.

This chapter also highlights the contrasting pattern of political incorporation for industrial workers versus teachers. In Mexico, which had an encompassing populist party that organized workers in all sectors, the pattern of worker and teacher incorporation was most similar. Still, it is important to note that teachers were affiliated to CNOP and not CTM. In other words, even though teachers were treated similarly to other workers in these three cases, even in Mexico there was a differentiation of teachers from industrial workers. In Argentina, labor in general was relatively autonomous from the state, with active mobilization and protest by various sectors, including teachers. However, this chapter has demonstrated that teachers were not connected to the PJ in the same way as other workers. Indeed, in Argentina and Colombia, teachers' unions developed much later than industrial worker organizations. They also differed in terms of partisan identities. In Argentina, workers generally supported the PJ, but teachers did not. They instead exhibited a strong tendency to assert their autonomy from party politics. In Colombia workers were generally affiliated to the traditional parties, but teachers were more aligned with the left. Blue-collar unions formed in the wake of the transition from an agrarian to an industrial economy, teachers' unions formed in the wake of mass public school systems, and these systems developed at different historical moments, depending on the aims of the regimes that pushed for public school expansion. The story of teacher incorporation differs from the account of worker incorporation in Collier and Collier's (1991) *Shaping the Political Arena*, and it is remarkable how differently teachers were treated than blue-collar workers.

A related thread in this chapter is that teachers struggled for labor codes and professional autonomy in all three cases. These labor struggles took different forms. Teachers in Mexico achieved labor laws for teachers the earliest, although these were partly a means to shore up the union leadership and control teachers politically. Ironically, labor laws in Mexico, rather than protecting education workers from abuses by politicians, opened the door for union leaders to become political bosses. Teachers achieved labor codes in Argentina in the 1950s. There were also provincial labor codes in Argentina, since the school system was more decentralized. Finally, teachers obtained labor codes quite late in Colombia, in the late 1970s. In all three cases, teacher labor struggles were protracted, often spanning decades, and teachers encountered political leaders who responded quite differently to demands for rules governing teacher hiring, promotion, and tenure.

The inequities of patronage politics in public schools and the education bureaucracy is another theme in this chapter. Patronage politics were a major issue for teachers in all three countries. And yet teachers' unions developed quite different relations to it. In Mexico, because of SNTE's close ties to the one-party state, clientelism became the modus operandi for SNTE. Patronage politics, clientelism, and political favoritism were a fact of life for teachers in Mexico since the revolution. Although Chapter 4 discusses how the more predatory clientelistic practices of Carlos Jonguitud generated resistance in the 1970s and 1980s, in general clientelism was used as an efficient and effective means to control dissident teachers. SNTE was a well-oiled political machine that was not prone to breaking down.

Argentina is a fascinating case that deserves more research because many analysts have noted that clientelism and patronage politics abound in the public administration, and yet little has been written about patronage politics in the education sector. There are, however, strong hints of provincial-level clientelism, especially in the poorer interior provinces. Alfredo Bravo described the Teacher Statute of 1958 as aiming to protect teachers from political favoritism. There are anecdotal accounts of malapportionment of teachers and patronage politics in public schools in the province of La Rioja, although these accounts fall short of definitive evidence.[21] What is clear is that within this context of widespread patronage, CTERA was an outsider union, like FECODE in Colombia, and it largely stayed out of regional political machine politics. Still, there is some evidence that in small provinces, such as Misiones, union leaders were able to leverage public sector jobs for political gain.

In Colombia, the union's exclusion from the National Front and its association with the opposition meant that it mobilized against clientelism. Teacher demands and protests for the Teacher Statute of 1979 stemmed from grievances related to patronage and clientelism, which was associated with regional political leaders who were from the Liberal or Conservative parties. The union, which had a leftist leadership, was not involved in clientelism. The Teacher Labor Code aimed to set rules for teacher hiring and promotion, so these were not based on political clientelism. It is important to note, however, that clientelistic practices did not go away completely in Colombia after 1979. Duarte (1998) notes that in rural departments in Colombia there were ways of using educational resources for clientelistic purposes, notably in the hiring of temporary teachers by department and municipal governments to keep schools fully staffed. My account of the different ways that teachers' unions were founded in part echoes Shefter's (1977) account of the difference between externally versus internally mobilized parties and their propensity to enact patronage politics or programmatic policy.

---

[21] See "Letter from Menemland." *The Economist* October 6, 1990.

Finally, this chapter has shown that restrictions on the political rights of teachers under nondemocratic regimes constrained mobilization. In Mexico, the one-party state forced teachers to vote for the PRI. Teachers were not supposed to vote for other parties, and other parties did not have a real chance of winning until the late 1980s. Teachers who decided to protest or align themselves with opposition parties routinely faced retaliation by union leaders who could transfer them to far-flung rural schools or block access to promotions and other benefits. Clientelism through the union was the primary way in which teacher rights were violated. In Argentina, teachers had to deal with military juntas, which severely cracked down on teachers. Indeed, repressive authoritarian rule in Argentina set back union organizing initiatives much more than the one-party state in Mexico or the consociational regime in Colombia. In all three countries, it would take democracy to enable teachers to fully express their political interests and mobilize in ways that were unconstrained. In Colombia, there was also clientelism, but it was organized around regional party bosses rather than through the union. Teachers had the right to vote, but there were obstacles to teachers becoming political candidates, and the only parties that teachers could vote for were the Liberals and Conservatives. Colombia was a consociational regime rather than full-blown authoritarianism, but teachers had limited options in terms of their political participation. There were also restrictions on strikes, with teachers who participated in them losing their jobs, going to jail, or being removed from their union leadership positions.

4

Organizational Consolidation in Mexico

Mexico has a teachers' union that became extremely hierarchical with a low level of factional competition. In this chapter and in Chapter 5, I argue that this organizational structure is most helpful in explaining the political strategy of SNTE, in which the union exchanged contingent support with various political parties for particularistic benefits. When the national organization tightly controls union locals, which in turn control the rank and file, the national leadership can shift positions quickly without having to worry about the reactions of its members or rival factions. The most spectacular illustration of this autonomy occurred in 2005, when the teachers' union broke its historic alliance with the PRI and entered into an alliance with the conservative PAN.

This chapter analyzes the organizational prerequisites for this strategy by charting changes in SNTE's organizational structure in the 1980s and 1990s. The consolidated organization of SNTE has its origins in the founding of the union in 1943–4, when it was integrated into the populist regime as a corporatist entity that delivered political support for the ruling party. For decades, national union leaders accumulated state resources and organizational benefits, which they used to build a dominant faction. This can be defined as a cohesive leadership that controls the national executive committee and the majority of the union locals, holding power for long periods of time. However, this corporatist organization of SNTE entered into crisis in the 1980s, when teachers experienced hardship from the debt crisis, but union leaders and the ruling party refused to voice teacher grievances. This lack of responsiveness to teachers generated a powerful dissident teacher movement that demanded a democratic political regime and a democratic union. Moreover, there was debate among policymakers about whether to push through a far-reaching decentralization reform that would break up the union or accommodate the union leadership and maintain policymaking authority at the federal level. By 1989, the union faced a moment of uncertainty. Meaningful change in the direction of shifting power from the union's national executive committee to the union locals and establishing a more democratic national union seemed possible.

However, a break with the corporatist model never happened. Policy decisions in the early 1990s by President Carlos Salinas de Gortari to address the labor grievances of teachers and shore up the union's national structure enabled a new group of union leaders to consolidate power. President Salinas decided to remove the old, corrupt union leadership. But at the same time, he supported an education reform package that kept the national organization of the teachers' union intact and compensated SNTE with new subsidies. These decisions paved the way for a new dominant faction led by Elba Esther Gordillo to take power. This faction, called the "hegemonic" or "institutional" group, reestablished hierarchical relations with teachers and gained full control over the national executive committee. Gordillo and her allies effectively demobilized and marginalized the dissidents, maintained the union's bureaucratic structure, and foreclosed the possibility for union democracy.

The opening sections of this chapter examine the threats to the corporatist model posed by the dissident movement and the regime response to help the union leadership regain control over the rank and file. President Salinas sheltered the union from the potentially disruptive effects of education decentralization policies and strengthened SNTE with policies to address teacher grievances. These concessions shaped the union's internal organization, providing the resources Elba Esther Gordillo needed to demobilize restive union locals and build a dominant faction that was more powerful than that of her predecessor, Carlos Jonguitud. The consolidation of power in the national union leadership was crucial for the strategy of instrumentalism.

THE DISSIDENT CHALLENGE

In the late 1970s, SNTE was controlled by the dominant faction of Carlos Jonguitud, Revolutionary Vanguard. Through this faction, the union had an organic link to the ruling party, the PRI. The union leader delivered teachers as a voting bloc to the party while controlling labor unrest by dissident groups, and in exchange the party granted him political candidacies and patronage positions to award to his allies. The teachers' union resembled other Mexican labor unions, such as the oil workers and social security workers, in terms of subservience to the ruling party and restraint in demand-making due to the corporatist mechanisms of control. However, because of its large member base and territorial extension, SNTE had organizational features that made it a "singular" labor organization in Latin America (Bensusán and Tapia 2011; Gindin 2011). SNTE was becoming bigger and more strategically important than other labor organizations.

While historical legacies had enduring consequences for the organizational structure of the union, the 1980s was a period of disruption and discontinuity. The debt crisis eroded the authoritarian regime and weakened the teachers' union. To stabilize the economy, President Miguel de la Madrid (1982–8) was forced to impose austerity measures on public spending, including education, after Mexico defaulted on its debt in 1982. There was a freeze on increases in teacher pay – even when inflation eroded purchasing power. President de la Madrid relied on SNTE leaders Carlos Jonguitud and his allies in the Revolutionary Vanguard faction to restrain the demands of the base. But with growing discontent, the oligarchic and bureaucratic leadership of SNTE lost control of rank-and-file teachers. At the same time, a rift emerged between technocrats in the SEP and Carlos Jonguitud over the union's influence in the education bureaucracy, and this rift created an opening for activist teachers to challenge the official union leadership (Cook 1996, 59–104).

The political and economic changes sparked a robust dissident teacher movement, the CNTE. This movement articulated teacher labor grievances and demanded democratic political reforms. Even before the economic crisis, in 1979, CNTE called for an end to the austerity measures imposed on education spending and also for democratic changes to the union itself (Foweraker 1993; Cook 1996). The head of SNTE, Carlos Jonguitud, faced a rebellion by teachers in several states in southern Mexico. While Jonguitud and his allies threatened to punish teachers who participated in protests by stalling professional advancement, transferring them to undesirable schools, and blocking access to social welfare benefits, these threats failed to stem the unrest owing to the deep discontent with the union leadership. Indeed, dissident protests spread throughout the country as teachers brazenly defied the union leadership.

Dissident teachers voiced economic grievances. President Miguel de la Madrid (1982–8), facing high inflation and negative economic growth, imposed harsh austerity measures on social spending. Teacher salaries declined precipitously and were often paid late. From 1982 to 1989, the average teacher salary declined from 2.5 times the minimum wage to 1.3, a decline of 52 percent in only seven years (Raphael 2007, 43). There was also a hiring freeze (INEE 2015, 22). Abysmal working conditions forced teachers to retire early or leave the profession to become taxi drivers, truck drivers, waiters, and informal sector workers (Raphael 2007, 129). As teachers' salaries declined, and teachers had to leave the profession or take a second job to supplement their income, the profession's prestige declined as well. According to one ex-union leader (Interview, Mexico City, March 25, 2012), teachers resented the union's failure to defend their interests: "After 1982 teacher salaries and bonuses fell and they were only a little bit more than the minimum wage … The union leadership [of Jonguitud] was more worried about getting political positions, and it neglected the issue of teacher salaries."

While teachers endured economic hardship, union leaders enjoyed conspicuous privileges. The growing gap between the standard of living of union leaders and the rank and file fueled discontent. The excesses of the union leadership, specifically the accessing of union coffers for personal consumption, were well documented. For instance, on July 12, 1987, the secretary general of SNTE, Antonio Jaimes Aguilar, used union funds for his daughter's *quinceañera* at a hotel in Michoacán, with 2,000 guests in attendance – including Carlos Jonguitud and the governor of that state.[1] The union also funded the political party that was imposing harsh austerity measures on teachers. On November 10, 1987, Carlos Jonguitud made a large contribution from the salaries of ordinary teachers to the presidential campaign of Carlos Salinas (Raphael 2007, 44–5). These episodes outraged teachers who had endured economic hardship, and they increasingly rejected union leaders who used the teachers' organization to pursue their own personal interests.

In addition to demands for better pay, dissident protests also called for union democracy. Union leaders violated teachers' rights. Teachers were automatically affiliated to the PRI and compelled to vote for the ruling party, even when this party did not respond to their labor demands. Moreover, the overwhelmingly male cadres of union leaders in Carlos Jonguitud's Revolutionary Vanguard faction were routinely accused of sexually harassing and assaulting female teachers who desperately

---

[1] In many Latin American countries, a *quinceañera* is a celebration of a girl's fifteenth birthday, marking entry into womanhood. Festivities often include a large gathering of friends and family. See "El Snte pago la fiesta de la hija de us lider," *Proceso* 1987.

needed help in resolving workplace problems (Cortina 1990). Teachers lacked legal recourse to counter these abuses. Such violations fueled anger against Jonguitud and demands to transform the union's authoritarian structure. Like the teacher movements that emerged in the 1980s against military regimes in Argentina, Brazil, Chile, and Peru, teacher protests in Mexico increasingly symbolized the struggles of ordinary citizens against autocratic rule and garnered widespread public sympathy.

Despite the harsh crackdown on teacher protests, repression failed. Governors deployed police against protesting teachers, and dissident leaders were arrested and imprisoned. Some teachers who were involved in the dissident movement, CNTE, were summarily fired. Others faced threats or acts of violence, since the dissident teacher movement sparked a "dirty war" within the union (Solano 2009, 98). For instance, on January 30, 1981, Misael Núñez Acosta, a dissident leader, was assassinated allegedly at the order of the official union leadership. However, with the regime crackdown, cycles of protests ramped up (Foweraker 1993; Cook 1996, 19). The killing of Núñez Acosta made him a martyr and a symbol of resistance, and his murder prompted solidarity protests in multiple states, including the State of Mexico, Guerrero, and Hidalgo (Solano 2009, 100). By the mid-1980s, Jonguitud had lost control over the protests. For example, in the states of Oaxaca and Chiapas, activist teachers mobilized against local union bosses who were not responsive to rank-and-file demands to push for higher teacher pay. The activists in those states were strong enough to win power in the local executive committee of these union sections and gain legal recognition for their victories (Cook 1996, 114–15). The dissidents expanded their influence into Oaxaca, Guerrero, Michoacán, the State of Mexico, Morelos, Hidalgo, and Mexico City.

With protests mounting, prominent leaders in the PRI saw Jonguitud as a liability since he exacerbated teacher discontent. Protests reached their peak in April 1989 when 500,000 teachers mobilized in Mexico City (Cook 1996, 316–19). As unrest threatened public order, President Carlos Salinas de Gortari (1988–94), the newly elected president, summoned Jonguitud to his office and asked him to step down. Salinas then named his replacement, Elba Esther Gordillo, who was at that time a relatively unknown union leader. Dissident teachers claimed credit for achieving a major victory, exerting pressure from below and forcing the regime to change the union leadership.

Still, the removal of Jonguitud did not resolve the crisis. On the contrary, leadership turmoil created hope for more transformative changes in the union's internal structure. The dissident movement disrupted the hierarchical relations that had afforded union leaders a tight grip on teachers, driving a wedge between the national leadership and the rank and file. Facing bottom-up mobilization and divided loyalties among union leaders, Elba Esther Gordillo was initially in a weak position. In 1989, she promised democratic changes to union statutes and acknowledged the legitimacy of the dissidents' demands for representation in SNTE's national executive committee (Ornelas 2012, 39). At the same time, Gordillo faced challenges from regional union bosses in several states who remained loyal to Carlos Jonguitud, even after his ouster, and plotted against the new leader (Cook 1996, 270). Facing challenges from both the dissidents and the entrenched old guard, Gordillo promised to usher in a new era of partisan pluralism and power-sharing. She promised to dismantle the old power structures in the union and bring about democratic changes.

PRESIDENT SALINAS' DECISION TO SHORE UP THE TEACHERS' UNION

During the period from 1989 to 1992, Elba Esther Gordillo, the recently anointed secretary general of SNTE, faced challenges on several fronts. The dissident teacher movement demanded union democracy, but the allies of Jonguitud were unwilling to pledge their loyalty to the new leader. Moreover, a far-reaching education decentralization reform threatened to fragment the union's organization. Indeed, there was a debate between President Salinas and his advisors about reforming education and what to do about the teachers' union. This period was marked by uncertainty and fluidity for Mexico, with widespread economic and political changes taking place that could have major consequences for what the union looked like and how it operated.

In 1989, in the wake of Jonguitud's removal, an emboldened group of technocrats proposed an ambitious decentralization reform. While Jonguitud had staunchly resisted policies that would decentralize decision-making authority within the Mexican public school system, his removal created hope that these policies would move forward. The technocrats proposed giving state governments a greater role in financing education, managing public schools, and making personnel decisions. Beyond managerial advantages, Secretary of Education Manuel Bartlett, a career politician who was a dogged reformer, argued for fragmenting the power structure of SNTE by fully decentralizing education to the state level. Since the founding of SNTE, a national system of collective bargaining for teachers had been in place. If collective bargaining took place at the state level, SNTE would effectively be broken into thirty-one small, politically weak unions.

President Salinas considered this proposal. It had an affinity with the market-oriented economic reforms he had supported for privatizing state-owned enterprises, even when these reforms generated opposition from organized labor. Indeed, while the austerity policies adopted by Miguel de la Madrid in the 1980s undermined organized labor, President Salinas went further and forced neoliberal economic reforms on unions in various industries. When privatizing state-owned enterprises in industries (e.g., telecommunications, television stations, banking, aviation, and mining), the government used coercive strategies, such as the elimination of labor contracts, forced bankruptcy and restructuring, and even the jailing of union leaders. In 1989, President Salinas ordered the military to arrest the powerful leader of the oil workers union, Joaquín Hernández Galicia, "La Quina." Other unions were pressured to negotiate the terms of more flexible policies for workers, which resulted in workforce reductions and less favorable labor contracts (Williams 2001).

A far-reaching education decentralization reform brought political risk, however. It might unleash a revitalized dissident teacher movement, which could capitalize on rank-and-file opposition to decentralization and produce a new round of disruptive protests. After the contested (i.e., stolen) election of 1988, in which Salinas had only won the presidency by resorting to thinly disguised fraud, with the PRI losing support among workers and peasants, the president wanted to shore up his party's political base. At the same time, President Salinas was negotiating concessions with the opposition to establish a federal electoral tribunal, the Federal Electoral Institute, which oversaw and certified the integrity of elections (Magaloni 2006, 241). In this context of declining support for the PRI and greater electoral oversight, Salinas considered another approach. By strengthening the position of Elba Esther Gordillo, who was a political ally, Salinas could simultaneously weaken the dissident teacher movement and strengthen teacher support for the PRI in the midterm elections of 1991 (Grindle 2004a, 66).[2]

---

[2] Grindle (2004a, 66) notes: "With congressional elections looming in 1991, the president was well-advised not to insist on a change that would further annoy the union. Its votes were needed."

Ultimately, President Salinas chose to enact new policies to shore up the teachers' union. Salinas removed Manuel Bartlett as Secretary of Education and appointed Ernesto Zedillo in his place since Zedillo promised a more conciliatory approach toward negotiations with the teachers' union. Salinas also jettisoned Bartlett's proposal for an ambitious decentralization reform. A close alliance between the teachers' union and the Salinas administration ensued. President Salinas supported a watered-down version of decentralization, with concessions to SNTE. In 1992, the government and the teachers' union signed the National Agreement for the Modernization of Basic Education. This agreement accommodated the union: Falleti (2010, 202) describes this agreement as the product of a "national-level (ruling) coalition formed by the national executive and the leadership of the national teachers' union." State governments were given relatively limited authority over education policy decisions; their primary role was hiring teachers and managing the teacher payroll. The most important policy domains remained at the federal level, notably control over the funding of education and teacher labor policy.[3]

This agreement laid the groundwork for the union to not only maintain but also rebuild and strengthen its centralized organizational structure. Crucially, it left in place the laws and institutions that established national teacher labor rights and national-level collective bargaining (Murillo 2001; Falleti 2010, 202–3; Ornelas 2012). These labor laws and institutions reinforced the union's organizational structure because teachers continued to be automatically affiliated to the union and national union leaders remained the central figures negotiating policy changes and salary adjustments. Decentralization did not change the automatic transfer of union dues from teacher salaries directly into SNTE's national executive committee's coffers. Although local union leaders negotiated adjustments to fringe benefits and salary bonuses with governors, these negotiations were less important than the national negotiations over base salary. Since national union leaders had discretion over the allocation of union resources and could withhold them from union locals, hierarchical relations remained in place. Maintaining key policy decisions at the national level helped national union leaders remain the highest-profile figures in SNTE.

While reinforcing the union's national structure, President Salinas simultaneously prioritized addressing the labor grievances that had energized the dissidents. With an improving economic picture in 1989, the

---

[3] The policy was called "federalization" rather than "decentralization"; see Falleti (2010, 188–230).

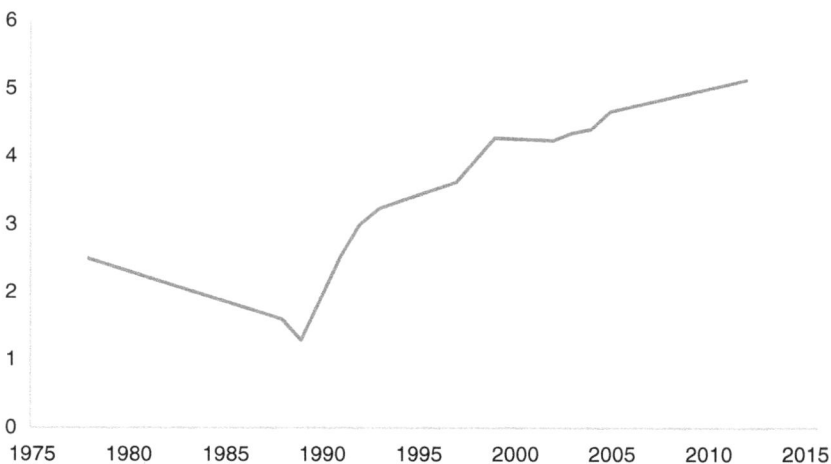

FIGURE 4.1 Starting teacher salary in minimum wages, Mexico
Sources: Wenceslao.com.mx, "Incrementos salariales porcentuales del SNTE," accessed February 24, 2023 via www.wenceslao.com.mx/snte32/salarios.htm

government had the revenue to reinvest in public education. In this context, Elba Esther Gordillo negotiated large increases in teachers' salaries with President Salinas' support (Cook 1996, 274). Figure 4.1 shows that teachers' salaries declined by 50 percent between 1982 and 1989 as a result of the impact of austerity measures on education budgets. Salaries recovered between 1989 and 1991, and as salaries improved by 150 percent, Gordillo and her allies claimed credit for delivering benefits to teachers. This credit claiming undermined support for dissident groups: "[A] strong economy and significant annual wage increases for teachers between 1989 and 1991 reduced discontent among the dissidents" (Hecock 2014, 67). Figure 4.1 shows that teacher salaries continued to rise steadily throughout the 1990s and 2000s, making strong gains against the minimum wage, which was the benchmark for measuring teacher salaries. Rising salaries yielded a windfall in union dues. By restoring teacher salaries, the government strengthened the union's national executive committee, as the state automatically transferred 1 percent of teachers' salaries into its coffers. The national executive committee had discretionary control over how union monies were spent.[4]

---

[4] INEE (2015, 76) estimates that in 2012 teachers earned 88–94 percent as much as other professionals; Elacqua et al. (2018, 20) find that teachers in Mexico earned 83 percent as much as other professionals for 2014–15, more than their counterparts in Ecuador, Chile, Peru, and Brazil.

Overall, from 1988 to 2012, starting teacher salaries increased from 1.6 of the minimum wage to 5.12, a dramatic increase.

The PRI also shored up SNTE by granting generous subsidies to the union leadership. In exchange for endorsing the 1992 National Agreement for the Modernization of Basic Education, the PRI gave SNTE leaders influence over a salary bonus program for teachers called Carrera Magisterial. This program purported to pay teachers a bonus based on professional merit, and these bonuses were large and permanent.[5] However, this program became highly politicized (Hecock 2014). It was governed by "mixed-commissions" composed of half union leaders and half officials from the SEP. Union leaders had discretion in deciding which teachers would receive these bonuses, and they used this discretion to reward political loyalty (Ortiz Jimenez 2003). Union leaders also used this program to punish dissident teachers and other would-be defectors by preventing them from gaining access to these benefits (Rodríguez 2014, 112).

Other subsidies improved teacher compensation and strengthened the union leadership. There were cost-of-living adjustments (*rezonificación*) for teachers who worked in large cities where basic goods were more expensive than in other parts of the country. These bonuses could amount to 40, 60, or even 100 percent of the base salary.[6] President Salinas also authorized the Teacher Affordable Housing Fund (Vivienda Magisterial, VIMA) on March 27, 1990. This fund provided low-interest, long-term loans to build housing for teachers. This fund received massive infusions of capital from President Salinas (as he was leaving office) and later from President Zedillo (also as he was leaving office). An audit report in 2002 showed that VIMA was used to funnel money to union leaders and their families.[7]

Finally, several initiatives that Elba Esther Gordillo and her allies wanted to launch were readily subsidized. SNTE secured land, property, and funds for union events. From 1989 to 1994, the federal and state governments donated, transferred, and offered long-term leases on land, buildings, and facilities to SNTE worth an estimated 2.8 billion Mexican

---

[5] Teachers who achieved the first level of the Carrera Magisterial program received 25 percent more than the base salary for teachers; those who reached highest level earned nearly 300 percent more (McEwan and Santibáñez 2005).

[6] The union leadership negotiated an expansion of cost-of-living adjustments to a large number of cities and states, even in the states of Oaxaca and Chiapas, where the cost of living was not as expensive as it was in large cities (Raphael 2007, 129–30).

[7] When the director of this program, Benjamín González Roaro, a close ally of Gordillo, stepped down, the fund was heavily indebted. Ultimately, VIMA became a symbol of union corruption (Raphael 2007, 131).

pesos (Raphael 2007, 238).[8] The Salinas administration also granted funds for SNTE to organize labor congresses, seminars, and events to strengthen the union organization.

In sum, the period from 1989 to 1993 was a turning point. As Mexico undertook bold reforms to the state and the economy, major changes to the union seemed imminent. Mexico also began its gradual path toward democratization, as cracks appeared in the dominant party regime. Against this backdrop, President Salinas made a political decision to reinforce the top-down model of unionism for teachers by empowering his ally, Elba Esther Gordillo, with subsidies. While Gordillo took over a union in crisis, the National Agreement for the Modernization of Basic Education paved the way for her to build a strong national leadership.

CONSOLIDATING A NEW DOMINANT FACTION

Gordillo took advantage of the influx of state resources and her popularity among rank-and-file teachers to build a new dominant faction. This became known as the "hegemonic" or "institutional" group (Ornelas 2012, 30). It gained undisputed control over the national executive committee and strongly influenced most of the union sections that operated in the states. This faction was organized around a core group of national leaders who made decisions and many operators, or staff, on the payroll of the national union leadership who carried out orders. Gordillo's status rose, and she became known as the boss (*cacique*) of the union.

Power consolidation took place in a series of steps. The first step was to make cosmetic changes so that the union appeared more democratic. In 1989, Gordillo paid lip service to the demands of the dissidents and invited several dissident leaders to serve on the national executive committee. She also condemned sexual abuse by the outgoing union leaders and recruited more women to serve in leadership positions. She changed union statutes to recognize political pluralism and the right of teachers to vote for any party.[9] In public, she distanced herself from the authoritarian

---

[8] The union was given modern buildings, including the Portal del Sol, the Library of the Teacher in Mexico City, and various resorts and hotels for teachers. President Salinas also subsidized SNTE's department stores and pharmacies. Moreover, the state subsidized the Fundación SNTE para la Cultura del Maestro, which was SNTE's think tank used to generate ideas for new education reforms (Raphael 2007, 238).

[9] Gordillo defended "freedom of partisanship," but she did so in a way that had a double meaning. Political rights meant that ordinary teachers were free to vote with their

practices of her predecessor, Carlos Jonguitud. As Mexico began its protracted transition to democracy and an open-market economy, symbolic changes made the union appear to be making reforms that were consistent with the times.

The second step was to weaken and undermine the dissidents. Gordillo devised a shrewd set of divide-and-rule strategies. The dominant faction incorporated some currents of the dissidents into its political organization. In 1989, Gordillo proposed a new broad front "that would incorporate the various currents found within the union" (Cook 1996, 274). This enabled Gordillo to establish allies among some dissident currents while she isolated currents that opposed her. Gordillo negotiated selectively with dissident leaders to fragment the dissident movement.

As the dominant faction coalesced, more divisions emerged among the dissidents, and Gordillo took advantage of these divisions. The dominant faction coopted charismatic dissident leaders. One particularly salient example is Blanca Luna, a dissident leader from Mexico City. In 1999, Luna led an occupation of the national union headquarters, protesting against the official leadership. After she was arrested and sent to jail, she engaged in marathon negotiations with Gordillo. Almost overnight, she was converted into a staunch loyalist, and Gordillo advanced her career in the union and in politics. Besides Luna, other dissident leaders who joined Gordillo included Rosendo Galíndez, Juan González, Joel Vicente, and leaders from the group New Unionism (Interview, August 22, 2012).[10] The dissident movement was thus vulnerable to divide-and-conquer strategies, as joining the dominant faction enabled rising dissident leaders to advance their careers.

The third step for Gordillo was to eliminate rivals in the national executive committee. In 1995, when Gordillo stepped down from the position of secretary general, her control over the union appeared tenuous.

---

conscience but also that union leaders had the right to support whatever party they chose, even if that was the PRI (Raphael 2007, 108). In other words, "freedom of partisanship" did not necessarily mean that SNTE would shift its support away from the PRI. In 1992, Gordillo founded the National Committee for Political Action (CNAP) in SNTE, which purported to provide campaign finance to teachers who ran for public office and invited presidential candidates to present their education platforms to the union. While CNAP symbolically ended old-style corporatist practices, Gordillo gradually weakened it and developed parallel structures to mobilize votes.

[10] A small faction that hailed from the left of the ideological spectrum, New Unionism (*Nuevo Sindicalismo*), which was headed by Emma Rubio and Miguel Alonso Raya, was affiliated to the dominant group. However, this faction split, with Raya defecting from Gordillo's dominant faction and Rubio remaining in it.

Because of Jonguitud's long tenure and abuses, union statutes at that time imposed strict term limits for the secretary general of SNTE. Gordillo relinquished power to Humberto Dávila, her principal rival, who became the secretary general. Davila plotted against Gordillo, seeking control over SNTE by allying with then-president Ernesto Zedillo, who also distrusted Gordillo. In the labor congress of 1997, Dávila challenged Gordillo by backing Raúl Morón against Gordillo's ally, Tomas Vazquez.

Gordillo still controlled the union, however. As a condition for stepping down, she had negotiated influential positions for her ex-husband Francisco Arriola, who became the finance secretary and continued to manage the union's complex finances in line with Gordillo's wishes. Moreover, Rafael Ochoa was the Secretary of Organization, and he packed union locals with leaders who were aligned with Gordillo (Raphael 2007, 171). As a result, in the labor congress of 1997, Gordillo rallied teachers for her preferred candidate, Tomás Vázquez, who was backed by the union's finances (i.e., Arriola) and by a capable operator who held the position of Secretary of Organization (i.e., Ochoa) (Raphael 2007, 177). Tomas Vazquez won 1,926 votes while Dávila's ally, Raúl Morón, won only 295 votes (Diaz de la Torre et al. 2013, 206). After this labor congress, there were no further challenges to Gordillo's power from within the union.

The fourth step was to gradually take down the window dressing of union democracy by adopting procedures for selecting new union leaders that emboldened the new dominant faction. SNTE did not hold direct elections in which rank-and-file teachers cast secret ballots for union leaders. Rather, union leaders were selected in labor congresses, where teachers selected union delegates who then decided the composition of the union leadership. These congresses took place on an uneven playing field. They were closed to the public, featured a token opposition, and were often announced at the last minute in a remote location. The dominant faction strategically decided when to hold new labor congresses, which limited the opportunities for rivals to protest or pose a challenge by participating. Gordillo's group had the advantages of incumbency, resources, and organization. Typically, new union leaders, who had Gordillo's backing, won supermajorities of support among delegates at labor congresses. A union advisor noted that "[labor congresses] were intended to prevent the intervention of outside political actors into the union" (Interview, October 8, 2012).

In addition, the dominant faction manipulated union statutes to weaken would-be rivals. Union statutes were ignored when they opposed the interests of the dominant faction. For instance, from 1998 to 2000, Gordillo served as a senator for the PRI while holding a leadership position on SNTE's Political Action Committee, even though union statutes forbade SNTE leaders from simultaneously serving the union and holding public office. Labor laws mandated that union leaders could only head a labor organization for a fixed period, at the end of which a new labor congress had to be held to choose new leaders. However, union leaders often remained in power after their legal term had expired if there was any threat that rival union leaders or dissident groups would seize power when a new labor congress was convened.

Concerned that union leaders might turn against her, Gordillo dismantled union statutes that imposed checks on her power and arbitrarily changed the structure of the national executive committee in ways that weakened potential rivals. For instance, from 1989 to 2002, the union was organized around union secretaries. Each secretary was responsible for a key function of SNTE: negotiation, union finances, organization, and so on. In 2003, the union secretaries were eliminated and replaced with multimember *Colegiados*, in which rival union leaders shared power and were jointly responsible for SNTE's key functions. This restructuring prevented any single union leader from developing a personal following (Interview, Mexico City, September 10, 2012).[11] Moreover, Gordillo initially retained term limits for union leaders, while she remained the power behind the throne. However, by 2004, she no longer needed the trappings of union democracy and created a position for herself, the president for life, with no term limits.[12] In 2011, the national leadership was reduced from seventy to thirty members, allowing her to purge union leaders she distrusted and ensure that only her closest allies held power.

In sum, by 1997, Gordillo had consolidated power in a new dominant faction that eclipsed the power of Carlos Jonguitud's faction, Revolutionary Vanguard. Gordillo was aided by the influx of resources and her popularity among rank-and-file teachers. She had created an evolving set of strategies that weakened the dissidents and all but eliminated internal rivals from her own institutional group. Gordillo cemented the position of her dominant faction in the national executive committee by using union resources to coopt rivals and by arbitrarily changing

---

[11] Wenceslao.com.mx, "Comités, Congresos y Consejos Nacionales del Snte," accessed February 24, 2023 via https://web.archive.org/web/20180325060032/.

[12] The union president superseded the secretary general, whom Gordillo feared might become a rival.

union statutes. In labor congresses, her faction delivered supermajorities to support her candidates and proposed changes to union statutes.

HIERARCHICAL RELATIONS WITH UNION LOCALS

While the dominant faction had undisputed control over the national executive committee of SNTE, it had to manage a complex and evolving set of relations with the union sections in the states. There were more than fifty union sections; historically there had been two in many states, one for teachers hired by the federal government and another for teachers hired by the state government. For national union leaders, exercising control across territory was challenging because of the combined effects of federalism, democracy, and education decentralization. This difficulty in exercising control created a patchwork of local political dynamics and opportunities for local union leaders to break ranks and form alliances with local party bosses. Nevertheless, the dominant faction had the resources to influence local leaders and strategies to weaken and deter would-be defectors. The union remained cohesive; national union leaders projected power and local union leaders largely followed national directives.

As Gordillo consolidated control over the national executive committee, her position to negotiate with local union leaders was strengthened. She was able to win the support of regional union bosses in the states of Chihuahua and Veracruz (Raphael 2007, 72). When regional union bosses who had been loyal to Carlos Jonguitud failed to support her, Gordillo pushed them out, in some cases by channeling union resources to dissident groups. For example, in Michoacán and Hidalgo, the dissidents, who had Gordillo's backing, ran rival regional union bosses out of power (Cook 1996, 216–65). As a result, most of the local union leaders who had supported Jonguitud flipped and became *Gordillistas*. Regional union bosses in Nayarit and San Luis Potosí, who had previously been part of Jonguitud's faction Revolutionary Vanguard, were also incorporated into Gordillo's dominant faction. As Gordillo's control over the union, financial assets, and political connections in the PRI grew, regional leaders rallied to her and supported her political initiatives.

Throughout the 1990s, Gordillo used her popularity among the rank and file, union resources, and control over union statutes to ensure that her allies populated the union sections in the states. Local union leaders sent Gordillo a list of candidates for leadership positions. She then flew these candidates to Mexico City and interviewed them personally to assess their loyalty (Raphael 2007, 121). If they passed this test, she invested in their political careers and helped them to advance through the ranks of the union. By 2000, Gordillo had cultivated allies in most states. Local union leaders avoided voicing opposition to her in public.

While most union sections aligned with the dominant faction, some governors tried – but failed – to cultivate union leaders who defied Gordillo. Indeed, with the National Agreement for the Modernization of Basic Education of 1992 and multiparty competition in state contests, regional party bosses, especially from the PRI (which had long-standing ties to teachers), attempted to weaken Gordillo's influence in their states. However, Gordillo had the tools to blunt these challenges.

The state of Yucatán, where a conflict developed between Governor Ivonne Ortega and Gordillo, is illustrative. In 2006, Gordillo supported the gubernatorial candidate of the PAN with the teacher-based party she created, New Alliance. But despite Gordillo's support for this party, Ivonne Ortega of the PRI was elected Governor of Yucatán in 2007. In response, Ortega made deals with leaders of both sections of SNTE in Yucatán in an effort to weaken Gordillo's influence in her state.[13] In plenary congresses of both sectional committees, Ortega put together a group of candidates opposed to Gordillo, among them Rigoberto Cervantes. Ortega's allies seemed on the cusp of winning power in the Yucatán sections of SNTE. In 2008, however, Silvia Alamilla Fuentes, the secretary general of Section 57 and a Gordillo ally, reacted by suspending the labor congresses altogether. Gordillo sent a special delegation and her "emissary" Silvia Luna to make sure that Ortega's allies did not win power. A stand-off resulted between Silvia Alamilla Fuentes and Rigoberto Cervantes, with each side accusing the other of making death threats. Ortega responded by supporting the formation of six parallel teachers' unions, one of which was headed by her ally Rigoberto Cervantes. In addition, she responded by withholding funding from the SNTE sections of Yucatán. SNTE's national executive committee retaliated by paying teachers who were in Section 57 with the bonuses from Carrera Magisterial but cutting off the bonuses to all teachers in the Yucatán who were in independent unions. In the end, Governor Ortega succeeded in fragmenting the teacher movement in Yucatán, but she failed to wrest control over the union sections of SNTE. This demonstrates how Gordillo responded to challenges to her control over the union. She suspended labor congresses and used other

---

[13] See Luis A. Boffil Gómez et al., "Revienta elección seccional del SNTE en Yucatán," *La Jornada* March 15, 2008.

closed procedures for selecting new union leaders to prevent governors and other political actors from intervening in her union's internal affairs.

The dominant faction used its control over state resources and capacity to advance political careers to maintain loyalty. Gordillo accumulated a vast share of financial resources over which she had discretionary control. At the same time, she advanced in the ranks of the PRI and cultivated close alliances with governors and other power brokers in the party. Gordillo's ability to leverage political advisors, financial resources, and political connections enabled her to promote local union leaders and offer them careers in the national executive committee and politics.[14] Gordillo strongly influenced which leaders advanced up the ranks of SNTE and subsequently moved into politics.

The dominant group developed strategies to manage the restive southern states of Oaxaca, Guerrero, and Michoacán, where the dissident group never fully demobilized. To counter the dissidents, the dominant faction projected power by deploying a group of veteran union organizers, Gordillo's emissaries (*los enviados*). *Los enviados* were paid by the national executive committee and sent by this committee (or Gordillo herself) to monitor state-level labor congresses, promote regional allies, and negotiate with dissident leaders. They also helped to sow divisions among the dissidents. In Michoacán, dissidents took a hardline position on the dominant faction, but had to collect their own union dues since the national executive committee withheld them. In Oaxaca, dissidents were more pragmatic. They took a militant position in public, but negotiated in private with the dominant faction to get their share of union dues (Interview, dissident leader, March 15, 2012). The emissaries were effective in dividing the dissidents and making sure that they could not form a united front against the hegemonic faction. They demonstrated the reach of the national executive committee and the ways in which the national union bureaucracy could be used to quell local dissent.

To summarize, the dominant faction used its resources, organization, and political connections to promote allies and establish hierarchical relations with union locals. It intervened in state-level sections at the subnational level to ensure that Gordillo's allies won power. Exercising control across territory was difficult because it involved projecting power to the

---

[14] When union leaders entered public office, Gordillo could fill new openings in the union with new allies. One union adviser described the dominant faction's capacity to reward loyalty: "[It] offers a very large number of opportunities and positions to many people" (Interview, Mexico City, February 23, 2012).

far corners of Mexico, hundreds of miles from Mexico City. The dominant faction faced challenges from dissidents, who gained strength as they criticized Gordillo for being a labor boss who was cut from the same cloth as Carlos Jonguitud. However, even if they succeeded in mobilizing rank-and-file discontent against Gordillo, the balance of power favored the national executive committee leaders. The national leaders used several strategies to assert control over union sections, and the overwhelming majority remained loyal to the dominant faction.

CONCLUSION

The early 1990s marked a sea change in Mexican politics. In the wake of the 1988 election, which was tainted by allegations of fraud, Mexico began a gradual political opening. Discontent with PRI rule was reflected in growing support for opposition parties, which began to win governorships and steadily increased their representation in the national legislature. At the same time, there was a transformation in labor politics (Middlebrook 1995; Bensusán and Middlebrook 2012). President Salinas confronted labor unions when adopting new economic policies. In general, labor unions were forced to swallow the bitter pill of neoliberalism and were politically weakened as a result. Moreover, in the broader context of democratization, there was pressure from both the government and grassroots activists to make highly corporatist labor unions more democratic and responsive to the rank and file, at least in rhetoric, although the official labor sector resisted these changes (Samstad 2002).

Within the context of democratization and transformation of state–labor relations, teachers' stand out as a deviant case. In the late 1980s and early 1990s, many labor unions in Mexico faced restructuring and neoliberal economic policies that were imposed on them, effectively weakening or "busting" them. But during this same period, teachers gained resources and maintained political power. While SNTE faced a challenge from the dissidents, who pushed for more powersharing, and technocrats, who pushed for education decentralization, in the end President Salinas decided to adopt education policies that bolstered Elba Esther Gordillo against her rivals and preserved the union's corporatist character. Gordillo's leadership faction revitalized the national union bureaucracy. The national executive committee was strengthened by limited decentralization, which meant that the primary locus of educational policymaking remained at the national level, and subsidies that strengthened national union leaders since they had discretionary control over how these resources were used. As Mexico transitioned from authoritarianism to a more open political regime, changes in the teachers' union went in the opposite direction. Elba Esther Gordillo rebuilt a dominant faction and reestablished a hierarchical organization by relying on cooptation and control.

In contrast to some scholars who focus on the similarities among the *caciques*, or union bosses, who headed SNTE (i.e., Jesús Robles Martínez, Carlos Jonguitud, and Elba Esther Gordillo) and continuity over time in the characteristics of the union organization, my analysis highlights at least some discontinuity. This chapter has shown that contingent decisions made at a moment of political turmoil and change produced this outcome. The coalition-building decisions of President Salinas after the critical 1988 election are crucial for understanding why SNTE's organizational structure not only recovered from the disarray of the 1980s but also grew stronger. Gordillo became even more powerful than past *caciques* of SNTE, establishing stronger hierarchical relations with union locals and a tighter consolidation of power in the national executive committee. The embattled regime shored up the teachers' union, making it an increasingly powerful organization that over time became impossible for party leaders to control.

In appeasing the teachers' union, the government allowed Gordillo and SNTE to control the education policy agenda. The government backed off from a far-reaching decentralization reform and accommodated the union's demands for maintaining a centralized collective bargaining arrangement and a national labor code. In other words, the decision to shore up SNTE reinforced the old corporatist model of public education. Big structural changes that might have weakened the union were deferred to a later date.

5

Instrumentalism in Mexico

SNTE's distinctive organizational structure explains its political strategy of instrumental alliances. A hierarchical organization enabled the union to remake its electoral operation. Even as the decline of the authoritarian one-party regime resulted in a de facto extension of political rights to teachers, the union maintained considerable influence over how teachers voted. The dominant faction continued to form teachers into a voting bloc because national union leaders had resources that they invested in sophisticated voter targeting, outreach, and media-based appeals. These new media-based appeals were layered over clientelistic practices inherited from the past. The dominant faction had influence over the leaders of union sections, who in turn wielded powerful control mechanisms over the rank and file. These hierarchical relations enabled the union to scale up teachers as a voting bloc, even when teachers had some leeway to defy the union leadership's political directives and vote based on their conscience.

The consolidation of power in the national executive committee is crucial to understanding how the union pursued strategic alliances with different political parties. Since the 1980s, with the emergence of multiparty competition in Mexico, new coalitional possibilities became available as the PRI's grip on power weakened and opposition parties sought alliance partners to shore up their position. However, for SNTE to take advantage of these possibilities, the union needed to be organized around a single faction that held power over the entirety of the national executive committee and most of the state-level union sections. A unified national executive committee guaranteed that new partisan alliances would not produce internal fracturing and dissent. The absence of rival factions enabled the dominant faction to issue directives to form a new teacher-based party, New Alliance (PANAL) in 2005, and to use the political support this party afforded as a bargaining chip. In other words, teachers largely stuck with union leaders when they embraced instrumental alliances because they had nowhere else to turn. The instrumental strategy – and Gordillo's political entrepreneurship – hinged on this consolidation of power.

The next sections examine how a hierarchical organization and a dominant faction in the national executive committee were crucial prerequisites for explaining the strategy of instrumentalism. They show how the union's hierarchical structure enabled it to mobilize teachers in elections and how its consolidation of power enabled negotiations with political parties from across the ideological spectrum. The last section analyzes the political backlash against instrumentalism in 2013, which resulted in leadership turnover and policy changes that weakened the union overall. Despite this backlash, however, the union's internal organization remained largely intact. The teacher voting bloc remains influential, and union leaders continue to be ideologically flexible, in line with the main argument in this book. In other words, even if the strategy of instrumentalism has receded to an extent since its high-water mark in 2006, it remains the primary means through which SNTE – and teachers in Mexico – represent interests.

BUILDING AN ELECTORAL OPERATION

Gordillo used her considerable financial resources, political connections, and control over the union to build a vast network of political brokers. Unlike her predecessor, Carlos Jonguitud, whose political maneuvering and coercion engendered rank-and-file discontent, Gordillo retained control over teachers and mobilized them to form a political bloc. Hierarchical relations were crucial for the dominant faction to modernize and expand the electoral operation, target voters, and scale up electoral mobilization.

Historically, SNTE coerced teachers to vote in lockstep for the PRI. Carlos Jonguitud, who led SNTE from 1973 to 1989, quipped that teachers were "electoral plumbers," doing the party's dirty work.[1] However,

---

[1] Union leaders reminded teachers of favors granted to them, such as help acquiring full-time teaching positions, loans, promotions, and advocacy in resolving problems with the education bureaucracy. In exchange, teachers were to vote for the ruling party, organize rallies, distribute fliers and campaign materials, and get family and friends to vote (Raphael 2007, 186).

after Jonguitud's ouster, the traditional modes of electoral mobilization were in disarray. Steps toward democracy imposed new constraints on how the union participated in politics. During the reign of Carlos Jonguitud, coercing teachers to affiliate to the PRI and conditioning benefits on loyalty fueled the dissident uprising and ultimately ended his rule. As the PRI embraced neoliberal economic reforms, many teachers wanted to vote for the center-left PRD, which splintered from the PRI. As Mexico established a competitive, multiparty system, a tug of war ensued among political forces seeking teacher support. Union leaders could no longer intimidate teachers to follow their lead. They had to develop new powers of persuasion.

When Gordillo took power, she rebuilt the union's political machinery in a way that effectively mobilized votes while engendering less resistance. She paid lip service to the political pluralism of teachers and showed respect for political rights, but at the same time invested in a new electoral operation. Hierarchical relations facilitated sweeping changes in the way in which the union mobilized votes. The dominant faction invested in human capital and technology, collecting information about voting patterns. Gordillo hired political consultants and operatives with advanced training in computer science, communication, and polling, such as Noe Rivera Dominguez and Luis Castro, who attended graduate school in Europe and the United States. In the 1990s, the union also invested in computers and cellphones to analyze and disseminate information about voting in real-time (Raphael 2007, 166–7). Because of its hierarchical structure, the union was able to develop new political practices and then rapidly adapt them through the union sections in each state.

The union's top-down structure enabled the union to redirect teachers on the ground during elections. After the departure of Jonguitud from the union, Gordillo made progress toward cleaning up the union's public image. She created the national political action committee, which guaranteed teachers the right to support any party they wished; she signed the National Agreement of Education Modernization as a means to signal her commitment to education reform. In a similar modernizing spirit, in 1994, national union leaders publicly proclaimed that they would help to change the roles of teachers from electoral plumbers to neutral electoral observers. Rather than seeking to influence the election outcome, the union trained teachers to oversee polling stations and to follow proper protocols in vote counting.[2] The union leadership refrained from

---

[2] After fraud in the 1988 election, Gordillo proposed to the Grupo San Angel, a group of business leaders, intellectuals, and politicians concerned about the future of Mexican

directing teachers to support a specific party. Indeed, this new role for teachers, as neutral election observers, was helpful for the PRI's presidential candidate, Ernesto Zedillo, who needed teachers to legitimize the election results after allegations of fraud in 1988 (Raphael 2007, 162). On August 21, 1994, the day of the election, the union had information about the results before other organizations, and Gordillo was one of the first to congratulate Zedillo on winning (Raphael 2007, 136). As a consequence of the union's hierarchical structure, union leaders retooled its political activities and coordinated an increasingly sophisticated political operation.

By the early 2000s, however, the union began to shift from a position of political neutrality to openly mobilizing teacher support for certain parties. The union sought to replace threats and intimidation, which were associated with the corrupt leadership of Carlos Jonguitud, with inducements and persuasion to win political support. The union turned to media-based strategies to mobilize votes. To counter public perceptions of the union as highly corrupt, Gordillo hired professional consultants to promote a public image of SNTE as a modern labor organization that supported democracy, an open economy, and better functioning public schools. The emphasis on public relations and media-based strategies continued in 2005, when the union formed the teacher-based party, PANAL. In addition to targeting teachers, the party also targeted disaffected independent voters who wanted to cast a protest vote against the three major parties (Interview, legislative advisor PANAL, March 14, 2012). The party used effective television ads with vague, catchall appeals, for example, calling on voters to cast "one of three votes for education" by supporting PANAL for either the president, senate, or lower house.

As the hope for union democracy faded, union leaders resorted to old-fashioned practices of clientelism. SNTE exercised top-down electoral control at two levels. At the first level, teachers followed the orders of local union leaders, since teaching positions were distributed through union locals, and school principals and regional directors were usually union cadres. Union control over teacher careers meant that SNTE leaders encouraged teachers to work in political campaigns in exchange for promotions up the pay scale and assistance resolving problems with the

---

democracy, to use teachers as neutral election monitors. The dominant faction launched the National Organization of Electoral Observation of the Teaching Profession (Raphael 2007, 161).

education bureaucracy (Muñoz Armenta 2020). At the second level, local union leaders followed the national union leadership's directives, since the dominant faction could promote the careers of local union leaders or withhold union funds from them.

The union exploited its hierarchical structure to mobilize teachers as voters. While it refrained from mobilizing voters for the PRI in 1994, it gradually reverted to traditional practices of clientelism. In the 2000 election, the campaign of Francisco Labastida, the presidential candidate for the PRI, thought that SNTE would remain loyal to the PRI. The PRI gave large sums of money to SNTE to mobilize hard-to-reach rural voters to compensate for his party's growing weakness in doing this (Raphael 2007, 184). The dominant faction took down the window dressing of union democracy and again called on regional union bosses to deliver the vote. Clientelism – based on promises of teaching positions, salary bonuses, and other union advocacy services – remained in place. Estimates of the size of this electoral operation vary. According to Noe Rivera, a union insider who defected from the dominant faction, the national executive committee headed a network of political operators that was 55,000 strong – in Jalisco, Puebla, Hidalgo, Morelos, Guanajuato, and the State of Mexico (Muñoz Armenta 2011, 101). In 2012, a census of the teacher payroll revealed that 41,000 "teachers" actually did not show up to work and instead were full-time union organizers.[3] Others have reported that the electoral base of SNTE included 320,000 teachers, which it could control politically.[4] Regardless of the precise number, which may vary year to year, what is clear is that there are many thousands of union operatives, a phenomenon with few (if any) parallels in Latin America. Moreover, hierarchical relations held the multipronged electoral operation together, providing evidence for the argument that these relations served as the basis mobilizing teachers as voters and negotiating partisan alliance.

Despite the tug of war that ensued between SNTE, the dissidents, the PRI, the PRD, and even the PAN in a few states, all of which sought to carve out a niche of support among teachers, the national union leadership of SNTE held on to most of the base. Even though some teachers (former dissidents) became staunch PRD supporters and others remained

---

[3] Lilian Hernández, "El SNTE comisiona a 41 mil profesores en primer trimestre de 2012," *Excelsior* July 4, 2012.
[4] Laura Poy Solano, "El SNTE controla políticamente 320 mil maestros," *La Jornada* August 12, 2009.

TABLE 5.1 *Vote share* New Alliance, *lower house (proportional representation)*

	2006	2009	2012	2015	2018
Vote Share as a percentage of national electorate	4.60%	3.40%	4.10%	3.90%	2.50%
Total National Votes	1,883,476	1,164,999	2,041,608	1,486,952	1,390,882
Party Registry	Yes	Yes	Yes	Yes	No

Source: Electoral Registry (IFE)

loyal to the PRI, in 2005, a large enough number of teachers rallied behind PANAL. The party positioned itself as a nonpolarizing alternative, to enable teachers with partisan identities to support it along with their own preferred party. In 2006, 2009, 2012, and 2015, PANAL mobilized more than a million votes and maintained its party registry, winning seats in the proportional representation (plurinominal) districts (see Table 5.1). This table demonstrates SNTE's high capacity for electoral mobilization. Even in the states where the dominant faction had a more tenuous hold on local union leaders, the party met the threshold of 2 percent. For instance, PANAL performed well in the states of Oaxaca, Guerrero, and Michoacán, where the dissidents were strongest, in Nayarit, San Luis Potosí, and Veracruz, where regional union bosses remained loyal to the PRI, and Yucatán, where a PRI governor sought to intervene in the union. The dominant faction mobilized votes where it had supporters, and also where local union leaders resisted the national union leadership.

In sum, the power of national union leaders over local union leaders and rank-and-file teachers explains SNTE's remarkable capacity to launch a complex electoral operation that involved both persuasion and coercion. Owing to hierarchical relations, the union embraced modern practices of electioneering involving technology, polling data, and media-based strategies. At the same time, hierarchical relations enabled union leaders to maintain traditional practices of clientelism, which never disappeared. The union's top-down structure was crucial for it to develop this multipronged electoral strategy that effectively mobilized votes across territory. This party outperformed expectations in 2006, 2009, and 2012, and continued to exist at the state level, albeit in a more diminished form, in 2018.

THE TURN TO INSTRUMENTALISM

The concentration of power in the dominant faction was a necessary condition for Gordillo to become a political entrepreneur who could negotiate strategic alliances with new political parties. If hierarchical relations enabled the mobilization of teachers as voters, then instrumental negotiations hinged on the consolidation of power. After Mexico's democratic transition, opposition parties gained ground and presidents governed without a legislative majority (Muñoz Armenta and Castro Maravilla 2019). In an environment of divided government, Gordillo's faction negotiated with parties across the ideological spectrum. The union courted the frontrunner candidates for president and governor during political campaigns, and then claimed credit for delivering victory to them. The consolidation of power enabled these negotiations to take place, since SNTE could credibly coordinate its support for a new party. SNTE promised to deliver political support to politicians at multiple levels of government and to make pacts related to national education policy.

In the 1990s, as the dominant faction coalesced, Gordillo experimented with instrumental negotiations with different factions of the PRI. She established her own political grouping (*camarilla*) in the party and her political endorsement became coveted. There were early indications of the instrumental strategy. In the PRI's 1994 presidential primary, both Donaldo Colosio and Manuel Camacho Solis sought Gordillo's favor (Colosio was assassinated later that year). When Ernesto Zedillo secured the party's nomination over Camacho Solis, Gordillo sought an alliance with Zedillo. Gordillo's relationship with Zedillo was complex. At first, she was rebuffed, as Zedillo kept her out of his administration, but he subsequently helped her to rise in the ranks of the party. Gordillo led the National Organization of Popular Organizations of the PRI from 1995 to 2001 and served as a senator from 1997 to 2000.

In 2000, Francisco Labastida lost to Vicente Fox of the center-right PAN in a watershed election, creating a power vacuum and infighting within the PRI. In the past, the President of Mexico had been the de facto party leader, who kept the party's fractious labor leaders and governors in line. The president chose his own successor through the "*dedazo*," and the president nominated most legislative candidates and governors, having the authority to remove those who displeased him (Weldon 1997). But the PRI, having lost the presidency for the first time in 2000, lacked a clear leader and was in turmoil. In the broader context of chaos and disarray, Gordillo became a powerful broker because her dominant faction remained highly disciplined. Her standing in the party increased, and she provided electoral support to PRI governors, who then became close allies. In the 2002 election for PRI leadership, Gordillo formed a strategic alliance with Roberto Madrazo, who had run a strong campaign in the 2000 PRI primary against Francisco Labastida, the handpicked successor of President Zedillo. Madrazo and Gordillo formed one group within the party; Labastida and Beatriz Paredes, who had support in the rural sector and among indigenous groups, formed another.

Within the election for party leadership positions, Madrazo and Gordillo narrowly defeated rival Beatriz Paredes by a margin of 1,518,063 to 1,466,217, in large part because Gordillo flexed her muscles and mobilized political resources. This party primary in 2002 was the first election in which Gordillo openly pressured the union to mobilize votes on her behalf, violating her stated support for teachers' political rights. To win, Gordillo expanded her network of electoral brokers from 50,000 (in the 2000 presidential election) to 150,000. She raised a tremendous amount of money to finance Madrazo's campaign – even going so far as to sell land and ask a wealthy business leader for a loan to pay for this expanded operation (Raphael 2007, 205–6). Miguel Alonso Raya, a leader of SNTE, described Gordillo as having ordered the entire union to support her bid. In an interview, Raya said that "everyone in the union had to support Gordillo as the Secretary General of the party" (Raphael 2007, 207). Madrazo became the president of the PRI and Gordillo the secretary general, the second-highest position in the party; Gordillo was also the PRI's legislative coordinator for the lower house.[5]

After Gordillo established full control over SNTE's national executive committee, she defied PRI leaders' directives and pursued her own interests. President Vicente Fox (2000–6) of the center-right PAN and Gordillo formed a close alliance, with ongoing negotiation and political exchange. President Fox gave Benjamín González Roaro, a Gordillo ally, the directorship of the Civil Service Social Security and Services Institute of Mexico (ISSSTE). ISSSTE was a massive public pension fund and social security agency that provided various subsidies to public employees for housing, health care, and other benefits. The fund was rife with opportunities for corruption and clientelism. In 2011, Humberto Moreira, a

---

[5] Members of the PRI caucus favored Gordillo by a vote of 124 to 92, because Gordillo secured the support of many PRI governors (Raphael 2007, 219). The PRI's loss in 2000 created a political opportunity for Gordillo and her allies, who ascended in the party (Langston 2017, 97).

teacher from Coahuila who went on to become the president of the PRI, claimed that Gordillo attempted to divert funds from the ISSSTE to fund her political party PANAL.[6] What is clear is that Gordillo remained a political insider during Fox's administration and continued to gain access to state resources.

Facing partisan turnover in the presidency, SNTE maneuvered to maintain a close alliance with the new administration. There were various instances of the union participating in new policy initiatives and getting access to state resources. For instance, President Fox convened a group of civil society actors, including SNTE, to discuss the state of education and the reforms necessary in a newly democratic regime. Fox signed a pact with these actors: the 2002 Social Compromise for Education Quality. This contained an abstract set of policy objectives, none of which challenged the union's political power; it demonstrates how the union was included in the Fox administration's policymaking process (Loyo 2008, 33–4). In addition, Gordillo and Marta Sahagún, the first lady of Mexico, worked on a joint project, a *Guide for Parents*, which resulted in lucrative contracts for the Fundación SNTE worth 53 million pesos.[7] Even as Gordillo remained in the PRI, SNTE established a close working relationship with the PAN government.

In exchange for these benefits, as the legislative coordinator of the PRI, Gordillo voiced support for Fox's conservative economic policies, even his proposed value-added tax on food and medicine, which were widely criticized for being regressive and hurting the poor. However, as she cut deals with the PAN president, she sparked conflict with Roberto Madrazo, the president of the PRI, who wanted his party to unite in its opposition to Fox's agenda. Gordillo could not sustain a leadership position in the PRI while also expressing open political support for President Fox; she was accused of betraying her own party. Gordillo's *camarilla*, or party faction, began to differentiate itself from the rest of the party. In 2005, she began to separate from the PRI, the union's partisan patron of more than sixty years. Rather than simply being ousted, Gordillo negotiated her exit with Madrazo, dragging her feet to prevent a new legislative coordinator from taking over (Raphael 2007, 227–9).

---

[6] Andrea Becerril, "Senadores de PRI y PAN rechazan toda alianza con Gordillo Morales," *La Jornada* July 10, 2011.

[7] However, this guide was denounced for its abstinence-only sex education unit, and because it was distributed based on the private initiative of the Foundation *Vamos Mexico* (headed by Marta Sahagun, wife of President Vicente Fox) and the SNTE foundation – rather than the SEP (Raphael 2007, 196–7).

Since power in SNTE was rooted in the dominant faction, the union could form a new teacher-based party, PANAL. The absence of rival factions in the national executive committee was critical to establishing this new party since defections would have undermined this effort, splintering the would-be party into fragments that were too small to sustain political representation. The partisan identity of the teachers' union was transformed from the top down. The dominant faction had already created a political organization, the Civic Association of the Teaching Profession. This association mobilized 72,000 signatures in 241 district-level assemblies in 7 weeks and achieved a party registry, which gave it access to public campaign finance and the right to appear on a ballot (Muñoz Armenta 2011, 102). For other parties that lacked the backing of SNTE's strong organization, this process was long and arduous, taking years to complete. Gordillo also forged an alliance with the university student association at ITAM, a leading private research university. She recruited student leaders, such as Xiuh Tenorio, who was the President of the Alumni Association of Students of ITAM and appealed to young people to freshen the party's face, even if the union provided the organizational muscle behind these candidates.

PANAL articulated the interests of Gordillo's faction; the party permeated the national leadership. The overwhelming majority of the national executive committee pledged allegiance in 2005. Gordillo did not formally occupy a leadership position in the party, but her daughter, Monica Arriola Gordillo, and other close associates were high-ranking party leaders. The relationship between the union and PANAL was remarkably close. According to one high-ranking union leader (Interview, Mexico City, March 27, 2012), "New Alliance as a party, or an electoral alliance, is indissolubly tied to our union and it is beneficial that it maintains its party registry, because that way it doesn't lose its local organizations. Losing its local organizations would obviously weaken it at the national level."

The leader described how the union leadership constantly invited union leaders from minority parties to participate in PANAL. Strategic planning meetings for PANAL were convened in SNTE's national headquarters with the same people who participated in the union meeting remaining to participate in the party meeting. "In SNTE's national executive committee, they talk about issues related to New Alliance. After finishing the union's agenda for the day, they say, 'OK, friends, you know you are welcome to stay,' and what comes next is the meeting of New Alliance" (Interview, Mexico City, March 27, 2012). Inside the union, there was constant pressure for union leaders to support the teacher-based party because it was the political expression of the union's interests.

My central argument is that the concentration of power in the national executive committee was decisive in explaining the capacity of SNTE to negotiate shifting alliances. Instrumentalism is a broad concept; it fits with any labor union that switches support from one party to another, regardless of whether they form a new electoral vehicle to do so. In Mexico, instrumentalism took a specific form because the teachers' union formed a teacher-based party, PANAL, which served as a bargaining chip in negotiations. To explain the formation of this political party, two factors were crucial: the aforementioned concentration of power in the national executive committee, and also the particular electoral rules in Mexico.

The teachers' union was the unintended beneficiary of electoral rules of proportional representation that were adopted in 1977. According to these rules, new parties needed only 2 percent of the national vote to maintain a legal registry, receive public campaign financing, and win guaranteed seats (Eisenstadt 2004, 39). Mexico had a hybrid electoral system. There were 300 single-member seats for the lower house and 200 "plurinominal" seats allocated through closed-list proportional representation, with 2 percent of the vote as the threshold for securing representation. This low threshold meant that SNTE could sustain a teacher-based party since, in presidential elections, 2 percent of the vote amounted to about 2 million votes. The union had 1.2 million members, and it could mobilize most of its base, not to mention the friends and family members of teachers. The remaining votes could be mobilized with media-based appeals.

PANAL was both an electoral vehicle and a bargaining chip in negotiations. It marked a full-blown shift toward instrumentalism. The party positioned the dominant faction to maneuver within the party system. With a legal registry, PANAL could formally serve as a partner in multiparty coalitions. Within a competitive political environment, Gordillo used the party to claim credit for delivering electoral victories to the presidents and governors who were her political partners. Because of the concentration of power in Gordillo's dominant group, SNTE leaders did not need to consult with or build consensus with rival factions. Politicians negotiated directly with Gordillo because she had undisputed control over the union. This facilitated pact-making since the discipline of the dominant faction made Gordillo a credible negotiating partner.

In the 2006 presidential campaign, Gordillo used PANAL to court both Felipe Calderón of the PAN and Andrés Manuel López Obrador of the PRD. Gordillo reached out to López Obrador, claiming that teachers were very leftist, although López Obrador sought to distance himself from Gordillo (Cano and Aguirre 2013). At the last minute, Gordillo offered to support PAN's Calderón (Raphael 2007, 276–7).[8] She sent mixed signals to leading candidates, as she had in the 2000 election, and after the results were announced, she claimed credit for delivering pivotal votes to the winner.

Gordillo claimed to have provided pivotal votes to Calderón. Some Mexican teachers – like their counterparts in other countries – undoubtedly supported the leftist candidate, López Obrador, because of the political socialization of teachers and because their policy interests were more aligned with the left. And yet Gordillo relied on her network of political operators to cultivate a differentiated vote.[9] Her directive was for union cadres to vote for Calderón as president and for PANAL for the lower house of the legislature. She also convinced PRI governors to abandon their presidential candidate Roberto Madrazo and support the PAN since the PRI candidate was far behind in the polls. Indeed, in an intercepted phone call made in 2006 with the governor of Tamaulipas, Eugenio Hernández, Gordillo claimed that a union poll of 6,364 likely voters showed that Felipe Calderón held a narrow lead in the presidential race (Raphael 2007, 299).[10] There were also allegations that Gordillo sought to suppress the vote tally of both López Obrador and Madrazo by calling on teachers, who served as polling station workers, to make small but systematic errors in the vote tally, resulting in fewer votes for those two candidates (Raphael 2007, 286–95). The key point is that Gordillo claimed credit for Calderón's victory and seemed to throw her political support behind him.

Analysts disagree about the number of votes that Gordillo delivered to Calderón. In the popular press, there has been a tendency to exaggerate and promote conspiracy theories about the far-reaching influence of

---

[8] Jorge Castañeda, "Amores y desamores," *Reforma* July 10, 2011.
[9] Raphael (2007, 281), quoting Guevara Niebla, notes that teachers vote for the left, with strong support for the PRD, even as the dominant faction does not reflect this leftward tendency among teachers.
[10] For a transcript of the intercepted calls, see Carmen Rangel Sánchez, "Grabaciones incomodas" *El Mexicano* July 10, 2006. See Ornelas 2012 on the negotiations between Gordillo and Calderón for the Alliance for Education Quality (Alianza Calidad Educativa).

her shadowy networks. Political analysts, using a novel empirical strategy to analyze poll station-level data for federal elections in 2000, 2006, and 2012, found that union leaders had a strong capacity to influence teachers as voters when poll stations were in schools. Indeed, the union had a huge role in mobilizing votes for PANAL: "[O]ur estimates of the electoral impact of the SNTE machine explain roughly half of the PANAL's vote share" due to the union's official endorsement of its party (Larreguy et al. 2017, 884). However, the finding was also that there was no evidence of split ticket voting in polling stations located in schools for Calderón and PANAL, suggesting "that teachers did not mobilize parents to vote for a party to which they felt no attachment" (Larreguy et al. 2017, 889). There is some indication that Gordillo was good at bluffing and claimed to deliver more votes than she really could.

What is clear is that the president rewarded the union with patronage and rents – either because Calderón believed that Gordillo had mobilized electoral support for him or because he believed that Gordillo could help him advance his education policies. Gordillo's son in law, Fernando González, was named the Sub-Secretariat of Basic Education, the highest-ranking position a union ally had ever received in that secretariat. Another Gordillo ally, Luis Ignacio Sánchez Gómez, headed the education administration in Mexico City, which was under the federal government (Ornelas 2012, 45). Gordillo's allies were also appointed to the National Lottery and the ISSSTE. Since they were interpreted as a cynical ploy of a president seeking to shore up support, these appointments generated criticism in the media and within the PAN, including from Calderón's Secretary of Education, Josefina Vázquez Mota. The dominant faction also received rents during Calderón's administration. Teacher's salaries increased steadily under President Calderón, as they had under President Fox. Calderón also continued to expand cost-of-living adjustments for teachers (i.e., *rezonificación*). Moreover, SNTE received a no-bid contract for an educational technology project (Ornelas 2012, 108). It also gained influence over a health program for low-income students, even though this program should have fallen under the jurisdiction of the Secretariat of Health (Ornelas 2012, 205).

Recognizing the union's decisive role in shaping education policy, Calderón negotiated directly with Gordillo. Other societal actors, such as parent organizations and business leaders, were excluded. Even the Secretary of Education, Josefina Vázquez Mota a dedicated member of Calderón's PAN, who pushed for ambitious education reforms, was sidelined. As tensions escalated between Vazquez Mota and Gordillo,

Calderón sided with Gordillo because of Gordillo's capacity to deliver political support to the PAN, especially in gubernatorial contests in Baja California and Michoacán, where elections were competitive (Raphael 2007, 315–16). Moreover, without Gordillo's support for education reform, it was widely assumed that implementing any reform was unworkable. In 2009, Vazquez Mota stepped down as Secretary of Education to take the position as the Legislative Coordinator for the PAN. This move was interpreted as the president seeking to accommodate Gordillo's interests. The president sought to move forward on a new education policy that would replace political discretion and informal institutions with rule-based procedures for teacher hiring and evaluation (Ornelas 2012, 17–33). At the same time, he sought to do so in a way that enabled him to maintain Gordillo's support.

Calderón signed a pact only with SNTE, the Alliance for Education Quality of 2008. It established a national competition for hiring new teachers based on a merit-based exam. In theory, this appeared to be a major reform that would prevent the union from influencing teacher hiring, which had been a key mechanism of political control. Since the 1946 Regulation of the General Conditions of Work for Teachers, the teachers' union had played a major role in managing the teacher payroll.[11] The Alliance for Education Quality aimed to change this and to substitute a political criterion for teacher hiring and promotions for technical and apolitical ones. On May 31, 2011, the SEP and SNTE signed another pact, the Agreement for the Universal Evaluation of Teachers and School Administers of Basic Education, which established merit-based teacher evaluations for moving up the pay scale. This put in place a merit-based evaluation that would replace promotions based on the discretion of union leaders and political favoritism. Rather than imposing these policies on the union, the president included the union in these policy decisions. Notably, in 2009, when creating the Independent Federalist Evaluation Body to establish the technical and administrative standards for the teacher hiring competition, the evaluation body had 50 percent representation from SNTE and 50 percent representation from the state and federal authorities (Santiago et al. 2012). President Calderón calculated that negotiation with the union was the only way to advance new policies, despite the political costs and criticisms he received for taking this approach.

---

[11] Gilberto Guevara Niebla, "Leyes que sustentan el poder del SNTE," *Nexos* June 1, 2012.

These reforms threatened an important source of union patronage, and supporting them was risky for Gordillo as well. The National Competition for Authorizing Teaching Positions purported to take power away from union leaders since the political machinery of the union was organized around the informal institutions that were used to buy and sell teaching positions. Moreover, the teacher competition threatened an older generation of near-retirement teachers who did not want to lose out on the profit they could earn from selling their positions. Retiring teachers stood to lose when policies would prevent them from cashing in on the sale of or bequeathing their teaching position.

Yet despite the risks of angering local union leaders and rank-and-file teachers, Gordillo voiced support for these policies for several reasons. There was mounting political pressure for some kind of education reform. If a teacher evaluation was inevitable, and there was growing public opposition to the buying and selling of teaching positions and other forms of corruption, then Gordillo wanted to set the terms of the negotiation. She made public comments condemning the practice of buying and selling teaching positions and called for an end to this form of corruption (Ornelas 2012, 49). In exchange for supporting these policies, she negotiated concessions from Calderón's government, namely rents and patronage, which she distributed through her dominant faction to buy the support of teachers. The union leadership was supposed to convince the rank and file that the benefits for accepting teacher evaluations and merit-based hiring outweighed the costs. Finally, Gordillo spoke out of both sides of her mouth. Initially, union leaders voiced support for these agreements, but as rank-and-file opposition mounted, they began to back away, resorting to tactics of delaying and blocking the reform by claiming that the government had not held up its side of the bargain.

Gordillo faced a backlash from dissident teachers who had held onto power in a few union sections for going along with these reforms. Even if the dominant group had an advantage in terms of financial resources, the dissidents posed an unexpected challenge in several states, notably Oaxaca, Guerrero, and Michoacán. Since the Alliance for Education Quality seemed to be imposed on teachers from the top down with the blessing of SNTE's national leadership and since it threatened teachers' labor rights, dissidents regrouped and articulated rank-and-file discontent. Major protests broke out in several states, notably Morelos (Ornelas 2012, 168–202). Dissident mobilizations proved difficult to control. In Morelos, after eighty-six days of teachers refusing to start the school year and open classes, the protest was finally brought under control by withholding the pay of teachers who went on strike. In the end, SNTE's national leadership regained control over these teachers and negotiated a resolution to the strike that got teachers back in the classroom (Ornelas 2012, 202). This major strike failed to block the national competition, but the resolution meant that teachers who participated in the protest were paid – even for days that they spent protesting; and it did not close all the loopholes for buying and selling of positions. Ultimately, the Alliance for Education Quality fell apart, never really achieving its stated aims because there was a lack of political will to implement these policies.

The instrumental approach depended on Gordillo's capacity to maintain the full backing of the national executive committee, which was her source of leverage. The clearest expression of instrumentalism can be seen in the strategic negotiations between Elba Esther Gordillo, Vicente Fox, and Felipe Calderón, from 2000 to 2012, during which Gordillo shifted her position so that she could accommodate the economic and education policy goals of right-wing presidents in exchange for concessions, patronage, and rents. During this period, the dominant faction's influence reached its high-water mark in its capacity to negotiate and deliver support and to present itself as a more viable interlocutor than the troublesome dissident teachers who made unreasonable demands. The control that Gordillo's faction exerted over the national executive committee allowed her to construct instrumental alliances. In some cases, these posed risks for the union, such as the ending of the practice of buying, selling, and bequeathing teaching positions, but the union nevertheless opened negotiations and made deals.

BACKLASH AGAINST INSTRUMENTALISM

SNTE's political strategy of instrumentalism set the stage for a sharp political backlash. The strategy of highly visible and shifting partisan alliances, which went hand in hand with pervasive corruption scandals and scathing media coverage, left Gordillo politically isolated. In the 2012 presidential campaign, the presidential frontrunner, Enrique Peña Nieto, rejected Gordillo as an ally. Indeed, he campaigned on merit-based teacher evaluations to improve learning outcomes and eradicate patronage and corruption in SNTE, notably in the buying, selling, and bequeathing of teaching positions. The union's highly visible role in politics, which contributed to teacher absenteeism and the illicit marketplace for teaching positions, became a major campaign issue. Peña Nieto argued that such practices were incompatible with a twenty-first century education system organized around performance-based standards and evaluations. In addition, rank-and-file teachers were disenchanted with Gordillo's leadership, and the negotiations that seemed to benefit her and her cadres more than the rank and file. Polls in 2013 from the newspapers *Excelsior* and *Reforma*, as well as the Lower House, showed support for Gordillo plummeting to new lows among teachers (Ornelas 2018, 218).

The election of President Enrique Peña Nieto (2012–18) marked a major shift in the union's relationship to the government and education policy. Peña Nieto had the support of Mexicanos Primero, a think tank with close ties to business leaders and an agenda to increase transparency and end union-based patronage. In December 2012, leaders of all parties in the national legislature signed the Pact for Mexico, a political agreement that aimed to strengthen the Mexican state, democratize politics and the economy, and increase opportunities for civic participation.[12] President Peña Nieto aimed to build on his predecessor's, Felipe Calderón's, incomplete education reform. In 2013, the legislature passed the General Law of Professional Teacher Service, which established universal teacher evaluations for teacher hiring, a merit-based system to promote teachers (rather than promotions based on political work for the union), and a dismissal procedure for teachers who failed the evaluation three times. The new law centralized the teacher payroll in the national Secretariat of Education. The aim was to weaken SNTE's ability to mobilize teachers as voters by preventing union leaders from distributing teaching positions (*asignación de plazas*) and granting teachers leaves of absence to work for the union full time (*comisionados*).

The reforms by Peña Nieto resulted in several important changes. First, there were punishments for teachers who failed to pass the evaluation (Muñoz Armenta 2020). Teachers could retake the evaluation multiple times, but those who failed on the third attempt were reassigned – they did not lose their jobs but were removed from the classroom. Teachers saw this possibility of losing their teaching position as a threat, even if think tanks such as Mexicanos Primero framed this as a rather gentle policy given that teachers could try multiple times to pass the evaluation. In addition, there was a census of teachers to clean up the teacher payroll: Some teachers who were politically connected earned two salaries (even if they did not work both jobs); some teachers whose names were on the payroll

---

[12] This reform advanced with overwhelming support. In the Lower House, 360 representatives voted in favor, with 51 in opposition, and 20 abstentions, only twenty days after President Peña Nieto took office (Muñoz Armenta 2020).

had passed away (and their children or someone who had bought their position taught under their names); and some teachers were on the payroll but never showed up to teach (i.e., ghost teachers). Third, there was the Law of the National Institute of Education Evaluation (INEE) which aimed to support INEE, the governmental agency charged with designing and implementing the teacher evaluation and increasing its autonomy from the union. This law shored up INEE's technical capacity and its ability to carry out evaluations without political interference. Finally, the law introduced competition for the hiring and promotion of teachers. Overall, these reforms aimed to increase transparency but were costly for the governors and union leaders of sections in the states, since governors and union leaders had had a wide latitude to engage in corrupt practices and patronage politics when information about the number of teaching positions and budgets was less transparent (Muñoz Armenta 2020).

There is no question that these new policies were aimed at SNTE because of the instrumental strategy it had adopted and its visible efforts to mobilize teachers as voters. In February 2013, Gordillo was arrested and indicted on charges of money laundering. Her arrest can be interpreted as President Enrique Peña Nieto seeking to deliver on a key campaign promise: to fight against corruption. This arrest was a demonstration of force by the PRI, which wanted to show it could still intervene in labor organizations and replace disloyal union leaders. It was also perceived as a necessary step to advance a broad set of education reforms that would end traditional practices of corruption and replace them with merit-based evaluations. Gordillo's highly visible political negotiations with multiple parties was hard to sustain over time because she became a political pariah.

While Gordillo was released from prison in 2018, because of mistakes by the prosecution, her reputation was tarnished and she no longer controlled the union. While she attempted a political comeback, she remained a marginal player in Mexican politics. In addition, turmoil in the national union leadership meant there was a partial breakdown in hierarchical relations, with several state-level union sections moving in the direction of the dissidents. The dissident movement that took center stage in the 1980s was quiet throughout the 1990s and 2000s, largely coopted by the national union leadership. However, dissident activists lived on in several states, notably Oaxaca, Guerrero, and Michoacán. Discontent with teacher evaluations fueled a renewed wave of protests, and the dissidents gained ground in states where they had previously been weak or nonexistent (Muñoz Armenta 2020). Dissident groups grew stronger because of the turmoil that came with Gordillo's removal.

These reforms, which stripped union leaders of their control over teaching positions, affected the internal operation of the union. Dissidents rallied ordinary teachers against the new union leader Juan Díaz de la Torre, whom they criticized for failing to represent the rank and file, and they maneuvered to make a deal with the president. Moreover, alongside the dissidents who opposed Díaz de la Torre, some union leaders remained loyal to Gordillo, even after she was deposed from the union leadership. Gordillo cast a long shadow and continued to influence several family members who served as political operators. Union leaders such as Díaz de la Torre lacked Gordillo's charismatic appeal, her largesse, and her media-savviness, and they did not have the same capacity to direct teacher mobilization from above and shift the union's political support from one party to another. Juan Díaz's power base was mainly in the national executive committee, as he lacked influence over the union sections in the states. The teacher-based party, PANAL, lost its national registry in 2018. An electoral reform in 2014 raised the vote threshold necessary to maintain a national party registry from 2 to 3 percent, and PANAL failed to meet this higher threshold.

Despite these political setbacks for SNTE and the ensuing changes inside the union, my argument stresses the continuities in the internal organization of the union. With Gordillo out of power, the union remained organized around a dominant faction. Indeed, Juan Díaz de la Torre had the blessing of President Peña Nieto; it was widely understood that Díaz de la Torre would ensure labor peace, advance education reform, and not interfere in the investigation of Gordillo (Fernández 2019, 136). In exchange, President Peña Nieto supported Díaz de la Torre's bid to head the union and agreed to make deals with him that would continue to improve teachers' salaries and subsidize the union. There were other remarkable continuities in SNTE's internal operation as well. In the 2018 labor congress, the old-style practices of secrecy, exclusion of opposition factions, and clientelism were used to rebuild a dominant faction. In the National Labor Congress of 2018 in Puerto Vallarta, union statutes were changed to eliminate the position formerly held by Elba Esther Gordillo. In this congress, Díaz de la Torre was the only candidate eligible to be the president of SNTE, and he named his new group Unity, Pride, and Commitment, resorting to the old practices for winning power.[13] In other

---

[13] Laura Poy Solano y Javier Santos, "Aprueban reforma en el SNTE para relegir a Díaz de la Torre," *La Jornada* February 13, 2018.

words, there was more continuity than change when Díaz de la Torre took over, and a dominant faction remained in power.

If the new education policies limited the union's ability to distribute and sell teacher positions, they also reinforced the internal organization of SNTE because the union continued to negotiate with the government to secure access to new subsidies. Díaz de la Torre built a new dominant faction, and many of the leaders from Gordillo's group joined him. Even with these reforms, Díaz de la Torre still had access to considerable discretionary union resources, which were collected from the union dues of teachers, and he had influence over changes to union statutes. He used these levers to build a dominant faction. Even as the dissidents mobilized protests against the unpopular teacher evaluations, they posed only a limited challenge since the dominant faction controlled union resources. As Bocking notes (2019, 70), "Torre and his allies still appeared to hold a tight grip on power in the majority of state sections and at the national level of the SNTE."

Moreover, President Peña Nieto could capitalize on the union's instrumental strategy, and he did not want to undermine the organizational foundations of the teachers' union that underpinned this strategy. It was much easier for the president to negotiate with the national union leadership than to negotiate with the fractious, militant, and fragmented dissidents. Indeed, Peña Nieto was careful that his language reflected a challenge to Gordillo and her corrupt leadership specifically. In interviews, there was broad agreement that Gordillo was being punished for her betrayal of the PRI, but Peña Nieto's aim was not to undermine SNTE or teachers in Mexico. Given the organization of the union, the best path for the government was to negotiate with the national executive committee of SNTE because that was where interlocutors had some ability to make good on agreements. In other words, the instrumental strategy benefited presidents who had reliable interlocutors, and presidents were reluctant to dismantle the organizational structure that sustained this strategy.

Thus, the union's overall strategy maintained crucial elements of instrumentalism. Even as fractures formed among the groups led by Gordillo, Díaz de la Torre, and the dissidents, teachers remained a powerful voting bloc and instrumental negotiations with different parties continued. Union leaders brokered agreements with President Enrique Peña Nieto. Díaz de la Torre supported the teacher evaluation policies, and, in exchange, the government offered him resources, including salary increases and subsidies (Ornelas 2018, 232–3). This assistance demonstrates continuity in the meetings that took place with the union leader and the government and the announcements on May 15, National Teacher Day, of new raises and generous subsidies. The high-ranking officials saw the dominant faction as a bulwark against the dissident teacher movement and a guarantor of stability.

The new policies that nationalized the management of teacher payroll and promotions weakened the power of union leaders and hindered their ability to redirect political support. Still, there are continuities in both the union's internal organization and its political strategy. SNTE still has a vast store of financial resources and mechanisms to control its member base. Teachers remain a coveted voting bloc, even if union leaders have lost some capacity to direct how teachers will vote. The dominant faction continues to be the main source of power in SNTE, and it can pivot its political support to new political parties. Hence, the union has adapted to political change by maintaining its strategy of negotiating with whoever is in power and relying on electoral mobilization.

CONCLUSION

The consolidation of power within SNTE by Elba Esther Gordillo and her hegemonic faction enabled union leaders to project power outwards, into the party system. Other labor organizations in Mexico were severely weakened by the economic reforms of the 1990s and they became politically marginal. In general, these unions either remained loyal to the PRI or began to gravitate toward the center-left PRD. But teachers were different. SNTE embraced a bold and highly visible strategy of shifting partisan alliances. The hierarchical, top-down organization of SNTE enabled the union to mobilize teachers as voters. While the one-party PRI regime came apart, with voters exercising political rights and defecting from the ruling party, teachers remained under the thumb of the union leadership. Teachers coalesced as a voting bloc in the 2000s as power became more concentrated in the national union leadership. The consolidation of power in the national executive committee, and the high level of discipline among union leaders, enabled the union to shift its support from the PRI to a new party. In 2013, after Gordillo was forced out of the union, the organizational structure remained largely intact, and SNTE continued to pursue an instrumentalist strategy. This demonstrates that within the broader context of democracy and regime opening, union organizations played a crucial role in interest intermediation and shaping how teachers were represented in politics. While ostensibly the transition to multiparty competition gave voters more choices, teachers remained largely contained within their powerful labor union.

The strategies that I have identified in this book generate a distinctive policymaking dynamic in the education sector. For Mexico, the instrumental strategy was effective for many years in terms of pushing up teacher salaries and giving the union access to policymakers. But over time it generated a sharp backlash. SNTE's shamelessness, lack of principles, willingness to form any sort of political alliance, and widely documented practices of patronage politics and clientelism made it a toxic political partner. In other words, the full-blown instrumental strategy generated mounting opposition from other political parties, public opinion, and teachers themselves. Therefore, instrumentalism has a major downside of drawing unwanted scrutiny and attention to the union, thereby setting the policy agenda for a course correction to limit the union's ability to mobilize teachers from the top-down and redirect policy, therefore limiting the union's role in the policy process.

6

Organizational Weakening in Argentina

The political strategy of the largest teacher organization in Argentina, CTERA, contrasts sharply with the Mexican case. While the Mexican teachers' union SNTE relied on coordinated electoral mobilization and strategic negotiations, CTERA was more fractious and rebellious. It had a stronger propensity to reside in the opposition and articulate interests through protests. While this pattern resembled that of the dissident teachers movement in Mexico, it covered a broader swath of the teaching profession. CNTE was relegated to a few Mexican states, but militant teachers were present in most Argentine provinces. A group of CTERA leaders gravitated toward the PJ, a tendency that is broadly observed among nearly all Argentine labor unions. However, the Peronist leadership was not able to bring the rank and file along with them. This is because a group of teachers resisted Peronism and demanded the union maintain its political autonomy. If SNTE's narrow and particularistic demands were entangled with the political ambitions and instrumental strategy of the union leadership, CTERA's demands that centered on labor policy were intertwined with a more restive base that national union leaders struggled to control. CTERA in many ways resembles a social movement union in its repertoire of contention, demands for policies to address labor grievances, and dispersion of power to the base.

This chapter, and Chapter 7, demonstrate how a different organizational model in Argentina produced this strategy of movementism. Movementism in Argentina is characterized by recurring protests and an inability to deliver votes to a given political party. This strategy stems from the weakness of hierarchical relations in CTERA. Divisions that separated the national leadership from provincial and municipal leaderships prevented the coordination of teachers across territory via top-down mobilization. Even if there was some bureaucratization in CTERA, national union leaders could not independently pursue their own political interests.

Elements of CTERA's loose organization can be traced to the 1940s, when teachers were a fragmented field of labor and professional associations. Recall that middle-class teachers asserted their political autonomy and rejected Juan Perón's efforts to incorporate them into unions that were affiliated to his populist movement (vom Hau 2009; Gindin 2011). But there was at least one important parallel with Mexico: In the 1990s, there was a moment of political uncertainty in both countries when education reforms were on the political agenda and teacher–state relations were changing. Indeed, if CTERA was weakened by military repression, by the late 1980s union leaders were taking important steps to consolidate power. Therefore, it is crucial to analyze political changes in the 1990s to explain why the national executive committee of CTERA did not ultimately consolidate power and establish control over provincial unions. This chapter shows that President Carlos Menem's decision in 1992 to impose decentralization on teachers and ignore labor grievances played a major role in undermining national union leaders and empowering militant groups in the provinces.

The decision to decentralize education weakened national union leaders, who were excluded from policy negotiations and denied access to state resources. This undermined organizational hierarchies. The national leaders of CTERA became weaker as they contended with a highly mobilized archipelago of local leaders and grassroots activists. These activists were energized by labor grievances, mobilized from below, and rejected efforts to influence their political engagement. The ongoing presence of local union leaders and grassroots activists constrained the national executive committee. National union leaders could support parties only if those parties made policy concessions that rank-and-file teachers supported; but even then, national union leaders had only a limited capacity to constrain protests. On the other hand, the union avoided involvement in the electoral arena. Grassroots activists rejected political endorsements because they had disparate partisan identities; there were enclaves of Peronism but also teachers who supported center-left parties that were staunchly anti-Peronist, as well as more radical left parties. National union leaders moved toward the PJ, to be sure, but they lacked the resources and political connections to bring along the rank and file.

Various factors created propitious conditions for teacher protests in Argentina: labor grievances stemming from the underfunding of education, and the hardship teachers endured, especially during the financial crisis of 1999 to 2001. Without denying the importance of labor issues, this chapter argues that the organizational structure of CTERA, with power rooted in provincial and municipal actors, is crucial in understanding why teachers engaged in ongoing protests – especially protests that took place during periods of economic expansion when teacher salaries improved. The opening sections look at the process of union rebuilding in the wake of democratization, after harsh repression during the military regime. Even if, with the return to democracy, newly elected leaders offered little support to the union because of the debt crisis, union leaders made some progress in consolidating CTERA through their own initiatives. The chapter then turns to decentralization under President Carlos Menem as a point of inflection. Decentralization undermined national union leaders, weakening their hold on the base. Once organizational hierarchies were weakened, movementism became the union's political strategy.

DEMOCRACY AND ITS DISCONTENTS

After teachers experienced trauma from severe military repression, the democratic transition in 1983 promised teachers better working conditions and stronger unions. At first, democracy seemed to create a favorable opportunity for teachers to influence education and labor policy. The newly elected president, Raúl Alfonsín (1983–9) of the UCR, enacted policies to "democratize" the education system. Teachers who had been arbitrarily fired during military rule were reinstated; new programs of civic education were launched; school enrollment and funding for education increased; and the government organized forums for dialogue between stakeholders in the education sector (Hanson 1996, 309). Indeed, education spending rose steadily from 1983 to 1986, recovering some from the austerity measures that had been imposed by the military regime (Rivas et al. 2010, 35). CTERA supported President Alfonsin's decision to roll back the retrograde education policies that were in place during the reign of the junta.

But President Alfonsín disappointed teachers because, unable to manage hyperinflation and the debt crisis, he had a limited capacity to respond to labor demands. Elected leaders largely ignored CTERA and did little to help build a strong union. The president was preoccupied with more pressing problems: stabilizing the economy during the turmoil of the debt crisis and prosecuting human rights violations perpetrated by the military. Education and teachers were secondary concerns. To be sure, in 1985 the government recognized CTERA as a legal entity, granting it a *personeria gremial* that enabled union leaders to collect dues and post union representatives in schools (Gindin 2011, 124, 131). This was an important step for CTERA in establishing itself as the primary labor organization for teachers. However, compared with teachers' unions in other Latin American countries, this legal recognition came quite late. Moreover, after recognizing CTERA, the government did not furnish the union with subsidies or material resources that could help it to build a strong organization.

Indeed, President Alfonsín was unresponsive to labor unions in general, and teachers were no exception. This stemmed from Alfonsin's ties to the UCR, which had a conflictual relationship with Peronism and workers. Throughout the 1980s, labor conflict broke out. The largest Peronist labor confederation, the CGT led by Saúl Ubaldini, opposed Alfonsín's administration and organized a series of thirteen general strikes (McGuire 1992). In response, the president proposed that unions hold more open internal elections (with the aim of weakening Peronist leaders) and appointed non-Peronist union leaders to positions in government (to sow further divisions among labor unions). For teachers, the president spurned Peronist leaders of CTERA by naming Alfredo Bravo, a former secretary general of CTERA – a socialist, who had been tortured under military rule – to the position of Sub-Secretary of Education. However, this policy of dividing unions only inflamed labor conflict, and Alfonsin proved unable to control labor unrest.

Education policies during the 1980s did not take teacher demands into account. In 1984, the president organized a National Pedagogical Congress that included civil society groups, but this congress disproportionately represented the Catholic Church. Teachers participated but were unable to exert influence owing to weak organization and internal divisions (Gindin 2006, 97). The final set of proposals, issued in 1988, consisted of conservative policies, including education decentralization (Falleti 2010, 89). Ultimately, these proposals were shelved and never enacted into law by Alfonsin's administration because the government faced mounting crises from hyperinflation and rebellions by military officers in 1987. Education policies were proposed and considered, but no concrete actions were taken.

As President Alfonsín faced record budget shortfalls and ongoing financial instability, he was unable to improve teacher salaries. From

1976 to 1988, there was a 23 percent decline in real teacher salaries, which made basic goods and services, such as food and public transportation, unaffordable (Migliavacca 2009, 132). Education spending fell sharply throughout the 1980s – the result of the failure of the president's heterodox stabilization package, the Austral Plan, and mounting hyperinflation. Spending per student declined from 900 pesos in 1987 to 600 in 1989 (Rivas et al. 2010, 34). In this regard Argentina was not unique; throughout Latin America, the combination of runaway inflation and austerity measures sharply eroded teacher salaries and created considerable hardship (Elacqua et al. 2018).

Teachers articulated discontent with both national and provincial governments over their handling of education policy. Because President Alfonsín was unable to improve the working conditions of teachers, CTERA organized ongoing strikes. In 1985, these protests lasted twenty-four or forty-eight hours (Migliavacca 2009, 6). Throughout the 1980s, teachers stood out as one of the most militant sectors of labor. Data on labor conflict shows that from 1984 to 1989 teachers accounted for 12 percent of all strikes, 24 percent of strikers, and 37 percent of workdays lost (McGuire 1996, 138–9; Murillo 2001, 165).

Plummeting education spending from 1987 to 1989 precipitated the White March of 1988, a strike that lasted forty-two days. This protest was historic not only because of its large size and national scope but also because it articulated demands for a comprehensive response from the national government to the problems of teachers. Protesters denounced the failure to pay salaries and pensions in a timely fashion, especially those on the provincial government payroll; the failure to pay substitute teachers; inequalities in salaries across different categories of teachers; the government's refusal to disperse funds that it owed the union; and underinvestment in social welfare funds (i.e., the Teacher Social Welfare Fund, OSPLAD) (Andelique and Tonon 2014, 7). Teachers marched, demonstrated, and organized public spectacles to demand national collective bargaining and federal funds (Migliavacca 2011).[1]

The White March did not convince the government to change course, however. Owing to the debt crisis and chronic budget deficits, the government lacked the resources to meet teacher demands. Not surprisingly, education remained a backburner issue, eclipsed by the ongoing economic crisis. Still, the White March established an enduring network

---

[1] SUTEBA, "23 de mayo de 1988: a 27 años de la marcha blanca," accessed July 19, 2020 via www.suteba.org.ar/23-de-mayo-de-1988-a-27-aos-de-la-marcha-blanca-12097.html.

of militant activists in CTERA who gained experience organizing protests. These activists were mobilized by labor grievances rather than by national union leaders, and so the protests they organized had a spontaneous quality. The official leadership could not control protests. Thus, the White March was a step toward establishing the "self-mobilized" (*auto-convocados*), a dissident teacher movement that would challenge the official leadership (Migliavacca 2011). This landmark protest, and the lack of government response to it, laid the groundwork for an activist base to become the driving force behind teacher mobilization.

STEPS TOWARD UNION CONSOLIDATION

In the wake of democratization, there were some initial signs that CTERA would consolidate power and affiliate to the PJ. While President Alfonsín ignored teachers and the White March stimulated grassroots activism, union leaders with ties to the PJ began to centralize power in CTERA through their own initiatives. However, rival teachers' unions maintained legal registries and continued to affiliate teachers. These included the "orthodox" Peronist union (UDA), the Argentine Association of Technical Teaching (AMET), the Argentine Union of Private School Teachers (SADOP), an independent union, the Confederation of Argentine Educators (CEA), and several small, regional ones (Perazza and Legarralde 2008, 19–21). Rather than being automatically affiliated to a union, teachers in Argentina had to file an application to join a union, and by the early 2000s only 55 percent joined CTERA – a majority, but not all teachers (Murillo et al. 2002, 210; Chiappe 2012, 2–3). CTERA faced other rival unions and did not have a monopoly on teacher representation. Still, union leaders began to bring some order to the fragmented field of teacher organizations and establish CTERA as the largest and most important teacher organization.

CTERA did achieve a degree of consolidation. In 1984, it had 150,000 members divided among 54 base organizations; by 2001, it had 233,585 members divided among 25 base organizations (Gindin 2011, 138). By the late 1980s, CTERA had established itself not only as the dominant teachers' union, but also as one of the largest and most influential labor organizations in Argentina. Within CTERA, union consolidation and the formation of a dominant faction went hand in hand. The Lista Celeste, a faction with a core of leaders from the Peronist left, was rapidly gaining power. In 1985, CTERA's third national congress selected Wenceslao Arizcuren of the UCR as the secretary general. In 1987, the Celeste ramped up its organizing and won enough votes in the fourth labor congress to make Marco Garcetti of the PJ the secretary general of CTERA; the Ministry of Labor recognized Garcetti as CTERA's official leader.

Because of the history of Peronism in Argentine labor organizations and the potential of the Lista Celeste to dominate CTERA, the rise of this group of leaders generated consternation among rival factions, which culminated in a leadership crisis. When Garcetti was named the new secretary general of CTERA, the incumbent, Wenceslao Arizcuren, refused to step down, and CTERA temporarily fractured into two organizations. During the White March of 1988, Arizcuren denounced Garcetti for failing to communicate the status of negotiations with the base, even though the base sustained the strike, and of being out of touch with the rank-and-file (Migliavacca 2011). In the end, Garcetti prevailed by gaining the support of teachers who were center-left Peronists, orthodox Peronists, and moderate sectors of the UCR. Arizcuren only had the radical sectors of the UCR and support from a handful of small, left parties, and he eventually relinquished power (Gindin 2006, 97; 2011, 140). A dominant group that established its control over the national executive committee had emerged.

Fears of the Celeste establishing a hegemonic faction, like the one in Mexico, were not unfounded. Celeste embarked on an ambitious project to "Peronize" the union by changing union statutes to its advantage. Since CTERA's founding in 1973, union leaders were selected through labor congresses based on a formula of proportional representation. This was used to guarantee power sharing among union leaders from different political parties, and it helped to bring together teachers with various partisan identities. However, having rival parties represented in leadership had the downside of exacerbating internal conflict and paralyzing decision-making – as became evident during the conflict between Arizcuren and Garcetti (Murillo 1999, 42). After the Celeste won power, this faction changed union statutes in a way that entrenched it in CTERA's national executive committee by ending the system of selecting union leaders in labor congresses via proportional representation and establishing a winner-takes-all formula. The new procedure for selecting union leaders involved, first, forming a list of proposed candidates for each of the leadership positions in the national executive committee. Then each list competed for the votes of union members in a union-sponsored election. The list with the most votes won and took over the national executive committee. The new procedure had the advantage of strengthening union democracy, since teachers directly elected the union leaders. But as the Celeste became the largest group, the winner-takes-all formula gave it an advantage over rivals. Indeed, in the ensuing elections in CTERA, the Celeste has continuously won and held power over the national executive committee and the largest provincial organizations. While there has been leadership turnover within the Celeste, with Peronists and non-Peronists holding power, the same faction has held power since 1987.

But if there was an impulse for union consolidation (and bureaucratization) in both Mexico and Argentina, there was greater resistance from the base in Argentina. In 1988, the Lista Celeste affiliated the union to the CGT, the Peronist Labor Central. As a condition for joining the CGT, labor law required that CTERA only recognize one local union in each province. It needed to combine various provincial unions into a single organization. But union leaders and activists from left parties spearheaded resistance against this consolidation effort, fearing that they would be excluded from power (Migliavacca 2011). In response to a perceived power grab, AMET and UDA, which had joined CTERA in 1985, permanently broke ties in 1988 (Gindin 2011, 141–3). Provincial unions in Chaco, Tucumán, Santiago del Estero, and Santa Cruz also withdrew, albeit temporarily (Gindin 2011, 142). Thus, efforts to restructure CTERA and align it with the PJ sparked a rebellion among union leaders and grassroots activists who staunchly opposed a centralized union that embraced Peronism.

By 1989, union leaders had made some progress toward consolidating power. The Lista Celeste, which was made up of union leaders mostly from the Peronist left, took over the national executive committee. Robert Michels' (1962) infamous "iron law of oligarchy," whereby even the most democratic political parties and social movements inevitably transform into hierarchical and bureaucratic organizations, seemed to be taking hold. Since the democratic transition, union leaders had more space to organize teachers and establish a stronger labor organization. The Celeste seemed to be outcompeting rivals and transforming CTERA into a labor organization with strong ties to the PJ.

IMPOSED DECENTRALIZATION AND ITS CONSEQUENCES

In Mexico, President Salinas' education package of 1992, which limited decentralization and subsidized SNTE, shored up Elba Esther Gordillo. By contrast, decentralization in Argentina during the same period weakened national leaders of CTERA. The economic reforms of President Menem marked a political realignment in Argentina (Levitsky 2003). Along with economic policy, education was also transformed, with major ramifications for teacher labor relations and school funding (Murillo 2001; Corrales 2004; Falleti 2010). Decentralization changed intergovernmental relations. It also had far-reaching consequences for the structure of the union organization and the contentious pattern of mobilization because this policy undermined the authority of national union leaders.

For CTERA, the 1980s was a period of rebuilding as the union recovered from military rule. On the eve of the presidential election in 1988, CTERA was establishing a more centralized organization and the Lista Celeste was strengthening CTERA's ties to the PJ. When Marco Garcetti stepped down, the next secretary general from the Lista Celeste was Mary Sánchez, an experienced leader who had led the White March. Sánchez was a Peronist. She supported Saul Ubaldini, the leader of the CGT, and endorsed the candidacy of Carlos Menem since Menem campaigned to adopt policies that would benefit workers. After May 14, 1989, Menem was elected with a mandate to adopt heterodox economic policies – he had made vague promises to create jobs and improve salaries, albeit with few details.[2]

But once in office, President Menem enacted "neoliberalism by surprise" (Stokes 2001), catching his allies and opponents off guard by embracing the neoliberal economic model. He privatized state-owned enterprises and adopted the Convertibility Plan, which pegged the Argentine peso to the US dollar (Murillo 2001, 134; Corrales 2002). These policies ended hyperinflation, which had stabilized by 1991, and returned the economy to growth (at least during his first term in office), but also contributed to rising unemployment, poverty, and the expansion of the informal sector. To enact these policies, President Menem reconfigured the PJ, shifting power to regional party bosses, business leaders, and technocrats, while labor leaders were demoted (Levitsky 2003). In the past, the PJ had connected to voters via programmatic exchanges with labor unions; Menem instead connected to voters through clientelistic networks that operated through territorial organizations (Szwarcberg 2013; Oliveros 2016). Menen's strategy of dealing with unions, like that of President Salinas in Mexico, was bifurcated. He leveraged a shared Peronist identity to pressure union leaders to support his economic reforms, even when they generated discontent among rank-and-file workers. In exchange for supporting his new policies, Menem compensated some unions (Etchemendy

---

[2] Shirley Christian, "Argentina's President-Elect in the Shadow of Perón: Carlos Saul Menem," *New York Times* May 16, 1989.

2011). But he also took a more repressive approach toward unions that opposed his policies, such as the dissident Peronist Saul Ubaldini, who split from the CGT. Menem replaced dissident union leaders, prevented union leaders from gaining access to union finances, and used force to put down striking workers (Dean 2022, 113–47).

As President Menem turned to the neoliberal economic model, a major education reform was on the political agenda. The Ministry of Economy, led by Domingo Cavallo, a technocrat, wanted rapid, far-reaching decentralization. While the military had decentralized preprimary and primary education in 1978, in 1987, the national government still operated 45 percent of secondary and 27 percent of technical schools (Murillo 2001,164). Under Cavallo's proposal, the national government would hand over the secondary and technical schools (and teachers) it managed to provincial governments without providing federal funding to cover the additional cost. Such a reform would reduce the national government's budget deficit, although it would sharply cut resources to teachers and schools.

One reason for pushing the unfunded decentralization policy was to reduce wasteful spending. In the less developed provinces in the interior of the country, the public sector was used to create jobs for political allies – and, indeed, in interior provinces such as Santiago de Estero 87 percent of the economically active population was employed by the provincial government (Gibson 2005, 123; Gervasoni 2018). The education sector was no stranger to patronage politics. Reducing federal transfers to the provinces would pressure governors to tighten budgets and control spending on public sector jobs. There were reports of problems with the public sector payroll in provinces such as La Rioja. Turnover in the governorship created political turmoil and a lack of continuity in the technical teams in the Secretariat of Education, suggesting patronage politics (Cruz Olmeda 2003, 34; see also McGuire 1996, 140). Indeed, on occasion, the national government had to intervene and bail out heavily indebted provincial governments that could not cover the cost of the provincial payroll (Nicolini et al. 2002). For the national government, reforms that would reduce a bloated public sector would help to tame unsustainable federal spending that contributed to inflation.

There was another way to decentralize education that would shelter teachers from harsh budget cuts. The Ministry of Education preferred a gradual decentralization that included more funding from the national government (González 2016, 213). In 1990, Secretary of Education Luis Barry proposed a bill to the national legislature based on the National

Pedagogical Congress that had been sponsored by President Alfonsín; this would decentralize education to the provinces but transfer the necessary federal funds to cover the cost of the teacher payroll (González 2016, 212). In other words, decentralization proposals with varying levels of federal funding were on the table.

However, Barry's bill died in committee because it lacked legislative support.[3] The president and his top economic advisers had already decided to prioritize cutting federal expenditures on education. President Menem sided with Minister of Economy Domingo Cavallo and supported his (unfunded) policy, outlined earlier (Perazza and Legarralde 2008, 17). This transfer of secondary, technical, and state-subsidized private schools to the provinces affected all teachers, including primary school teachers, since the operating cost of the entire school system in each province increased without additional revenues.

To pass the Federal Law of Education, President Menem relied on his technocratic cadre to negotiate with governors. Education decentralization was a difficult reform to enact because governors voiced concerns about revenue shortfalls for schools: They did not want to be responsible for covering the additional cost of public schools that the national government wanted to impose on them. However, there was a political opportunity to enact reform in 1991, at a time when President Menem could capitalize on his popularity for having stabilized hyperinflation along with improved fiscal conditions as the economy returned to growth. The president and his ministers pressured and ultimately convinced reluctant governors to support this law without addressing concerns about its future ramifications; they negotiated side payments and argued that rising growth would give provincial governments more revenues to offset the added cost (González 2016, 213). One by one the governors signed off, and Menem announced the new policy in a national television address, arguing that restructuring the education sector was necessary to modernize and rationalize state spending. A bill was rushed through Congress. The Minister of Economy, Domingo Cavallo, put the decentralization of secondary schools in a budget submitted to Congress in 1992. The Federal Law of Education was passed in 1993 because governors

---

[3] According to Falleti (2010, 90): "The proposal called for a gradual and funded transfer of schools. It was presented to Congress in February of 1990. In this proposal, authored by Secretary of Education Luis A. Barry, the transfer of schools was only one step in the process leading to the decentralization of education, whose main objective was to improve the quality of education. But the proposal was shelved at the congressional Education Committee and never reached the floor."

pressed the national legislators from their provinces to support the bill, and Menem already had agreements with the governors before the bill reached Congress (Falleti 2010, 90–2). In other words, Menem got the decentralization law he wanted because national legislators serve as the agents of governors, and the Peronist governors fell under the authority of a Peronist president (Calvo and Abal Medina 2001).

The president, having engaged in protracted and difficult negotiations with the governors, refused to negotiate with CTERA. When teachers protested, Menem sought to suppress dissent, adopting an approach that echoed the strategy he used on dissident unions that opposed his neoliberal economic policies (Dean 2022). He encouraged governors to adopt a penalty for teachers who participated in protests, with the Orwellian name of an "attendance bonus" (*presentismo*) – a bonus for perfect attendance that was, in practice, a penalty on teachers who missed even a single day of class to engage in protests. These bonuses varied considerably in size; on average, they accounted for 6 percent of teacher pay, but in some provinces such as Santa Cruz, the attendance bonus represented 33–50 percent of the base salary of teachers (Delgado 2002; Murillo and Ronconi 2004, 95). Many teachers were afraid to lose such a large share of their take-home pay. In addition, the bonuses were determined by gubernatorial decree, and were implemented at the discretion of governors whenever they needed to discourage teachers from protesting.[4] In the short term, threats and hardline measures contained protests, especially at national level. From 1992 to 1994, there was a decrease in the number of teacher protests, with just over twenty per year (Murillo 2001, 165). Over the long term, however, as grievances festered and pressure built up, these measures would not deter protests.

Menem negotiated compensation with other Peronist unions who supported his economic policies, often in the form of union control over social welfare funds. But he continued not to negotiate with CTERA, and he did not compensate the union (Murillo 2001, 152; Falleti 2010). Instead, Menem took advantage of the fragmented field of teacher organizations, playing one union against another. In 1989, Menem put UDA, the orthodox Peronist teachers' union, in charge of administering social funds (OSPLAD and Caja Complementaria) – even though UDA was smaller and less representative of teachers than CTERA (Perazza

---

[4] For example, in the province of Buenos Aires, the bonus was suspended in 1994, then reapplied in 2002, when teachers took the streets in the wake of the financial crisis (Murillo and Ronconi 2004, 81).

and Legarralde 2008; Nardacchione 2014, 18).⁵ As a result, CTERA had limited access to state resources and subsidies, which are crucial if union leaders wish to consolidate power and establish hierarchical relations with the base.

Decentralization had sweeping consequences for the public school system in Argentina. It also strongly shaped how the teachers in that system were represented in politics. Decentralization was imposed on the union and CTERA did not get concessions. President Menem's policy decision had an element of contingency since alternative proposals were on the table. These may well have promoted a stronger national union leadership, without dispersing as much power to the provincial and municipal unions. But Menem pursued a bold unfunded decentralization policy, and because of this approach teacher grievances festered and grassroots activists were energized.

UNION CONSOLIDATION, DISRUPTED

President Carlos Menem's decision to impose decentralization on CTERA disrupted the incipient process of union consolidation. This policy decision had three consequences for the internal life of CTERA and how teachers were represented in politics: (1) provincial union leaders gained policy authority and resources vis-à-vis national union leaders, weakening organizational hierarchies, (2) labor grievances strengthened grassroots activists at the municipal level, and (3) political dealignment caused by CTERA's split from the PJ reinforced a multiparty identity in the union.

(1) *Weakening organizational hierarchies*: In Argentina, decentralization broke down the chain of command connecting the national executive committee and provincial unions. This policy reversed efforts by national union leaders to consolidate power because the Federal Law of Education effectively transformed CTERA into a loose confederation of provincial unions. After this law was passed, provincial union leaders were responsible for negotiating changes to teacher policy and pressuring governors to improve teacher salaries. In other words, weakening hierarchies meant that leaders in CTERA's national executive committee

---

⁵ CTERA was excluded from the policy process: "CTERA complained of the government manipulating union competition by granting registration to competing organizations, favoring other unions as bargaining partners, and trying to grant them the control of the teachers' welfare fund" (Murillo 2001, 166).

were not supreme; rather, they deferred to provincial leaders and grassroots activists who were the de facto representatives of teachers. In some junctures, local and provincial union leaders had interests that aligned with the national leadership, to be sure, but national leaders lacked the capacity to control the base. As predicted by Tiramonti (2001, 17), with education decentralization, power in CTERA resided below the national executive committee, in the provincial organizations and in the municipal union sections.

As a consequence of federalism, there were a variety of labor laws and collective bargaining arrangements across Argentine provinces. Some teachers' unions engaged in collective bargaining at the provincial level, but a significant proportion of provinces had not legalized collective bargaining for teachers. In the absence of the right to bargain collectively, the only recourse for these unions was to stage disruptive protests to pressure provincial authorities to negotiate salary increases. Power resided in the provincial union leaders who presented lists of demands to governors, while national union leaders stood on the sidelines (Gindin 2011, 143).

Control over union resources further strengthened the union leaders in the provinces. Whereas SNTE's vertical structure was partially a function of the national executive committee's control over union dues, for CTERA union dues were transferred to the coffers of provincial unions, which in turn deposited 10 percent in the account of the national executive committee. But provincial unions also had the authority to withhold dues from national union leaders. Therefore, CTERA was a loose confederation and leaders in CTERA's national executive committee were deferential to provincial union leaders. Leaders of large provincial unions, such as Robert Baradel, the secretary general of the largest provincial union in the Province of Buenos Aires, the Union of Education Workers (SUTEBA), were identified as having the strongest de facto influence in CTERA.

Even though, officially, the highest-ranking leader of CTERA, the secretary general, led the confederation, the secretary general was more of a figurehead and less of a power broker. Throughout the 1990s, the decentralization policy created an existential crisis for national union leaders because the national government did not set labor regulations, nor did it engage in collective bargaining. Moreover, during Menem's administration, national policymakers refused to meet with union leaders. CTERA leaders only had authority over functions that were of lesser importance to teachers, such as teacher training and continuing education (Perazza and Legarralde 2008, 21–2, 33). Pushed out of the policy process, national leaders had limited authority to articulate the interests of the rank and file.

National union leaders had limited access to state subsidies. Whereas SNTE's national executive committee received generous subsidies, CTERA's national executive committee received little support. The teachers' union played an uneven role in managing social welfare benefits for teachers. In 1989, a rival union, UDA, took over the social welfare fund for teachers (OSPLAD), which provided health services and other benefits. CTERA would later regain influence on the boards of these social welfare funds, but the funds suffered from chronic state underinvestment. CTERA leaders were not able to secure resources from these funds to establish political control. Indeed, decentralization halted the process of organization building and weakened the national executive committee. Overall, national union leaders had little leverage over their provincial counterparts, since the provincial leaders played a larger role in managing union finances and providing services to teachers.

(2) *Labor grievances*: If national union leaders lacked the resources and policy authority to consolidate power, even provincial union leaders did not fully consolidate power. Consider Robert Baradel, who led the largest provincial teachers' union in Argentina, SUTEBA, with 116,000 members. Baradel was widely regarded as one of the most powerful leaders in CTERA. He was militant, challenging any governor of the province who refused to negotiate large salary increases by staging massive teacher strikes. He was a staunch Peronist, a part of the Lista Celeste, and would become a close ally of President Cristina Fernández de Kirchner.

However, even powerful regional union leaders such as Baradel contended with a militant base. Baradel exercised control over much of SUTEBA, but there was ongoing contestation over who had influence in the municipal level base organizations. Indeed, in 2013, nine union locals of SUTEBA – in La Matanza, Tigre, Quilmes, Ensenada, Escobar, Bahía Blanca, Marcos Paz, General Madariaga, and Berazategu – supported left parties and rejected Baradel's faction, the Lista Celeste (De Luca 2018). This grassroots support for militant, leftist union leaders stemmed from ongoing labor grievances. Even Baradel was unable to resolve many of the underlying issues of salaries that did not keep pace with ongoing inflation and the rising cost of living. While Baradel accumulated substantial resources, he faced constant pressure from grassroots activists. In other words, even the highest profile provincial leaders of CTERA lacked the capacity to control union base organizations and mobilize teachers

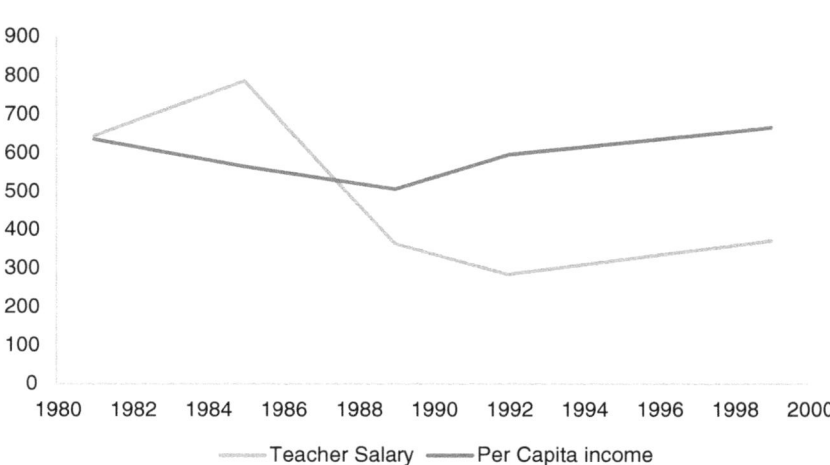

FIGURE 6.1 Teacher salaries versus income per capita, Argentina
Source: Rivas et al. 2010, 41

from the top down; an activist base in union locals and schools operated autonomously. Governors could not count on provincial leaders to restrain contentious actions by these militant groups.

In Mexico, ongoing negotiations between SNTE and the government resulted in continuous increases in teacher salaries. By contrast, in Argentina, labor grievances festered. The government responded to teacher complaints about low salaries intermittently, and often in a partial way, because of strained budgets and because teachers were a low priority. This lack of responsiveness energized militant activists. The militant base first emerged in the White March of 1988. It became even more powerful when teachers experienced ongoing hardship due to the unfunded decentralization reform. Since governors lacked the resources to cover the cost of the teacher payroll, they resorted to underhand tactics to balance budgets, such as paying salaries late and freezing salary adjustments. Figure 6.1 shows that teacher salaries fell sharply from 1985 to 1992, and they fell below per capita income. Although teacher salaries recovered some from 1992 to 1999 (in the run up to Argentina's financial crisis) they remained well below per capita income. The fall in teacher salaries was attributed to the dearth of federal funds for provincial governments (Rivas et al. 2010, 41). The late payment of salaries coupled with low pay enraged teachers. Provincial leaders were unable to solve these problems, which created an opening for militant activists to give voice to teacher discontent.

A variety of indicators show how dramatic the decline in teacher pay really was. From 1985 to 1998, teacher salaries (including bonuses and other benefits) fell by 31 percent in the province of Buenos Aires and 33 percent for the City of Buenos Aires (Migliavacca 2011, 100). The Buenos Aires metro area made up 43 percent of all teachers in Argentina. Forty percent of female teachers were the primary breadwinners in their households (with two to five dependents on average), and 50 percent of these households fell below the poverty line (CTERA 2003). "Pauperization" created a shortage of teachers, since meager pay discouraged entry into the profession (Donaire 2009).[6] Indeed as late as 2020, a shortage of teachers forced officials in Buenos Aires to hire 1,300 non-Argentine teachers (largely Peruvians, but also Venezuelan refugees) to keep classrooms staffed.[7] Difficult working conditions made teachers sympathetic to militant activists who took a hardline position vis-à-vis the government.

In addition to low salaries and late payments, decentralization also resulted in unequal pay across provinces. This policy was regressive, disproportionately affecting the poorest provinces, where teachers earned much less than those living in wealthier ones. The absence of the national government exacerbated inequality. National and provincial union leaders alike struggled to address this, and the inequality further fueled the militant base.

During the debt crisis of the 1980s, labor grievances contributed to a robust dissident teacher movement in Mexico. Elba Esther Gordillo demobilized this movement because she negotiated improvements in teacher pay. By contrast, in Argentina, prolonged labor grievances festered well into the 1990s (after the debt crisis) because of the unfunded decentralization policy and other efforts to control education spending. This policy fueled a militant teacher movement that national leaders were unable to control. Low pay enabled activists to criticize national and provincial union leaders for not doing enough to address teacher grievances and to establish deep roots in the base. These activists became a permanent fixture in CTERA and continued to agitate for spontaneous protests in the 2000s, even as progress was being made in improving teacher pay.

---

[6] Ricardo Donaire, "Acercamiento empírico al reclutamiento de los docentes," Documento de Trabajo No. 28, 2001.
[7] Maximiliano Fernández, "Por la falta de maestros, 1.300 docentes extranjeros ya están inscriptos para dar clases en la ciudad de Buenos Aires," *Infobae* January 22, 2020.

(3) *Political dealignment*: President Menem's decision to reconfigure the Peronist coalition and impose decentralization on the teachers' union is an instance of what Roberts (2014, 112–13) calls "programmatic dealignment," in which labor unions reject labor-based parties that embrace neoliberal reforms. Facing pressure to adopt new policies to address high inflation and stagnant growth, labor-based parties embraced bait-and-switch strategies and supported neoliberal policies that went against the interests of rank-and-file party members. This type of dealignment tends to weaken support for populist parties and empowers leftist groups. Roberts' insight is helpful for understanding the political identities of teachers in Argentina. Menem's education policies strengthened anti-Peronist groups and reinforced CTERA's multiparty identity. While CTERA had been moving in the direction of the PJ, another consequence of the decentralization reform was that no single political party established control over CTERA. Rather, a powersharing arrangement was institutionalized.

Teachers were pushed out of Menem's coalition, and many felt betrayed by the PJ. Education decentralization halted "Peronization," which had been taking hold in the late 1980s. Indeed, teachers moved into the opposition, along with other center-left Peronist factions. Mary Sánchez, the secretary general of CTERA, withdrew from the PJ and joined the Broad Front (Frente Grande), a group of ex-Peronists who became disaffected with Menem and formed their own, small political party, which resided in the opposition. In addition to Mary Sánchez, many leaders of CTERA played a key role in the founding of this party.

In 1991, CTERA withdrew from the Peronist labor central, the CGT, and helped to launch a new type of labor central, the CTA. The founding of the CTA represented a new form of social movement unionism in Argentina, one that was more internally democratic and aligned with broader social issues.[8] Teachers and public sector workers were the backbone of this confederation. The Lista Celeste, which had been a Peronist faction, incorporated non-Peronist leaders. The next secretary general of CTERA, Marta Maffei, was from the Intransigent Party, a small leftist party that had defected from the UCR in the 1960s and was aligned with the Celeste. Another influential leader, Eduardo Macaluse, was an independent. The Celeste became a multiparty vehicle for power-sharing, rather than an exclusively Peronist faction.

---

[8] Garay (2017, 43) describes social movement unions as labor organizations that "press for workplace, social, and political issues that affect their members and broader communities."

Anger with Menem temporarily eased tensions among rival leaders, aligning union leaders with disparate partisan affiliations. The decentralization law brought various teacher organizations together: CTERA, AMET, UDA, CEA, and SADOP all opposed the austerity measures imposed on education. In CTERA, non-Peronist provincial unions in Chaco, Tucumán, Santiago del Estero, and Santa Cruz, which had withdrawn in 1988, rejoined in 1992 because of Menem's policies. Partisan differences were less salient because of teacher polarization against Menem. Unity was achieved since teachers rejected neoliberal policies no matter their partisan identity. However, this convergence of different groups was triggered by opposition to the government, rather than the capacity of union leaders to leverage union resources to exert discipline over teachers.

To summarize, the unfunded decentralization policy had three crucial effects. First, it weakened the national executive committee and strengthened provincial union leaders, since policy authority and union resources were devolved to the provincial level. Second, it galvanized rank-and-file activists with labor grievances, strengthening a militant base and preventing provincial leaders from consolidating power. Third, it drove a wedge between CTERA and the PJ of Carlos Menem, and thus cemented a power-sharing arrangement among various parties. The result was that no cohesive group of union leaders consolidated power; national, provincial, and local leaders acted independently of one another.

CONCLUSION

This chapter has shown what happens when governments neglect unions and enact policies that generate labor grievances. The outcome is a militant labor movement that is unruly and unresponsive to the official union leadership. Major policy decisions, namely unfunded decentralization, can set back union-building efforts, and produce a many-headed hydra. In interviews, leaders of CTERA, such as Secretary General Stella Maldonado, recognized the fluid power relations within CTERA:

We believe that we have the most democratic labor union of any in Argentina. In our labor congresses, union leaders come with a popular mandate from the base, they cannot come and vote however they want ... I go to all the provinces and meet with local leaders and also the delegates from the schools and I speak directly with the teachers ... There is a very fluid contact between me and the rank and file, and there is the same thing with the provincial union leaders and the base. (Stella Maldonado, interview, November 14, 2012)

Rather than having a rigid, hierarchical organization for articulating interests, CTERA is a union in which power is dispersed. Union leaders touted CTERA's internal democracy and the ways in which all teachers had a space to participate in internal union elections.[9] However, this chapter has demonstrated that union democracy in part reflects the political weakness of national union leaders. Political decisions by President Carlos Menem played a major role in dispersing power in CTERA and cementing a bottom-up mobilizing structure. While CTERA was headed by a dominant faction, the Lista Celeste, this faction did not have control over the union. Powerful activist networks challenged the dominance of this group.

> Within CTERA there are minority groups that question the leaders of the Celeste, and these opposition groups are independent, Marxist, and anti-bureaucratic. For example, Tribuna Docente, is a group in CTERA which has a presence in the provinces of Neuquén, Buenos Aires, Entre Ríos and Santa Cruz. Tribuna Docente is linked to the Trotskyite Workers Party, which is highly critical of the Lista Celeste, which it considers to be made up of union bureaucrats. (Asciutto 2013, 202)

Among Argentine labor organizations, CTERA was not unique. Other public employees, such as the Association of State Workers (ATE) and health worker unions also had a militant base that regularly protested. In many ways, CTERA reflects the broader pattern of dissident Peronist unions that rejected Menems' neoliberal reforms and party discipline. The government's spurning of CTERA during the 1990s had implications for the labor movement, especially public sector unions. Leaders of CTERA played a major role in the founding of the CTA, a rival labor central to the CGT, which was made up of Peronist unions that were disaffected with Menem's leadership of the PJ. The CTA would grow to become a major player in Argentine politics that represented workers in various sectors, beyond education.

---

[9] While CTERA was more internally democratic than SNTE, there were disagreements about how internally democratic CTERA really was, because internal union elections were not monitored by outside observers and it was difficult to verify how transparent the electoral proceedings were.

7

Movementism in Argentina

The organizational structure of CTERA, in which relations between national union leaders and the base were less hierarchical than in Mexico, generated movementism. The weakness in hierarchical relations created space for a militant base to establish itself. This base was not responsive to the political endorsements of the national executive committee. The militant base was one of several factors that shaped recurrent protests, but this chapter argues that it played a crucial role in sustaining them. Certainly, a highly mobilized base accounts for the propensity of teachers to engage in ongoing provincial-level labor conflict – even when prolabor Peronist governments were in office – and the tendency for teachers to express opposition to right-wing governments with high levels of strike activity. The restiveness of the base also helps explain CTERA's limited role in electoral politics, especially its refusal to mobilize its members to vote for the PJ. Building on Murillo (2001), Burgess (2004), Caraway (2012), and other scholars who have shown that leadership and union competition generate oppositional repertoires, my argument stresses the consequences of a breakdown in vertical relations in the same union (i.e., CTERA) at different levels (i.e., national, provincial, and municipal) on the propensity of worker protests to become a routine and enduring part of political life.

The tenuousness of hierarchical relations in CTERA also prevented the union from organizing an effective electoral operation. The union's organizational structure limited its capacity to mobilize teachers from the top down. While CTERA was formally organized around the Lista Celeste, a faction with strong ties to the PJ that continuously held the national executive committee, this faction was not uniformly Peronist and it lacked discipline. It was unable to mobilize teachers in the political arena. Because the union lacked access to the abundant state resources that SNTE enjoyed, it was unable to influence how teachers voted; nor did CTERA establish clientelistic relations.

As in Mexico, democracy and multiparty competition in Argentina created new coalitional possibilities for union leaders to participate in the formation of new political parties and negotiate alliances. But the new parties that union leaders helped to found had weak support from CTERA because teachers were politically divided and did not follow the union leadership. To be sure, the governments of Nestor Kirchner and Cristina Fernández de Kirchner created unprecedented opportunities for national leaders of CTERA to gain representation in a prolabor government. The Kirchners provided policy concessions, and several union leaders were recruited to serve as political candidates for this political group. Still, union leaders did not deliver teachers as a cohesive voting bloc to the Kirchners. The characteristics of the union organization, then, explain a great deal of why CTERA had a small electoral footprint and avoided entanglements in party politics. The union engaged in political exchanges on policy issues, but national leaders had a limited capacity to deliver votes or even strike restraint.

The next sections examine how the bottom-up organization of CTERA was crucial for movementism. The mark of the activist base on protests is reflected in the fact that protests were organized primarily at provincial and municipal levels, were widespread across provinces, and recurred over time. Patterns of protest by Argentine teachers look quite different from those of their Mexican counterparts, and there are contrasts between Argentine teachers versus other workers such as the Teamsters. The next section examines the union's role in electoral politics. While some union leaders became politicians, the union was not beholden to any political party, and it lacked a coherent partisan identity. The last section analyzes the policy dynamics that ensued from movementism and the extent to which the creation of a new policy, a national institution of collective bargaining for teachers, transformed the union's political repertoire.

THE REPERTOIRE OF MOVEMENTISM

Teacher labor relations in Argentina have been conflictual, especially at the provincial level. CTERA was a loose confederation of provincial unions that had relatively democratic procedures for selecting its leaders.

Effectively, it was a many-headed hydra, with its energy in provincial union leaders and municipal activists. The union's political strategy centered on oppositional collective action. Protests are a recurrent feature of provincial politics throughout Argentina; they also took place at the national level when conservative governments were in power. This idea is in line with Murillo (2001, 11–26) and others who have shown that more divided unions, where there is a replacement threat and problems of coordination among rival union leaders, tend to be more militant. My analysis extends this framework to explain militancy that is sustained over time. Tensions in union organizations, among leaders at different levels, contribute to ongoing protests. CTERA's lack of hierarchy generated a tendency for many protests to occur each year. In the 1990s, President Menem's crackdown on teacher protests induced fear among union leaders who wanted to avoid retaliatory decrees, fines, and prosecution for protests that were declared illegal. But pressure built up from below and then boiled over as the activist base established itself. Activists did not care about punitive decrees or the legality of protests. By the mid-1990s, there was an explosion of activity.

The contrasts between teacher protests in Mexico and Argentina highlight the importance of the rank and file. In Mexico, protests were intermittent and relegated to a few union sections. To be sure, the dissident teacher movement, CNTE, had a strong capacity for organizing disruptive protests. CNTE gained attention in the early 2010s, with an uptick in protests resulting from teacher evaluations and new policies for hiring teachers by Presidents Felipe Calderón and Enrique Peña Nieto. But protests were a response to specific policy changes, that is, teacher evaluation and merit-based exams for hiring teachers. In most states in Mexico, especially in the northern and central parts of the country, CNTE was nonexistent, and teacher protests either never or almost never occurred. Even after Juan Díaz de la Torre took over SNTE in 2013, most union sections in Mexico remained affiliated to the institutional group that almost never protested. CNTE was relegated to the poorer, southern parts of Mexico, with its strongest presence in the states of Oaxaca, Guerrero, and Michoacán. Teacher strikes were generally not widespread.

By contrast, in Argentina, the scope of teacher militancy was broader. There was no institutional group in CTERA that restrained militancy and delivered strike restraint. On the contrary, since democratization, protests had been a routine, ongoing phenomenon. In most years, students in multiple provinces were not able to return to classes at the start of the academic year because of teacher unrest. Newspapers regularly printed maps of Argentinian provinces showing where classes would begin normally and where protests would prevent them from starting owing to disagreements over salary adjustments.[1] In other words, teacher protests in Argentina were the most central feature of education politics and they received the majority of national political attention.

Teacher protests were frequently mentioned in interviews. For critical observers, the union's strategy of movementism had negative connotations. Teacher protests were a sort of extortion racket. Many of them took place in violation of the law. The fulcrum of CTERA's political power resided in its capacity to engage in permanent conflict with the government to instill fear into ministers of education. In other words, teacher strikes were a way in which CTERA coerced the government to come around to its positions. For sympathetic observers, teacher protests were about underpaid workers demanding labor rights and recognition, challenging governments that neglected them, and calling out officials on broken promises.

The pattern of teacher protests, compared with contentious mobilization by other Argentine workers, also highlights the distinctive organization of CTERA. Quantitative measures of teacher protests show that teachers were the most militant sector of labor in Argentina (Chiappe 2012). The activist base was the primary driver of recurrent protests. National-level protests were coordinated from the center by the national executive committee, and only when conservative governments enacted major policy changes that angered the rank and file. In general, national-level collective action was less common. Rather, teacher protests typically took place at provincial or local levels, with these actions occurring frequently. Provincial and local union leaders were the key actors behind these protests.

Since democratization in 1982, teacher protests have been a remarkably routine feature of Argentine politics. Teachers protested regularly throughout the 1980s (McGuire 1996). While the number of teacher protests declined after the decentralization reform in 1993, there was a new cycle of protests from 1996 to 2000 (Murillo 2001; Murillo and Ronconi 2004). In the 1980s, 1990s, 2000s, and 2010s, teachers were the most militant group of workers. Labor grievances (in the form of low salaries and late payment of salaries), which generated anger and discontent, are one set of factors that contributed to labor unrest. However, even in years

---

[1] Ricardo Braginski, "Por los paros, los alumnos pierden 3 meses de clase durante la primaria," *Clarin* April 2, 2019.

when teacher salaries were improving and in provinces where teacher salaries were relatively higher, such as Neuquén and Tierra del Fuego, there was militancy.[2] What is remarkable about teacher protests in Argentina is that they were widespread across provinces and recurrent year to year. Many provinces had a high level of labor conflict: Neuquén, Tierra del Fuego, Santa Cruz, Jujuy, Entre Ríos, Río Negro, and Tucumán (Chiappe 2012; Jaume 2020). This speaks to the broad scope of the activist base, which had more territorial coverage than in Mexico.

Protests were mobilized by various actors in CTERA. Although national union leaders sometimes played an outsized and publicly visible role in protests, most were led by provincial union leaders and grassroots activists. One such group of activists, which emerged during the 1990s, was the "self-mobilized" (*autoconvocados*). Migliavacca (2009) describes how this group of activists organized in the wake of the White March of 1988. In the late 1980s, Peronist union leaders were consolidating provincial organizations. Leftist activists who were opposed to the Lista Celeste developed their own networks, outside CTERA's formal organization. They operated independently of CTERA's leadership with ties to both unionized and nonunionized teachers (Migliavacca 2009, 126, 134). When the official leaders of CTERA were more reluctant to protest, fearing punitive presidential decrees or legal actions for unlawful strikes, activists criticized them and developed new methods to express dissent.[3]

Innovations in union tactics were developed locally and then adopted nationally. CTERA's most high-profile protest, the White Tent encampment (1997–9), had crucial antecedents in the provinces of Buenos Aires,

---

[2] Secretaria de Evaluación e Información Educativa, "Informe indicativo del salario docente," June 2022.

[3] One indication of the activist base was the tendency of teachers to develop alliances with public sector workers, university students, and *piqueteros*; that is, groups of informal sector workers or community associations from lower class neighborhoods. CTERA used its affiliation to the labor central, the CTA, to mobilize with public sector workers against austerity measures. They protested with university students against reductions in education spending and also in solidarity with *piqueteros* and unemployed workers, since many teachers worked in neighborhoods with high levels of poverty and unemployment. Teachers were part of a broad front that was opposed to austerity measures. In 1995, unemployed workers organized – along with teachers and left activists – to demand food from the mayor in La Matanza, a county in the province of Buenos Aires (Svampa and Pereyra 2003). In the province of Neuquén, teachers protested alongside *piqueteros* and blocked a bridge on a major highway. When the police were deployed and a young woman, Teresa Rodríguez, was killed on April 12, 1997, teachers organized another wave of protest against police violence that scaled up to the national level.

where teachers used humorous public spectacles to voice demands. In 1996, a protest in the province of Buenos Aires, "the circus of education reform," parodied the absurd policies of this period (Suárez 2005, 28–9).[4] Immediately preceding the White Tent, there was also a harsh repression of teachers demanding higher pay in Neuquén (Campo 2020). National union leaders such as Marta Maffei then began to tap this local energy to build a national protest movement. In other words, the protests that were organized at the national level were based on experiences organizing protests at provincial and municipal levels.

The White Tent encampment was one such protest that put teacher labor grievances on the political agenda. Teachers pitched a large white tent in front of the National Legislature and demanded better pay and working conditions, especially for underpaid teachers in the poorest provinces. This protest had broad resonance and attracted national media attention.[5] While the secretary general of CTERA, Marta Maffei, claimed credit for leading this protest, it was the activist base that sustained it. A rotating group of activists from the provinces maintained a hunger strike for 1,003 days (Suárez 2005, 27–8). This reinforced a broader pattern: The activist base developed tactics and sustained protests, while the national union leaders negotiated with government officials to resolve the conflict.

This protest shifted the policy agenda and made improving teacher salaries a top priority. If teacher grievances were ignored during the White March of 1988 and the Federal Law of Education of 1993, by 1997, there was growing pressure to address them. Protests by teachers traveling long distances from the poorest provinces to camp in front of the National Legislature created a spectacle. Gender may also have mattered, as female teachers, who were the primary household breadwinners, generated public sympathy. Moreover, the grievances were not fabricated – teacher pay really did lag behind that of other workers (Rivas et al. 2010, 41). CTERA pressed for national regulations to address the problems associated with the unfunded decentralization reform. Facing this pressure, President Menem created a new federal fund to bolster teacher pay, the National Fund for Teacher Incentive (FONID), which increased the salaries of teachers in the provinces with the lowest salaries. However, to

---

[4] SUTEBA, "1986–2016."
[5] Intellectuals, artists, activists, priests, media personalities, and athletes voiced their solidarity with the teachers. This protest attracted positive media attention because it did not disrupt the academic calendar. The protest involved 1,400 teachers, 86 civic groups, 475 cultural events, 46 radio shows, and 29 television shows (Corrales 2004, 344).

generate revenue, the government levied a new tax on vehicles, which was especially hard on the middle classes, with the hope of dampening public support for teachers (Paglayan 2014).[6] Concessions were granted grudgingly, and FONID was only a partial response to labor grievances: Salaries remained low and irregular payments continued.

After the White Tent, the deteriorating political and economic context from 1999 to 2002 created further hardship for teachers but an even more favorable environment for activists. A protracted economic and political crisis sparked an outburst of popular mobilization. When President Fernando de la Rua (1999–2001) imposed austerity measures to stabilize the economy, there were massive protests by the lower and middle classes that he violently repressed, leading to his ouster. Interim President Rodríguez Saá then defaulted on the national debt and stepped down, prompting a period of extreme political instability (see Levitsky and Murillo 2003; Lupu 2016).

As the financial crisis deepened and popular mobilization ramped up, teachers became a particularly energetic segment of labor. These conditions were ripe for activists to flourish and expand contentious actions. In 2001, Minister of Economy Domingo Cavallo proposed a 13 percent across-the-board pay cut for public sector workers to avoid defaulting on debt payments. Provincial governments followed suit, imposing harsh austerity on public spending, with major cuts to education. Federal transfers to FONID were suspended. Teachers across provinces were paid late and issued IOUs (*patacones*) (Migliavacca and Blanco 2011, 150).

The ensuing outrage further stoked the movementist repertoire. By 1999, major episodes of teacher unrest threatened governability in some provinces. In Corrientes, protests by militant activists spiraled out of control. In that province, there were mounting irregularities in the public sector due to mismanagement, corruption, and soaring debt. This prompted public sector protests in which teachers – and the self-mobilized in particular – played a leading role. Teachers demanded salaries that they were owed, contributions to social welfare funds, funding for hospitals, and the payment of pensions owed to pensioners. In June 1999, massive protests forced the legislature to impeach Governor Pedro Braillard Poccard (Rivas 2003). Teachers remained on strike. By December, they were owed four and a half months of salary, and their salaries were still among the lowest in the country. Teachers organized tent encampments, hunger strikes, and demonstrations – chaining themselves to the cathedral

---

[6] Jorge Rosales, "El impuesto docente llega ahora a los usados," *La Nación* May 29, 1999.

and blocking highways.[7] Ultimately, these protests forced the governor to step down. Corrientes demonstrates the intensity of protests that were sustained by bottom-up mobilization.

Corrientes was not unique. Labor conflict in the province of Entre Ríos also spiraled out of control, along with conflicts in thirteen other provinces. The conflict between the provincial government and public sector workers began in 1999, when austerity measures were imposed – including a 19 percent pay cut for public sector workers. By 2001, teachers and other public sector workers (i.e., the union of public employees, ATE) were in a state of "permanent mobilization" (Suárez 2005, 134). Governor Sergio Montiel, facing riots and mounting public sector protests, responded with police repression, the summary firing of 4,000 public sector workers, threats to deduct the pay of workers who participated in protests, and the imprisonment of union leaders. The unions challenged these decrees in court while continuing to organize marches, demonstrations, and caravans. The governor's inability to pay teacher salaries caused this conflict to escalate into what he described as "urban guerrilla warfare" (Suárez 2005, 135). The intensity of sustained protests again demonstrates the role of an activist base.

Activists continued to use social movement tactics, showing solidarity with other groups. Solidarity protests occurred in several provinces, but the Province of Buenos Aires stands out (Suárez 2005, 88–170).[8] In July 2000, the self-mobilized teachers who controlled local unions in the province joined the Big March for Work, which was led by leaders of the CTA, the labor central that CTERA had helped to form: Union leaders collected signatures and marched with the aim of securing unemployment insurance for workers who had lost jobs as a result of the financial crisis.[9] Protesters blocked roads in solidarity with unemployed workers who demanded basic subsidies (Migliavacca 2009, 174–6). The deteriorating labor conditions of teachers – who were not paid or were issued IOUs – fostered a broader movement. Teachers also organized protests in which they opened schools but used instructional time to talk to students and parents about the problems they faced and to develop new forms of protest.

---

[7] However, teacher conflict severely disrupted the operation of public schools. Students lost seven months of class and were automatically promoted to the next grade. See "Todos pasan de grado aunque no hubo clases," *La Nación* December 2, 1999.
[8] Migliavacca (2011) provides a detailed account of teacher protests in the province of Buenos Aires in 2001.
[9] SUTEBA, "10 de agosto: Marcha grande por el trabajo."

With the presence of grassroots activists, teacher protests articulated a broad set of demands in line with popular sector interests. On August 10, 2001, the "self-mobilized" blocked roads along with the *piqueteros* to protest cuts to school cafeterias and scholarships, which harmed students from low-income households.[10] On July 19, 2002, teachers organized a demonstration that lasted forty-five days called the Education Farm (Granja Educativa). They made common cause with university students and *piqueteros*, protesting the harmful effects of austerity measures. One of the demands was to halt the inclusion of schools in rural areas in the austerity package to eliminate hardship pay bonuses for teachers who worked in remote locations (this hardship pay was a major portion of their salaries).[11] Teachers also protested cuts to school cafeterias, which affected students who went hungry.[12]

LIMITED POLITICAL ACTION

A robust activist base not only contributed to ongoing protests and oppositional behavior but also to the union's limited role in the electoral arena. To be sure, activists were not always resistant to party politics. In some countries, such as Uruguay and Bolivia, militant activists created movement-based political parties that had hybrid elements of social movements and more institutionalized political parties (Anria 2018). But among Argentine teachers, there was a more oppositional relationship to party politics in general, because of the polarization engendered by Peronism, the broad distrust of politicians, and resistance to union leaders who sought to transform CTERA into an electoral machine. To be sure, some prominent leaders of CTERA were outspoken Peronists, but they did not speak on behalf of all teachers.

While many prominent leaders of CTERA had a strong Peronist identity, including Robert Baradel (secretary general of SUTEBA), Stella Maldonado (secretary general of CTERA), and Hugo Yasky (secretary general of CTERA and later of the CTA), this partisan identity did not permeate the whole union. A crucial feature of CTERA was that power was dispersed in the base, and there was resistance to appeals by union leaders who sought to mobilize political support. In Argentina, some union leaders went into politics and appealed to teachers as voters,

---

[10] SUTEBA, "2000 / 2001 / 2002."
[11] See "Protesta por la reclasificación de escuelas," *Clarín* June 7, 2002.
[12] SUTEBA, "2000 / 2001 / 2002."

but large swaths of teachers resisted voting for them. In other words, when union leaders went into politics, they did not bring teachers along with them, in contrast to SNTE, where union leaders had more tools to compel teachers to follow their directives. Programmatic dealignment, resulting from Menem's decision to impose neoliberal economic policies and unfunded education decentralization, helped to cement an attitude of distrust and skepticism among teachers because politicians and union leaders who purported to represent them had betrayed them. There was a fear that this would happen again.

In the 1990s, some union leaders did become political candidates and appealed to teachers as voters. Teacher hostility to Menem's neoliberal policies helped to bring them together in the opposition. In 1995, when Menem ran for reelection, CTERA campaigned against him: "[W]e told our base not to vote for Menem" (Stella Maldonado, interview, November 14, 2012). The unfunded decentralization policy that was imposed on the union helped teachers to overcome their diverse partisan identities and rally in opposition. A handful of CTERA leaders, harnessing the frustration and anger with President Menem, entered the national legislature. Argentine union leaders leveraged their leadership experience to become politicians. Indeed, many prominent leaders from the union became elected leaders (see Table 7.1). The most salient cases include CTERA's secretary general, Mary Sánchez, who helped found a new opposition party, the Broad Front (Frente Grande), which rejected Menem's neoliberal agenda.[13] In 1993, Sánchez was elected as a National Deputy. Sánchez helped to negotiate FONID in 1998, articulating the interests of the White Tent protesters. Other prominent leaders of CTERA, Marta Maffei and Eduardo Macaluse, who led the White Tent protest, followed Sánchez's lead, and became National Deputies through the center-left party Front for a Country in Solidarity (FREPASO) in 1999. Table 7.1 shows that various union leaders were indeed able to enter politics. The electoral rules afforded union leaders opportunities to become politicians; the pathways into power were not closed to teachers.

As political candidates, union leaders appealed to teachers for their votes by claiming credit for defending labor rights and organizing protests. Indeed, the White Tent gave CTERA leaders media attention. CTERA Secretaries General, such as Mary Sánchez and Marta Maffei,

---

[13] For more on the Broad Front, see Abal Medina (2009).

TABLE 7.1 *Former union leaders (CTERA) who became national deputies*

	Years	Position in union	Political party	District
Delia Bisutti	2005–9	Sec. Gen. UTE	ARI, Sol. e Igualdad	Buenos Aires (Cd.)
Alfredo Bravo	1991–2003	Sec. Gen. CTERA	Socialista, Alianza	Buenos Aires (Cd.)
Jorge Cardelli	2011–15	Sec. Gen. UNRC	Mov. Proyecto Sur	Buenos Aires (Cd.)
Eduardo Macaluse	1999–2011	Leader of SUTEBA, CTERA	Alianza, Coal. Civica	Buenos Aires (Pr.)
Marta Maffei	2003–7	Sec. Gen. CTERA	ARI	Buenos Aires (Pr.)
Mary Sánchez	1995–9	Sec. Gen. CTERA	Frente Grande	Buenos Aires (Pr.)
Horacio Piemonte	2009–13	Leader SUTEBA	ARI	Buenos Aires (Pr.)
Elsa Quiroz	1999–2011	Leader SUTEBA	ARI, coalición Civica	Buenos Aires (Pr.)
Mabel Marelli	1997–2001	Leader CTERA	UCR, Alianza	Misiones
Marilú Leverberg	2007–15	Sec. Gen. UDPM	Frente para la Victoria	Misiones
Carmen Nebreda	2009–13	Sec. Gen. UEPC	Frente para la Victoria	Córdoba
Antonio Riestra	2011–15	Leader AMSAFE, CTERA	Pares	Santa Fe
Verónica Benas	2007–11	Leader AMSAFE, CTERA	Pares	Santa Fe
Nélida Belous	2007–11	Sec. Gen. SUTEF	Social Protagónico	Tierra del Fuego

Source: Author's data

elevated their leadership profile by gaining favorable media attention through CTERA (Hugo Yasky, interview, December 5, 2012). Upon entering public office, former union leaders sponsored education legislation and sat on education committees. During the late 1990s, the former secretary general of CTERA, Mary Sánchez, who was a national deputy, advocated for teacher rights in Congress, voiced solidarity with protesters, and even participated in union rallies.

Union leaders, as candidates on party lists, appealed broadly to lower- and middle-class voters based on a broad set of policy objectives that included education, along with issues related to the environment, human rights, social policy, and gender equity. Party leaders recruited CTERA leaders as political candidates because of their policy expertise and leadership profiles, which appealed to large swaths of the electorate. Most leaders of CTERA were described as *cuadros*, or experienced political leaders with a strong background in policy and innovative proposals, rather than *operadores*, or political brokers who used clientelism (Gabriel Nardacchione, interview, November 23, 2012). Indeed, CTERA leaders had a deep understanding of education policy and were recognized as human rights activists; party leaders recruited them to shore up the party's platform on education or human rights. CTERA leaders running for office made broad appeals to voters beyond teachers.

But the political support of teachers for union leaders did not endure. CTERA had a multiparty identity, with union leaders and rank-and-file teachers hailing from the radical, Peronist, communist, socialist, and anarchist camps. Polarization against President Menem brought teachers together only temporarily, and partisan divisions returned after President Menem left office. The largest faction in CTERA, the Celeste, had prominent Peronist leaders, but it was really a loose coalition that also contained center-left parties opposed to Peronism (Gindin 2011, 127). This group lacked the organizational muscle to transform the restive teacher movement into a coherent voting bloc. If union leaders became political candidates, the union could not back their candidacies without engendering resistance. Specifically, union leaders who affiliated to the Broad Front and FREPASO (i.e., non-Peronist, center-left parties) alienated rank-and-file activists who supported the PJ. Partisan divisions undermined the possibilities for concerted political mobilization through CTERA.

When prominent union leaders, such as Eduardo Macaluse and Marta Maffei, joined center-left parties, such as the Broad Front and FREPASO, the activist base began to reject these parties because they formed strategic alliances with right-wing parties. The center-left, anti-Peronist parties such as FREPASO were too small to challenge Peronism on their own. The only option was to ally with center-right parties, such as the UCR, to build a broader coalition (Garay 2010, 58; Roberts 2014; Lupu 2016). In 1999, a pact was forged between FREPASO and the UCR, in what became known as the Alliance. But the incompatible agendas of these parties sharpened the divisions among teachers. Peronist and leftist teachers felt betrayed by an alliance with a conservative party, and they rallied against the former union leaders who had become politicians for these parties. Teachers criticized leaders who were in center-left parties that were anti-Peronist for betraying teachers.

In interviews, union leaders acknowledged the resistance of the base to campaigning through the union. To be sure, union leaders appealed to teachers with shared partisan identities. However, owing to the electoral system in Argentina that aggregated votes in provincial districts, most union leaders cum politicians targeted broad swaths of provincial voters; the party lists that union leaders ran under appealed to lower- and middle-class voters, rather than narrowly targeting teachers (Laura Tuñón, interview, November 21, 2012). Indeed, former leaders of CTERA who became politicians relied on parties to organize campaign events, while they avoided involving the union in their campaigns. One former union leader who became a National Deputy described the union's role in his campaign as follows:

We tried not to involve the union in my political campaign. We did meet with teachers, but not through the union. I don't think it's good to involve the union in party politics. I think it's good for teachers to be politically involved ... but I disagree with bringing the union into a political party because this creates internal divisions within the union and distrust of the representatives ... it creates the possibility that the whole union will become erroneously associated with a small group of people. (Eduardo Macaluse, interview, November 16, 2012)

Union leaders in Argentina – unlike Mexico – avoided politicizing the union. This perspective was shared by high-ranking CTERA leaders, who rejected the idea of endorsing political candidates or parties:

We haven't asked our base to go out and campaign for a given candidate ... it would be looked down upon if CTERA, as a union, did this ... we have never allied with a political campaign of any candidate, we have only mobilized against political options that were clearly opposed to public schools. (Stella Maldonado. interview, November 14, 2012)

THE POLICY RESPONSE TO MOVEMENTISM: NATIONAL COLLECTIVE BARGAINING

If instrumentalism by SNTE led to a policy backlash against the union, movementism generated a different policy dynamic. Education politics centered on establishing an institution of national collective bargaining to address teacher labor grievances. Movementism made the resolution of teacher protests a priority on the national political stage throughout the 2000s and 2010s. Disruptive teacher protests were a problem that politicians could not ignore. Because of these ongoing protests, there was mounting pressure to establish a national institution of collective bargaining, the Paritaria Nacional Docente (National Institution of Teacher Collective Bargaining, PND), where union leaders, cabinet ministers, and governors could negotiate salary adjustments. This institution was designed to resolve teacher unrest, but the activist base did not stop protesting. A peaceful resolution of the issue of teacher salary adjustments became the axis of political conflict over education, and the logic of movementism is crucial for understanding the origins and persistence of labor conflict.

President Nestor Kirchner (2003–7) courted labor unions in general and teachers in particular. Kirchner faced widespread mobilization from the popular sectors when he took office, and he needed to court labor unions with the capacity to mobilize disruptive protests, especially teachers, to calm social unrest (Schipani 2021). Thus, the prolabor government included labor unions in policymaking and developed neocorporatist relations with them (Etchemendy and Collier 2007). A national policy response to teachers had its roots in a provincial labor conflict in Entre Ríos. In that heavily indebted province, the government issued IOUs and teachers were owed five months' back pay. The resulting labor conflict led to a stalemate between militant teachers and the governor. The Kirchner government stepped in, bailing out the indebted province. The president and the minister of education Daniel Filmus signed an agreement with CTERA to use national funds to pay teachers in Entre Ríos, with the teachers agreeing to return to the classroom (Etchemendy 2011, 97–8).[14] This intervention was significant, since it marked a major federal policy shift to demobilize protests.

Kirchner sought to address the problem of teacher protests by recentralizing labor relations with the teachers' union. The government fostered a close relationship with Hugo Yasky, CTERA's secretary general. Teachers joined the governing coalition. President Kirchner addressed unrest by directing national resources to education. In December 2003, Law 25,864 guaranteed 180 days of class in schools across the nation as the first part of a broader package to ensure that schools would remain open (i.e., teacher protests would not disrupt the academic calendar) in exchange for higher teacher salaries. In 2004, Law 25,919 set a minimum salary for teachers. In 2005, the Law of Education Finance set national

---

[14] Yet even after this intervention and a labor agreement between the union and the governor, conflict in Entre Ríos resumed (Suárez 2005, 145–6).

education spending targets of 6 percent of GDP. These reforms demonstrated a commitment to national teacher regulations and more funding for education. Even militant activists who were critical of President Kirchner supported these policies.

In 2006, a proposed National Law of Education generated a conflict between the CTERA and former union leaders in the national legislature. The national executive committee strongly supported the bill since union leaders had written key sections of this landmark piece of legislation (Stella Maldonado, interview, November 14, 2012). But former CTERA leaders in the national legislature – Elsa Quiroz, Marta Maffei, and Eduardo Macaluse – were affiliated with ARI and Civic Coalition, political parties that were offshoots of the Broad Front and FREPASO. They decided to vote against the bill, arguing that it did not go far enough to overturn the Federal Law of Education. CTERA leaders accused the legislators of opposing a bill that would benefit teachers for petty political reasons: ARI and Civic Coalition did not want President Kirchner to achieve a legislative victory. Marta Maffei, who was a respected CTERA leader, was described as betraying CTERA and following party leaders:

When it came time to vote for the [National] Education Law, we had more support from National Deputies who were not from CTERA, than from those who were. This is extremely odd because in the [National] Education Law that was passed, there were at least forty-five articles that were written by CTERA, but Marta Maffei privileged opposing the government [of Nestor Kirchner] and voted against the bill. (Stella Maldonado, interview, November 14, 2012)

The Law of Education Financing created the PND, which enabled national-level collective bargaining (Etchemendy 2011, 96). It was an "organizational" victory for CTERA since it strengthened the national executive committee (Valdez Tappatá 2015, 25). Kirchner not only improved teacher salaries but also formalized collective bargaining and national teacher regulations. From 2003 to 2009, real teacher salaries increased by 40 percent. When the PND was convened for the first time in 2008, CTERA was included in the policy process, and the national union leadership refrained from protesting (Etchemendy 2011; Valdez Tappatá 2015). The government formed an alliance with prominent CTERA leaders – Hugo Yasky, Robert Baradel, and Stella Maldonado – and achieved a degree of cooperation with these leaders. Some scholars, such as Sebastián Etchemendy, describe this arrangement as neocorporatist. In some ways, CTERA became more centralized, and power became more concentrated in the national executive committee. With the governments of Nestor Kirchner and Cristina Fernández de Kirchner, union leaders became more involved in managing state resources, negotiating national salary increases, and being represented in government. There were prominent union leaders who became staunch Peronists – arguably, the prolabor Kirchner government realigned CTERA with the PJ.

There is no question that the prolabor government marked another major change in teacher–state relations. The question is the extent to which these changes upended the weak hierarchical relations. My argument stresses the important continuities in the union's organizational structure and its political repertoire. Even while acknowledging that there was a close alliance between the Kirchner faction of the PJ and a prominent group of CTERA leaders, it is important to note that an alliance with the national leaders of CTERA was not the same as an alliance with the restive base. There was still a robust activist base that refused to obey the national leaders. The 2006 National Law of Education did not fully reverse the 1992 Federal Law of Education (Migliavacca et al. 2015); the school system remained decentralized to a considerable degree; and the power base of provincial union leaders remained intact. Protests continued in the provinces and activists refused to restrain demands.

Collective bargaining did not realign teachers with the prolabor Peronist government. CTERA leaders supported the government but acknowledged the right of provincial unions to strike and even to reject the salary adjustments that national leaders had negotiated (Stella Maldonado, interview, November 14, 2012). National leaders feared being accused of pressuring provincial union leaders and activists to accept the agreements that they negotiated. Moreover, in 2012, there were ongoing tensions between teachers and President Cristina Fernández de Kirchner on reaching an agreement on salary increases, with the president accusing teachers of working few hours and having three months of vacation.[15] Even if there was communication and coordination with high-ranking union leaders such as Hugo Yasky, relations between the government and the union remained tense and marked by disagreement.

Negotiating improvements in teacher pay was complicated and difficult. Teachers struggled to coordinate demands. Although CTERA, as the largest teacher organization, had the most representation, there were representatives from four other teachers' unions. Within CTERA, there were many different groups. Union activists remained unsatisfied with the salary adjustments that the national executive committee negotiated,

---

[15] Delfina Corti, "CFK dijo sobre los docentes: 'Trabajan 4 horas por día y tienen 3 meses de vacaciones,'" *Chequeado* September 25, 2019.

expressing frustration with incremental improvements (Migilivacca and Blanco 2011, 170–1). CTERA's secretary general lacked the capacity to negotiate on behalf of union members; instead, decisions were made through deliberation with provincial union leaders.

On the government side, governors, finance ministers, and education ministers raised concerns over whether they could afford salary adjustments. Even though the president and national CTERA leaders wanted to reach a deal, they struggled to bring other officials and union leaders along. Negotiated salary increases tended to be short-term solutions that did not decisively resolve labor conflict. National agreements set nonbinding guidelines or norms for governors to follow on teacher pay. According to the former minister of education, Juan Carlos Tedesco, union fragmentation made it all but impossible for PND to function:

> In the PND, five different union federations that all have different provincial organizations meet together. Therefore, this fragmentation, alongside the tendency to be more oppositional, makes dialogue very difficult. Other countries do not have this problem. If you go to Mexico, despite all of the critiques of the Mexican teachers' union, which is extremely powerful in political and economic terms, it is united and it can solve problems … there is union machinery that enables deals to be reached, and these deals are more or less stable.[16]

Government officials such as Juan Carlos Tedesco, an academic and the minister of education during the administration of Cristina Fernández de Kirchner, have criticized the union for organizing too many strikes and not showing enough restraint, even when teacher salaries were improving dramatically.[17]

The activist base organized persistent protests; national leaders were unable to restrain provincial and local unions. Data for 2006 to 2009 show that teachers remained the most militant sector of labor. They were responsible for the 53 percent of workdays lost. Teachers had the highest proportion of strike participants, making up 40 percent of total strikers. They organized 13 percent of all strikes, which was the third-highest number after other public employees (34 percent) and health workers (15 percent) (Chiappe 2012, 18). After the national government began to engage in collective bargaining with teachers and improve salaries, teachers in the provinces did not demobilize.

---

[16] See Gabriel Latorre, "Entrevista a Juan Carlos Tedesco sobre la Integración de TIC en la Educación Argentina," *Insurgencia Magisterial* April 9, 2016.

[17] See "Un debut con tizas afiladas," *Pagina12* November 16, 2007.

FIGURE 7.1 Individual workdays lost to teacher strikes, Argentina
Source: Labor Conflict Database, Ministry of Labor, Argentina

The PND did not end labor conflict. To be sure, there was a decline in national strike activity; national union leaders who were allied with the government of Cristina Fernández de Kirchner (2007–15) showed some restraint. But at the provincial level, labor unrest persisted, even as teacher pay increased. Negotiations between CTERA and the national government were difficult to hammer out; even temporary agreements of just one year were hard-fought victories (Etchemendy 2011, 101–2). There was a gap between the union and the government's proposals for salary adjustments. Conflict between the union and government broke out in 2013, when the prolabor government, seeking to control inflation, refused to negotiate salary adjustments with teachers (Etchemendy 2013). Data on the number of individual workdays lost show that, at the provincial and local levels, teacher protests declined in the wake of the adoption of national collective bargaining, reaching a low of less than 1.5 million in 2011 (see Figure 7.1), but then ticked back up and reached a peak of more than 6 million in 2017. This figure demonstrates the huge magnitude of teacher mobilization year to year, despite 2011 and 2015 when labor conflict eased.

The national institution of collective bargaining became the primary axis of conflict over education policy. Teacher protests drew criticism because they negatively affected learning in the classroom: Public school students fell behind when schools were shut down and the academic calendar was interrupted. If the White Tent encampment engendered public sympathy, frequent protests eroded public sympathy for teachers. Indeed, retired union leaders noted the dangers of protests that occurred too frequently, were narrowly centered on salaries, and had a negative effect on students and families. Mary Sánchez (Interview, November 30, 2012) criticized the activist base for recklessly organizing too many protests.

> We are in a crisis because organizing a protest is now something ordinary, or normal and this makes me nervous. It is used like a war of 48 hours, and then comes the discussion of how much is being asked. The political agenda is very narrow, only demands for higher salaries ... I am a union leader who is convinced that strikes have to be used as instruments to damage bosses or authoritarian governments, but not the students.

Media outlets portrayed teachers as perpetually unsatisfied despite large salary improvements. Teacher protests had the potential to push middle-class parents to send their children to private schools, which remained open when public schools were closed (Narodowski et al. 2013). Sustaining frequent protests was a costly strategy, and it drew growing criticism.

A CONSERVATIVE GOVERNMENT DISMANTLES COLLECTIVE BARGAINING

The failure of national collective bargaining to resolve labor conflict prompted President Mauricio Macri (2015–19) from the right-wing Cambiemos party, made up of an alliance between Macri's party, Republican Proposal, and the UCR, to confront the teachers. As a businessman, Macri's government offered strong representation to the business sector. Upon taking office, the president took a hardline position on CTERA. His education agenda prioritized improving Argentina's scores on international standardized tests such as PISA, with his proposed "Plan Maestro," which included a merit-based pay program and greater emphasis on teacher training. In addition, he proposed more rigorous teacher evaluations and subsidies to private schools. But the centerpiece of his education reform agenda was, like Menem's, the implementation of a program of fiscal adjustment that was incompatible with raising teachers' salaries. In other words, he shifted the focus of education policy from recentralizing teacher labor relations to improving the quality of education with performance-based measures, while holding down costs.

CTERA opposed these measures. To advance them in the face of union opposition, Macri began to dismantle collective bargaining with teachers. In 2017, negotiations involving the PND were suspended. Then, in January 2018, he used an executive order (Decree 52) to weaken the institution of collective bargaining, by reducing the representation of CTERA and freezing negotiations over salaries. Previously, CTERA had had five seats on the PND because it was the largest union; the other teachers' unions – UDA, SADOP, CEA, and AMET – had one seat each because they were small. President Macri's decree gave each union one seat on the PND, regardless of size. Moreover, his decree left the issue of teacher salaries outside the scope of national negotiations.[18] President Macri argued that since Argentina was a highly indebted nation near the point of default, the country could not afford higher salaries for teachers. His decree modified the Law of Education Finance (Ley 26,075). He also broke the agreement from 2016 that teacher salaries be 20 percent higher than the minimum wage. Macri's decree froze national salary negotiations; although the institution was not eliminated, it was rendered toothless on matters of salary. This institution aimed to address other issues of teacher work, namely school infrastructure, training, and professionalization, while leaving teacher salaries to the provinces.

The response to this decree highlights the continuities in CTERA's repertoire of movementism. There were more protests. There was an alignment between CTERA and opposition, but mostly at the national level. The union remained autonomous from parties and militant. This executive order prompted massive strikes by CTERA and its affiliated unions. The union filed a complaint with the International Labour Organization and threatened to prevent classes from starting on time for the 2019 academic school year. These protests were highly disruptive and hurt Macri's ability to govern, but he held the line. While during the presidency of Cristina Fernández de Kirchner national strikes had fallen sharply, President Macri's policies sparked national teacher protests, which the government could not control. The number of strikes by CTERA during the first fifteen months of Macri's government exceeded the previous twelve years, during the Kirchner governments.[19] The union set up an itinerant school in front of Congress to showcase the problems

---

[18] Nadia Nasanovsky, "Paritaria nacional docente: ¿cuáles son los cambios que hizo Macri?" *Chequeando* February 15, 2019.

[19] Ariel Riera, "Clarín: 'Los docentes [de CTERA] le habrán hecho a Mauricio Macri en 15 meses más huelgas que al kirchnerismo en 12 años,'" *Chequeado* March 28, 2017.

of teachers, and the education sector more broadly (Feldfeber et al. 2018).[20] While union leaders were repressed at first, they were ultimately allowed to set up this encampment, demonstrating strong continuities in the role of the activist base in mobilizing protests.

This weakening of the PND has not put an end to movementism. On the contrary, CTERA continues to organize recurring protests and has not lost its disruptive capacity. Because of movementism, national collective bargaining for teachers has been a central axis of conflict in education politics. Even though the union claimed credit for helping to bring about the founding of a major institution for collective bargaining, this institution did not resolve labor conflict. However, weakening this institution did not solve the problem either, as labor conflict with teachers only worsened.

CONCLUSION

This chapter has shown that there was a political repertoire in place in Argentina, movementism, and it has linked this with the union's organizational structure. Within CTERA, power resided in the provincial unions and the base. This generated recurrent protests. The organizational model also helps to explain CTERA's limited role in the party system, and the tendency of union leaders to separate from the union when they go into politics. Movementism generated a distinctive policy response: The prolabor government of Nestor Kirchner developed a national institution of collective bargaining to ease labor unrest, but provincial protests continued. Moreover, when a conservative government dismantled PND, ongoing protests created pressure to reestablish the national institution.

The organizational structure of CTERA was quite different from the organization of some prominent Peronist unions, which were more corporatist. Consider the Teamsters, headed by the colorful union leader Hugo Moyano. The union leadership had a hierarchical relationship with the rank and file, and the Teamsters union delivered votes to the PJ. But in 2012, a rift between Moyano and Cristina Fernández de Kirchner over Moyano's influence over union leaders as candidates for the PJ caused Moyano to defect and start his own party. Many labor organizations in Latin America established hierarchical relations, which went hand in

---

[20] CTERA, "Se inauguró la 'escuela pública itinerante' de Ctera frente al congreso de la nación," April 13, 2017.

hand with state corporatism, and afforded them some capacity to deliver the vote. But CTERA had a different history and internal organization, which engendered a more adversarial relationship with party politics; support was contingent, depending fundamentally on a shared interest in specific policies.

Teacher protests in Argentina had their roots in labor grievances, but protests outlived the original grievances that sparked them. The driving force behind persistent protests was an archipelago of local leaders and grassroots activists. Imposed decentralization was a critical policy decision that established deeply rooted networks of activists in the provinces. Provincial and local activists mobilized protests, voiced solidarity with various societal actors, and embraced social movement tactics. These activists were the central structure of interest representation for Argentine teachers.

Teacher protests became a routine part of political life and an essential feature of education politics. In the 1990s and early 2000s, teacher protests generated public sympathy. Teachers voiced solidarity with public sector workers, students, and popular sector groups that had been hurt by austerity policies. It took time for pressure to ratchet up on governments to respond to teacher labor grievances. However, in the end, movementism produced major new labor and education laws that addressed long-standing irregularities in the education sector. Since 2003, as teacher salaries have improved, teacher protests have come under scrutiny. While the Kirchner government made concerted efforts to forge an alliance with the teachers' union through national labor regulations, collective bargaining, and more federal funding, these concessions failed to ease labor conflict. The union maintained its oppositional identity and rejected an institutionalized role in politics, even as teacher salaries improved dramatically. Movementism therefore helps to explain why collective bargaining has become a central axis for political conflict.

8

Factionalism in Colombia

The Colombian FECODE represents a third pattern: leftism, or electoral mobilization for parties with a more rigid ideological profile. The union was easy to locate in Colombia's party system owing to its opposition to the traditional parties and its support for left-of-center parties. Unlike their counterparts in Argentina, union leaders in Colombia turned from protests to delivering teachers as a voting bloc. A different combination of organizational traits – a hierarchical organization paired with feuding factions – generated this outcome.

This chapter analyzes how these organizational traits were established in the Colombian context. In parallel with Mexico and Argentina, policy decisions during the early 1990s in Colombia marked in new phase in state–teacher relations. Recall that Mexico underwent a protracted transition to democracy, while in Argentina there was a sharper discontinuity when the military junta stepped down and elections were held. Colombia, which had a long-standing electoral regime, also saw a discontinuity with the adoption of a new Constitution. This political change was akin to a political opening because, by including new political and societal groups, the new Constitution expanded the definition of the political community. In this context, the Colombian teachers' union moved closer to the state and union leaders took part in policy decisions. The macrolevel political change of the new Constitution affected the internal dynamics in FECODE. The national executive committee established its supremacy over the departmental unions because national union leaders wielded more resources and had stronger political connections than their departmental counterparts, making relations in the union hierarchical. In line with my argument, the union formed teachers into a national voting bloc, and protests became less central to the political repertoire.

But while the union became more hierarchical, the political opening also reinforced factional divisions. In the 1970s, left factions linked to communist parties with ties to the Soviet Union, China, and Cuba challenged union leaders from the traditional parties (mostly the Liberal Party). But in the 1980s there was bitter turmoil among left parties, and a new cleavage emerged between the center and radical left. This stemmed from the contradictory dynamics of ongoing political violence, paired with an unprecedented opportunity to participate in politics. Specifically, an electoral reform that created incentives for union leaders to form personalistic electoral vehicles deepened the divisions between union leaders who supported participating in elections and those who abstained. There were competitive dynamics for union leaders to secure the political support of teachers. The political opening also motivated FECODE to adopt new procedures for selecting the national executive committee, making the union more internally democratic and reinforcing power sharing. In other words, the political opening in Colombia did not produce a hegemonic faction: Instead, there were deepening factional rivalries.

This chapter analyzes the evolution of the union organization in the 1980s and 1990s, to show how and why factionalism took hold. It first examines the Pedagogical Movement (MP) in the 1980s, a teaching-oriented social movement that revealed a fundamental split between the radical and moderate lefts. This sheds light on why the union was initially included in policy negotiations. It then examines broader changes in teacher–state relations that culminated in FECODE's role in negotiating an education decentralization package that strengthened the national executive committee. The last section analyzes how the political opening contributed to more hierarchical relations and deepening political divisions.

THE MP SPLITS FROM THE RADICAL LEFT

In the 1980s, throughout Latin America, the debt crisis and regime transitions made for a prolonged period of tumult and instability. For teachers in many countries, political and economic changes energized new social movements. In Mexico, a combative dissident movement, CNTE, challenged the official union leadership and the authoritarian regime itself. In Argentina, teacher protests culminated in the White March of 1988, and an activist base took over the provincial unions. In parallel, Colombian teachers witnessed new forms of teacher activism. But in Colombia the teacher labor struggle was outshone by the MP, which pressed for popular education, curricular changes, and pedagogical innovations. This section describes how this teaching-oriented movement came about and what it reveals about union divisions.

In the 1980s, Colombian teachers, along with other citizens, experienced a deteriorating political situation. The uptick in violence from a multisided war involving drug cartels, paramilitaries, leftist guerrillas, and the military produced instability and fear. Governments engaged in peace negotiations with leftist guerrillas, but demobilizing them and achieving a lasting peace proved elusive. While the Conservative President Belisario Betancur (1982–6) negotiated with the Armed Revolutionary Forces of Colombia (FARC) and allowed a political party formed by guerrilla leaders, the Patriotic Union, to participate in politics, this party was subsequently decimated by paramilitary groups in what became known as the "political genocide." In 1989, instability ramped up. When the government threatened to extradite cartel kingpins to the United States, cartels responded with a rampage of bombings, shootings, and kidnappings (Lessing 2015). Leah Carroll (2011) describes this period as "violent democratization": Political reforms and institutional changes (i.e., direct elections for governors and mayors and a proportional representation formula for the Senate) brought new groups into politics, but these reforms generated a violent backlash from conservative elites.

Teacher activism in Colombia took various forms in the 1980s. Teachers were thrust into this fraught moment and were among the victims of the violence. The lines between politics and armed struggle blurred. Many union leaders were affiliated with left parties, and there was a debate among these parties about whether to support the armed struggle, electoral politics, or both. There were, indeed, some union leaders who had an ideological affinity with guerrilla groups. Because of this association, right-wing paramilitary groups targeted teachers as a group, assuming wrongfully that all teachers were guerrilla sympathizers. In rural areas and in departments such as Antioquia that had a strong paramilitary presence,[1] teachers faced violence and death threats for engaging in any sort of political activism and for any association with labor unions or community organizations – and this violence has continued to the present.[2] In 1987, Luis Felipe Vélez, a militant union leader in the

---

[1] In the department of Antioquia, between 1978 and 2008, 334 members of the union were killed, according to reports from the Association of Instructors of Antioquia.
[2] Escuela Nacional Sindical, "Violencia Antisindical en Colombia: entre el exterminio y la violación a la libertad sindical," September 2020.

department of Antioquia who agitated for labor rights and a stronger teachers' union, was gunned down as he entered the union headquarters in Medellin.[3] This violence ramped up in the 1980s, and it has been ongoing ever since, taking place throughout the nation (CINEP 2010).

During the 1980s, the onslaught of political violence radicalized one group of union leaders who struggled for labor rights and revolutionary projects. Even after the Teacher Statute of 1979, the economic situation of many teachers remained precarious. While Colombia was one of the few Latin American countries that did not restructure or default on its debt, the economy was stagnant throughout the 1980s with rising unemployment. Inflation hovered at 20 percent, and after negotiating the Teacher Statute and establishing a pay scale, the government did not adjust teacher salaries upward. The professional status and salaries of teachers in Colombia remained low, as they did in other Latin American countries during the 1980s. Moreover, the violent persecution of union leaders who spoke out against these labor problems further pushed some teachers toward extreme ideologies. One group of union leaders embraced militancy, among them Luis Felipe Vélez, and continued to take up the banner of a stronger labor movement, better salaries, and in some cases revolutionary change.

But not all leaders of FECODE prioritized better salaries, building a stronger union, and revolution. In the 1980s a group of teachers organized a new social movement centered on issues of pedagogy, the professional status of teachers, and the broader role of teachers in society. The salary scale that was established in 1979 awarded raises based on earning undergraduate and graduate degrees. This created incentives for teachers to enter teaching colleges and universities in greater numbers. Even if the motivation for pursuing advanced degrees was to improve salaries, teachers encountered researchers and professors with new ideas related to pedagogy and education reform (Díaz Ríos 2016). As teachers enrolled in higher education, they articulated new demands related to pedagogy, the practice of teaching, and changes to the curriculum.

In addition, there was turnover in the union leadership. In the 1960s and 1970s, the union was divided between the traditional parties – Liberals and Conservatives – and leftist parties in the national executive committee. These left parties were ascendant, and union leaders from the traditional parties were being steadily displaced. The left parties adhered

---

[3] Nicolás Sánchez, "Luis Felipe Vélez: un profesor que incomodó a los paramilitares," *El Espectador* May 17, 2018.

to the revolutionary slogan "The only way to change education is to change the system." They pursued a strategy of confrontation and combative demands focused on labor issues. For these parties, teachers were proletariat workers who struggled against oligarchic elites. Some currents of the radical left were skeptical of "bourgeois" democracy, and instead focused on class struggle and overthrowing the exclusive regime. Indeed, even in the 1980s, some union leaders from communist parties still thought that the classroom should be used to indoctrinate students with revolutionary ideology (Bocanegra Acosta 2010, 36).

But in 1982, a new leader came in. Abel Rodríguez, who assumed the presidency of FECODE, was a former member of the pro-China communist MOIR who had become disaffected with the rigid orthodoxy of the old left. Instead, he fought for innovations in teaching and democratic change. In the same year, at the twelfth FECODE congress in the city of Bucaramanga, the teachers' union launched the MP. This marked a generational and ideological shift that divided the radical and center left. It rejected leftist propaganda in the classroom and sought to elevate the professional standing of teachers, moving away from a narrow focus on labor demands. In other words, it represented a less combative approach to politics, with more emphasis on professional expertise and proposals to reform education. The movement raised questions about how the curriculum shaped the quality of education, the role of teachers in society, and the resources needed to transform education. It embraced lofty rhetoric, embodying democratic, nationalist, and humanist values. The MP questioned the idea that policy elites and technocrats, with ties to international organizations, knew best. The dominant teaching paradigm of educational technocrats at the time, called education technology, aimed to standardize teaching in line with a mechanical criterion of efficiency and best practices. The MP was an expression of resistance to this approach. It valued the experiences of Colombian teachers and sought to invent new teaching practices that were developed in the classroom. For the movement's leaders, academic excellence was critical for the development of Colombia in the areas of language, art, social studies, and especially science and technology. Teachers were reimagined as cultural agents and citizens with a duty to defend democratic rights (Castro de los Rios 2015, 100). Teachers focused on popular education, making teaching practices and the curriculum appropriate for students from various backgrounds and bringing social justice issues into the classroom.

The significance of the MP can be interpreted in different ways. On the one hand, it produced ideas that shaped publications, congresses, and institutions. FECODE created its own Center of Study and Research on Teaching (CEID), a working group within the union, to pursue pedagogical projects; organized study circles to improve the practice of teaching; and launched the journal *Education and Culture*, which established a large readership. In 1984, this movement organized the First National Forum for the Defense of Public Education, and in 1987 it convened the National Pedagogical Congress, sponsored by President Virgilio Barco. In other words, at the very least, the MP was effective in convening a large number of teachers and intellectuals who generated new ideas and proposals. However, many of these ideas and proposals were vague, hard to translate into policy, and impossible to implement at scale. The MP achieved more in the way of discussion and process than concrete learning outcomes or new policies; it was more rhetorical than substantive. For policymakers concerned about the quality of education in Colombia, as measured by low performance on international standardized tests, such as PISA, the MP's proposals did not seem to offer viable solutions.

There is little question that the MP bolstered FECODE's legitimacy in society, and it made the union a protagonist for education reform. It lent FECODE the trappings of a reformist social movement – the values, identities, and ideas of which gained broad support and connected teachers to intellectuals and reformers. Indeed, the movement united primary and secondary school teachers with university professors, including Antanas Mockus, a respected math professor at the National University who went on to become a reformist mayor of Bogotá (1995–7, 2001–3) and a founder of the centrist Green Party in 2009. By building ties with professors, researchers, and intellectuals, teachers enhanced their policy credibility. To a greater extent than teacher movements in Mexico and Argentina in the 1980s, the MP focused on professional expertise and the practice of teaching. If in the 1970s FECODE had influenced policy by presenting a list of labor demands to government officials and threatening to take to the streets, the MP sought to engage in dialogue and negotiations within democratic institutions. It gained legitimacy with broad segments of society as a movement that took education seriously, and this positioned FECODE to be included in policy negotiations.

THE POLITICAL OPENING AND INCLUSION IN POLICY DECISIONS

By the 1980s, the exclusive electoral regime, in which the Liberal and Conservative parties shared power, faced a severe legitimacy crisis. While the arrangement had achieved a degree of political stability in the 1960s and 1970s and prevented violence between these parties, it excluded many political currents and groups in society. The political regime was still organized around landed elites and traditional families, while labor organizations and the popular sectors were shut out (Hartlyn 1984). By the late 1980s, reformist elites understood that the regime was fueling the guerrilla insurgency and broader discontent. Along with rural violence, there were protests in cities. University students and the civic movement demanded decentralization and more opportunities for ordinary citizens to participate in politics. Colombia embraced sweeping reforms to make the regime more inclusive and to recognize groups that had been kept out of politics, among them teachers. These broader changes set the stage for a transformation in state–teacher relations.

In the 1980s, the MP added issues to the political agenda related to the practice of teaching and a more nationalist and democratic school curriculum. These proposals gained attention, but political elites did not immediately respond to them because their agenda was centered on addressing the existential problems of violence, terrorism, and public security. Education issues were not the main priority, in parallel with Mexico and Argentina, where throughout the 1980s new education laws were also on hold. FECODE, having secured its legal registry in 1962, had already gained a modicum of state recognition. However, under the regime that was dominated by the traditional parties, teachers lacked representation in the national legislature and in the Ministry of Education. Thus, before 1990, FECODE had a limited role in policy decisions related to education and social programs for teachers.

But in the 1990s, the MP influenced policy. With the regime under siege, reformist elites invited previously excluded groups to participate in politics. The political conditions were propitious for the teachers' union to gain a seat at the negotiating table. There was a growing consensus that more inclusive institutions were the only solution to the crisis of violence. Before the constitutional convention of 1990, there were several steps toward political reform and broader inclusion. In 1986, President Virgilio Barco established direct elections for mayors, ending the practice of presidential appointments. In 1991, governors (who had also previously been appointed) were popularly elected (Falleti 2010, 125). In this context, political elites responded favorably to FECODE's demands, especially those related to social protection for teachers. In 1989, teacher protests pressured the government to enact Law 91 of 1989. President Virgilio Barco signed decree 1775 in 1990, which put this law into effect and created the teacher pension fund (Fondo de Prestaciones del Magisterio) (Bocanegra Acosta 2013, 316). Both the union and the national government named representatives to the fund's board, which aimed to shore up confidence in a teacher pension system that had been chronically underfunded by departmental governments. Hence, by the late 1980s, political elites had embraced various political reforms and responded to long-standing teacher grievances.

But escalating violence and mounting protests generated pressure for bolder change. In 1989, facing protests by university students who demanded political change (Dugas 2001) and the ongoing threat of violence, President César Gaviria (1990–4) called a referendum on a National Constitutional Assembly. Voters approved this referendum, and the ensuing Constitutional Assembly sought to bring in political outsiders, namely the guerrilla insurgents, to strengthen regime legitimacy. The Constitutional Assembly of 1990 used alternative electoral rules in which delegates were elected in a single national district to create incentives for broader civic participation. While the traditional political parties secured strong representation, this assembly included new groups and expanded the political agenda. The largest guerrilla groups, the FARC and the National Liberation Army (ELN), declined to participate and continued the armed struggle, but smaller guerrilla groups – the 19th of April Movement (M-19), Workers Revolutionary Party, Popular Liberation Army, and the Quintin Lame Armed Movement (made up of indigenous rebels in the department of Cauca) – laid down arms and took part in the assembly. In addition, Afro-Colombians (Paschel 2010) and indigenous groups (Van Cott 2002) gained recognition and representation, in part because of the demobilization of the Quintin Lame Armed Movement. Teachers also participated. The MP made FECODE an attractive partner to reformist elites because it had ideas for reforming education.

FECODE leaders influenced the articles that were proposed in the Constitutional Assembly relating to education. Two FECODE leaders, German Toro and Abel Rodríguez, were among the seventy delegates elected to the Constitutional Assembly. Both had been active in the MP and both were elected delegates from the M-19, the largest demobilized guerrilla group. As such, they articulated a new vision for public education and social rights. These leaders helped to bolster the universal right to education for all Colombian citizens (Article 67). The state, society, and family were responsible for defending this right, and compulsory education was mandated for children from age five to fifteen, regardless of economic means. Increases in education spending were "hard-wired" into the Constitution (Cárdenas et al. 2006, 3).

In addition to teacher influence on the articles of the Constitution, changes to the electoral system also created space for teachers, as a professional group, to secure political representation. Leaders of FECODE were the unintended beneficiaries of this reform. If the Teacher Statute protected teachers from political clientelism with labor rights and enabled teachers to vote their conscience without retaliation, then the Constitution of 1991 expanded the rights of union leaders to participate in politics as political candidates. The Constitution, as the highest law of the land, superseded the conservative labor code (Codigo Sustantivo del Trabajo), that had been in place since 1950. This had mandated that public employees, including teachers, step down from their positions to register as political candidates. The 1991 Constitution eliminated arbitrary restrictions on candidacies and cleared a path for FECODE leaders to enter the electoral arena.

The political opening included FECODE in politics, but this opening was fraught with contradictions. On the one hand, the MP helped propel union leaders into the Constitutional Assembly of 1990, where they shaped articles of the Constitution and subsequent legislation. On the other hand, radical groups criticized the Constitution for including ambiguous language that allowed the private provision of public education. Moreover, the Constitutional Assembly did not resolve the armed conflict. In the countryside, the largest armed groups, the FARC and ELN, maintained territorial control and continued to wage war against the military. While teachers and some left groups began to participate in electoral politics, violence by guerrilla and paramilitary groups persisted, and the traditional elites remained dominant in national politics. These contradictions were reflected in divergent views among union leaders on whether the Constitution fundamentally changed the political regime, whether to participate in politics, and how to negotiate with the government.

For teachers, the new regime was characterized by a change in teacher–state relations toward greater cooperation and opportunities for union leaders to play more institutionalized roles in defining education policy. In the wake of the Constitution of 1991, there were major education reforms. The policy process during the administrations of Presidents César Gaviria and Ernesto Samper was the high-water mark of FECODE's influence on education policy. Both presidents negotiated with FECODE. These negotiations could be testy, as cabinet ministers decried the union's unreasonable demands and ongoing protests.[4] Yet both presidents ultimately went along with policies that strengthened the union as an organization and responded favorably to teacher demands.

President Gaviria negotiated with FECODE's national executive committee, led by FECODE president Jaime Dussán, to design new policies. Teachers were not the only group in society included in policy negotiations. In the aftermath of the Constitutional Assembly, reformist elites engaged with various societal groups, including Afro-Colombians and indigenous communities, to turn vague language about rights into concrete policy proposals. For example, Law 70 of 1993 granted collective land rights and established legal mechanisms for protecting the rights of black Colombians (Paschel 2010, 738). In parallel, FECODE shaped pending legislation for teachers that formalized abstract language in the Constitution into more specific education policies. Even after FECODE leaders played a constructive role in the Constitutional Assembly, the union's proposals still needed to be enacted into legislation. Moreover, by the early 1990s, teacher salaries had stagnated. They had not been adjusted since the 1979 Teacher Statute, while in 1991 inflation hit 30 percent.

The decision of President Gaviria to negotiate with FECODE was unexpected because of the ideological distance between the president and the leftist leaders of FECODE: The president was from a conservative wing of the Liberal Party. He imposed neoliberal economic reforms on other sectors of labor and his "plan to open education" included market-oriented education policies (Bocanegra Acosta 2013). However, this plan was set aside in favor of policies that were a response to union pressure. Initially, in 1992, technocrats in the Planning Department and the Finance Ministry presented a bill to congress that would decentralize education to the municipal level and fragment the union (Díaz Ríos 2016). But FECODE organized a strike that blocked this proposal, seeing far-reaching decentralization as a threat to the 1979 teacher statute. While President Gaviria preferred market-oriented policies, education was not a high priority. Ultimately, Lowden (2004) hypothesizes that President Gaviria shelved the technocratic proposal owing to the ongoing problems of narcoviolence and "reform fatigue"; after enacting unpopular economic reforms he decided to avoid a protracted conflict with FECODE.

After the 1992 teacher strike, the government negotiated a major education reform package that was aligned with the interests of the union.

---

[4] See "No hay razón para el paro, dice el gobierno," *El Tiempo* February 4, 1991.

The union simultaneously negotiated two major laws: Law 60 of 1993 and Law 115 of 1994. Law 60 decentralized education by giving departmental and local governments administrative authority over education decisions, such as the hiring, firing, and the transferring of teachers. But this decentralization policy preserved the national character of education policy, with parallels to education federalization in Mexico. The national labor code for teachers remained in place and the integrity of FECODE as the national union that represented teachers was reinforced. Moreover, the national government was responsible for generously funding education – no matter the economic conditions. In contrast to Argentina, where decentralization was implemented with fiscal transfers that were based on the number of students enrolled in a province, in Colombia, fiscal transfers were based on the cost of the teacher payroll in a department – regardless of the student to teacher ratio (Lowden 2004). This decentralization reform preserved the broad contours of the unitary state in Colombia while providing generous funding for education, despite concerns about inefficient spending and the malapportionment of teachers.

In 1994, the union negotiated the General Law of Education, Law 115. In line with the demands of the MP, the main policy proposal was curricular autonomy for schools, with each school developing a special pedagogical project based on the needs of its students (Díaz Ríos 2016). The law also protected teachers from punitive evaluations. Both laws were the outcome of negotiations between national union leaders and government officials (Falleti 2010, 125–6). While leaders of FECODE purported to carry the banner of the MP and to advance its core principles in this law, the law was negotiated by the majority faction, led by Jaime Dussán.

After President Gaviria left office, a similar dynamic of negotiation continued with President Ernesto Samper (1994–8). But whereas President Gaviria was more supportive of neoliberal economic policies, President Samper was from a progressive wing of the Liberal party that was ideologically closer to the union. However, he was weakened by a campaign scandal. After his inauguration, President Samper's political survival was in doubt because of revelations that he received large (and illicit) campaign contributions from the Cali Cartel. With impending impeachment proceedings, Samper strengthened his alliance with teachers. He named Abel Rodríguez vice minister of education. Samper and Jaime Dussán, now the former president of FECODE, who had been elected to the Senate, formed a pact, in which they negotiated the "three eights," or three separate 8 percent raises of teacher salaries from 1996 to

1998. Jaime Dussán quipped that he nearly bankrupted the government (Interview, July 29, 2013): "I remember that a finance minister accused me of taking advantage of the weak government of Samper. We had made the teacher payroll extremely expensive." Moreover, Decree 1381 of 1997 created a special vacation bonus for teachers and called for five vacation centers exclusively for teachers. Spending more on education strengthened the union, since union dues were automatically deducted from teacher salaries as a proportion of their salary.

The education policy decisions enacted from 1989 to 1998 endowed FECODE with a strong national organization. For union leaders, this marked a period when the government finally addressed festering labor grievances, recognized the union as a legitimate organization, and made important strides toward improving the professional status of teachers. For critics, this was a period of state largesse for teachers, rent seeking, and policies that were more aligned with the narrow labor interests of teachers rather than the broader goals of better-quality education. Decentralization of education did not change the national labor code – FECODE's national executive committee continued to present governments with lists of demands on behalf of all teachers. The formula for funding education centered on the national government and it fully covered the cost of the teacher payroll. Union dues were automatically deducted from teacher salaries and new subsidies, such as the creation of the teacher pension fund, further empowered national union leaders.

CHANGES IN THE UNION: HIERARCHICAL RELATIONS AND FACTIONALISM

In the wake of political inclusion, there were changes in the union's internal dynamics. As the union moved closer to the state, gaining representation in the Constitutional Assembly, securing access to state subsidies, and playing a more institutionalized role in politics, it became a more hierarchical and bureaucratic organization. In particular, the president of FECODE became a high-profile leader on the national political stage, because he or she claimed credit for negotiating new education policies that benefited teachers and because new electoral rules created a direct pathway from the presidency of FECODE into the Senate. The national executive committee cemented its position as the locus of political representation for teachers; in general, departmental-level union leaders did not play a major role in policy negotiations and lacked a political following. Departmental-level union leaders, facing competitive internal union elections, sought alliances with national union leaders to bolster their position. National union leaders commanded authority and a significant share of the union's finances, which further elevated their standing, since these resources served as the basis for union factions and brokerage networks. As relations in FECODE became more institutionalized and hierarchical, the MP demobilized.

After FECODE was included in policy negotiations and gained access to state resources, power radiated out from its national executive committee. A top-down logic ensued. FECODE was a "federation" that brought together unions in Colombia's thirty-two departments and the capital; it was not a national union as SNTE was in Mexico. After the 1993 decentralization reform, the national government transferred funds to the departments, which were responsible for the teacher payroll. The departments deducted union dues and deposited them in the accounts of the departmental unions. These departmental unions in turn deposited 15 percent of the funds they collected with the national executive committee.[5]

However, de facto power in FECODE had a centralized character for several reasons. First, because of the national teacher labor code, major policy decisions affecting teachers continued to be negotiated by FECODE's national executive committee and the national Ministry of Education. National union leaders had policy authority, as their departmental counterparts did not, since they were privy to labor negotiations that most affected ordinary teachers. In the early 1990s, FECODE president Jaime Dussán cemented the authority of the national executive committee by pressuring President Ernesto Samper to improve teacher salaries. FECODE had a national organizational logic that reflected the fact that the national government set teacher policy – similar to Mexico. By contrast, in Argentina, teacher policy was set at the provincial level, which empowered provincial union leaders.

Second, national union leaders had strong political connections. Electoral rules created a pathway that enabled presidents of FECODE to become viable candidates for the Senate. By contrast, departmental-level union leaders had more tenuous pathways into politics – it was harder for them to win office, and the positions available were not as important. As a consequence of the likelihood that union presidents would become national political figures, they had political credibility,

---

[5] FECODE, "Conclusiones de la xx asamblea general federal," Medellín October 25–28, 2017.

and departmental-level union leaders followed their lead. Moreover, the union factions in FECODE had links to left parties, such as the communists and Maoists, which had a rigid, hierarchical structure. These parties were organized around a powerful cadre of national leaders who counted on party discipline and passed down orders to subordinates. The top-down logic of left parties permeated FECODE. Departmental union leaders operated under the national union leaders, as subordinates, with limited latitude for independent action.

Third, national union leaders had access to more resources. Departmental union leaders stood in the shadow of the national union leadership because they had fewer state subsidies. A key factor behind the centralized character of FECODE was the national executive committee's role in providing state-sanctioned services to its members. By the 1990s, FECODE provided various health and financial services to union members. The union's more hierarchical organization was closely related to its role in providing social programs to teachers.[6] In managing the teacher pension fund (Fondo de Prestaciones del Magisterio), FECODE leaders authorized contracts for health service providers for teachers and funds for affordable housing, and they also played prominent roles in financial cooperatives. Union leaders were involved in kickback schemes, and those who sat on the teacher pension fund had influence over the allocation of lucrative contracts.[7] The power and resources that national union leaders got from sitting on the board of that pension fund reinforced the top-down logic of the union. Departmental union leaders, by contrast, had access to fewer resources.

The growing clout of FECODE's national executive committee went hand in hand with the MP's separation from FECODE and demobilization. Demobilization occurred after a change in the union's leadership in FECODE effectively pushed out key leaders of the MP. FECODE president Abel Rodríguez, who had been a leader of this movement, was replaced by Jaime Dussán, who became union president and focused on labor priorities, not pedagogy. The union became politically active and changed its focus to pursuing public office. The academics and researchers in the MP distanced themselves from FECODE, and Jaime Dussán packed the editorial board of the journal *Education and Culture* with

---

[6] Recall that whereas in Mexico SNTE operated and managed a vast arrangement of housing funds, health service providers, car loans, grocery stores, and other services for teachers, the Argentine union, CTERA, was initially denied a role in managing the social welfare funds (Obras Sociales) for teachers.

[7] Mariela Guerrero, "La rosca decide," *Alternativa* No. 9 1997.

loyalists (Santamaria Fajardo 2017). As the union organization strengthened, the MP unraveled. FECODE president Jaime Dussán excluded MP participants from negotiations with the government related to the language in the 1994 General Law of Education – even though this law purported to reflect the principles of the MP. There was a split, as leaders of the MP left the union (or were forcibly removed) and formed their own autonomous movements, although these did not endure (Tamayo Valencia 2006, 110–11).

Taking the Colombian case in comparative perspective, then, shows how inclusion in policy decisions and closer ties to the state made the union more hierarchical and less prone to movementism. There are telling parallels with Mexico in this regard. In both cases, education decentralization packages were negotiated with union leaders and there were major concessions. These concessions made the union less likely to protest and more engaged in politics. However, in Colombia, there was no strong dissident movement that did not recognize national union leaders as legitimate. FECODE was the only game in town.

While there was factionalism before the Constitution of 1991, several factors indicate that inclusion in politics intensified factional competition. In Colombia, elites sought to make the regime more inclusive. The aim of President Gaviria was to shore up the legitimacy of the regime, so he shifted education policy to reflect the demands of FECODE to achieve this goal. Because he was from a conservative faction of the Liberal Party, he had no means to intervene directly in the union's internal affairs. This was consequential for the ensuing dynamics of factionalism in FECODE.[8] As in Argentina, where the ruling party also did not intervene in the union's internal affairs, multiple competing forces remained in the union and no faction established its supremacy. Presidents Gaviria and Samper might have preferred a more moderate faction in FECODE to take power, to avoid dealing with radical leftist leaders, but the success of the moderate faction did not benefit them directly – at least not in winning the political support of teachers – because few leaders of FECODE were from the Liberal Party. Therefore, the union's inclusion in politics did not tip the balance of power in favor of one faction or another.

---

[8] In Mexico, President Salinas had a stake in shoring up the dominant faction in SNTE, since this faction was a political ally. The president included SNTE in policy decisions to shore up Elba Esther Gordillo. After securing state resources and strengthening her political connections, Gordillo consolidated a hegemonic faction in 1997 and reined in the restive dissident teachers.

On the contrary, the political opening intensified factionalism. While factional dynamics in FECODE had been present since the 1960s, these divisions became more pronounced after the 1991 Constitution. With the rise of the MP in the 1980s, a new center-left current emerged. Even if the movement was demobilized, it marked a new ideological split in the national executive committee. Indeed, this was a period of turmoil and change for left-wing political parties in countries around the world, as the end of the Cold War fractured the left into two ideological blocs: one centrist and one radical (Handlin 2017). By this point, different currents of the left had emerged and were engaged in a bitter ideological fight. One strand was more comfortable with liberal democracy and more moderate in its outlook. The other strand had a more radical economic program and called for revolutionary change. In FECODE, a new generation of center-left union leaders who embraced a more pragmatic and flexible ideology was ascendant. But if the old left lost financial support from the Soviet Union and China, it maintained a cadre of activists with a rigid ideology. By the early 1990s, there were various groups aligned with either the center or radical left. There was a process of fissuring, as defections produced new, more personalistic factions.

If the political opening created opportunities for union leaders and teachers to participate in politics, not all factions embraced participation – at least not initially. The question of whether to participate in politics, and if so on what terms, sparked renewed divisions. With fresh memories of the political genocide in the 1980s, some factions feared that organizing public campaign events would encourage violence against them. The communist parties criticized the entrenched power of the oligarchy in democratic institutions while highlighting the unresolved grievances that sparked the guerrilla insurgency. But for emerging groups that were more moderate, the political opening marked a new opportunity to gain a voice in government and political power. In other words, there were contradictory interpretations of FECODE's incursions into electoral politics, with some union leaders vividly recalling the political violence against leftist activists and others recalling the effective interventions of Abel Rodríguez and German Toro in the Constitutional Assembly. Factional divisions hardened with the center left supportive of participation and the radical left suspicious.

Despite the grumblings of some union leaders, the new electoral rules created a strong inducement to participate. The electoral system in Colombia directly shaped dynamics in the national executive committee because it created incentives for party fracturing. The Senate of the Republic was a case in point. One hundred Senate seats were distributed among candidates through a D'Hondt formula, which was a way to assign proportional representation to various parties. Candidates could launch their own party lists and mobilize votes in a single national district (Crisp and Ingall 2002). This system induced candidates to pursue office as political independents, by organizing "micro electoral enterprises" (Pizarro 2006). The rules fragmented the vote and empowered union leaders to become politicians. This electoral system reinforced factionalism because the best way for union leaders to launch competitive bids was by creating new factions. Institutional reforms positioned union leaders with personal followings to launch candidacies for the Senate. The electoral laws allowed these parties to obtain legal registries that put them on the ballot, which enabled union leaders to pursue office without the backing of a major party. Union leaders could break from existing factions and create their own in anticipation of a run for public office, in which they targeted teachers as core constituents.

The political opening also reinforced factionalism by changing the procedures that FECODE used to select union leaders. Recall that teachers' unions in Mexico and Argentina adopted new union statutes and procedures, at least paying lip service to the idea of union democracy. By contrast, in Colombia, the procedures FECODE adopted to elect the national executive committee reinforced factionalism. In 1993, in line with the democratizing impulse of the new Constitution, FECODE (as well as the Unitary Central of Workers of Colombia (CUT)) eliminated labor congresses, where teachers selected delegates who then attended a national labor convention to select national union leaders. These congresses were replaced by direct elections, organized and monitored by the union itself, in which the rank and file voted for their preferred candidate. In contrast to Argentina, where CTERA adopted a winner take-all formula for union elections, in Colombia, FECODE union elections followed a proportional representation formula. Teachers voted for their preferred candidate, and the fifteen with the most votes won secretariats. Since multiple candidates organized political campaigns, only a few thousand votes were needed to win a leadership position. Winning factions negotiated who got which secretariats (i.e., president, secretary general, treasurer, etc.) by forming an eight-member majority. This procedure institutionalized distinct factions that shared power. Moreover, since national leaders had resources and political authority, they established a vertical chain of command in which national leaders had a following of departmental and local leaders.

CONCLUSION

This chapter has located FECODE in my analytic framework and placed Colombia within the broader comparative panorama. The internal dynamics in FECODE changed in the 1990s because the union was included in policy decisions, and there was a major shift in teacher–state relations. To explain how and why this shift happened, it is critical to trace the history of the MP and the divisions among union leaders in the 1980s. The political moment of inclusion in Colombia was crucial. Union leaders participated in the constitutional convention of 1990, and shortly thereafter, they were included in negotiations about education decentralization. Thus, the state recognized FECODE as the official entity that represented teachers and included union leaders in policy decisions. Decentralization was negotiated with union leaders and protected the union's key interest: maintaining a national labor code. Meanwhile, union leaders negotiated generous salary increases and acquired additional subsidies for the union.

Consequently, the union became more hierarchical, in that the status of the national executive committee was elevated vis-à-vis the departmental unions. By the mid-1990s, the MP had demobilized and there were deepening factional divisions among union leaders. Union development unfolded differently in Colombia than in Mexico and Argentina. The changes in teacher–state relations produced a competitive and factionalized union leadership, rather than one controlled by a hegemonic faction or one in which power resided in the activist base.

9

Leftism in Colombia

Factionalism generated leftism. As a political repertoire, leftism in Colombia featured the electoral mobilization of instrumentalism and the oppositional behavior of movementism. The mechanisms here are the competitive dynamics among rival factions. The Colombian teachers' union organized an energetic electoral operation because rival factions launched competing political organizing efforts to ramp up voter turnout.[1] In other words, electoral mobilization in Colombia stemmed from factional competition rather than coordination through a single national grouping. At the same time, competing organizing efforts by union leaders hardened the union's ideological association with left parties. The political outreach that leftist factions conducted crowded out the remaining union leaders linked to the traditional parties. Any union leader who moved toward the government and pursued instrumental alliances was accused of selling out and faced a backlash from an energized group of rival factions.

In the 1970s, union leaders from left factions seized power in the national executive committee and mobilized massive protests. That was the initial moment when factionalism and leftism began to take hold. However, transforming FECODE into a leftist union was a slow-moving process. The decade of the 1990s marked a fuller expression of leftism and an inflection point – when left parties cemented their hold on the base, formed teachers into a leftist voting bloc, and moved away from a strategy centered on disruptive protests. Teachers were affiliated to left parties based on their union membership. There was an ideological

[1] "El poder de Fecode," *Semana* June 8, 2007.

hardening and sorting of teachers into factional camps. More intense factionalism contributed to greater politicization and sharper divisions between center- and radical-left currents.

This chapter establishes how the internal organization of FECODE (i.e., a leadership riven with factional divisions) shaped electoral mobilization through the union and ideological rigidity. The first section examines the repertoire of leftism and how it was linked to factionalism. As demonstrated in Chapter 8, factionalism resulted in part from the political opening and the distinctive institutional context created by the 1991 Constitution. But this chapter shows that the proximate cause of teacher mobilization was the political activities of factions; political institutions did not shape teacher mobilization in a direct or deterministic way, and when these institutions changed in 2003, teachers remained rooted in the left. Contrary to the Argentine tendency for ongoing and disruptive protests, protests by FECODE were easier for the government to manage owing to the political priorities of union factions. The next section shows how factionalism and ideological rigidity produced rival negotiating strategies that limited the ability of union leaders to intervene in the policy process. The final section shows that leftism remained the central tendency of political mobilization for the union throughout the 2010s.

THE PROPERTIES OF LEFTISM

The factional dynamics in FECODE shed light on the union's repertoire of leftism. The proximate cause of teacher mobilization was the political activities of union factions – specifically, their competing outreach and organizing efforts. This section lays out how electoral mobilization through the union and adherence to left parties was put in place. Competition among rival factions – which had hierarchical organizations and left-leaning ideological commitments – generated a robust electoral operation. Ideological competition hardened the partisan identities of union leaders. Union leaders then recruited teachers into their political groups and effectively split the union into rival camps. The remaining union leaders who were from the traditional parties were crowded out. In this way, strong ties to left parties were locked in.

To understand factionalism in FECODE, it is necessary to examine how a project to consolidate control over the national executive committee failed. By the early 1990s, a new center-left faction was gaining power, led by Jaime Dussán. This faction had a hierarchical structure. Dussán was from the rural department of Huila, and he earned a reputation as a political operator who built clientelistic networks, rather than a *cuadro* who had ideas and proposals for education reform. His political behavior resembled that of Elba Esther Gordillo of Mexico in some ways, as she was also from a rural state, Chiapas, and was an expert in building brokerage networks. Both leaders used the union as a political instrument and leveraged union resources to promote allies and squeeze rivals. In 1992, Dussán packed the editorial board of the journal *Education and Culture* and the research unit of FECODE, CEID, with loyalists. Moreover, as president of FECODE, Dussán used resources from the teacher pension fund to award contracts for services that were given to friends and family members, thereby establishing networks of patronage. Dussán was a political boss. He recruited brokers in the union to work under him, and had a penchant for establishing a personal following through clientelistic relations and corruption.

Dussán used his faction to build a small political party, or electoral vehicle, Education, Work, and Social Change. This group had a center-left orientation and it was created in 1994 out of necessity. Dussán requested a position on the list of the left party, M-19, but the party leader, Antonio Navarro Wolff, refused the request because Dussán showed little loyalty to the party; he seemed to want to use it to advance his political career. After this rejection, Dussán built his own organization. Recall that the electoral rules for the Senate in Colombia, in the wake of the Constitution of 1991, enabled political candidates to launch campaigns through their own party lists, which amounted to personal electoral vehicles. Serving as president of FECODE raised Dussán's leadership profile and he claimed credit for negotiating Law 60 (i.e., decentralization) in 1993 and Law 115 (i.e., the General Law of Education) in 1994. Education, Work, and Social Change was a personalistic electoral vehicle since Dussán was the only major candidate who won office from the list.[2] The driving force behind this party was Dussán's control over the union – union resources and member services – which he used to direct mobilization from the top down. He promoted allies through his faction, and was the first political entrepreneur to untap the electoral power of FECODE. Like Gordillo, Dussán sought to use his political position to engage in negotiations with presidents who were from

---

[2] After this election, Dussán changed the name of his political grouping from Education, Work, and Social Change to the Social Democrats, which was loosely modeled on the Social Democratic party of Sweden. FECODE received support from Lärarförbundet, the Swedish teachers' union.

different political parties, demanding particularistic benefits. Clientelism was not a stranger to FECODE; as union leaders became politicians, some emulated the practices of traditional politicians.

In the 1994 legislative election, two former FECODE presidents competed for Senate seats: Dussán, who had served as union president from 1990 to 1994, and Adalberto Carvajal, who had served as union president from 1962 to 1970. Carvajal won only 12,094 votes, and his failed bid ended his political career. Dussán won 33,175 votes across the departments and was elected to the Senate (Crisp and Ingall 2002). Dussán's coattails extended into FECODE's national executive committee: In 1994, nine of fifteen of the members of the national executive committee were from his political group.[3]

Despite some similarities between Dussán and Gordillo, SNTE in Mexico and FECODE in Colombia were different sorts of unions. Gordillo consolidated power because she controlled SNTE's labor congresses. By contrast, Dussán was unable to control internal elections in FECODE. Factional competition was rooted in the direct elections that FECODE adopted for the national executive committee in which rank-and-file teachers voted for their preferred union leader. Seats were allocated to the fifteen who won the most votes, which amounted to proportional representation. Given these rules, multiple factions could secure representation, which prevented any union leader from establishing a hegemonic faction.

Internal union elections helped factions to organize teachers into a voting bloc. Indeed, in 1993, after FECODE adopted direct elections, internal union elections became a dress rehearsal for campaigns for public office because they produced factions with strong organizations, resources, and sophisticated campaign operations. They were akin to a party primary, revealing to prospective political candidates how much support they had. Union elections gave factions an opportunity to gain experience by conducting outreach to teachers and mobilizing support. Left factions built parallel national organizations that aimed to compete with Dussán's political group at national and departmental levels. Moreover, union elections provided information about the level of support for a given union leader. Like a party primary, internal union elections assisted would-be politicians in assessing their viability as political candidates. Celio Nieves, a vice president of FECODE who became a city

---

[3] See "Las elecciones de fecode: Derrotado el Samperismo," *Tribuna Roja* January 26, 1998.

council member in Bogotá, described how union elections influenced his foray into politics (Interview, June 5, 2012).

CCJ: So, were these results [from internal union elections] important for your decision [to go into politics]?

CN: Of course, because here in Bogotá, I had 3,700 votes [in FECODE's internal election]. That is an important base because in the elections for city council and the lower house my vote share multiplied almost six times because in addition to the teachers, the family members of teachers also voted for me.

Competitive union elections for the national executive committee, in which there was a proportional representation formula for allocating seats, afforded factions an opportunity to build rival organizations and challenge Dussán's control over teachers. As Dussán flexed his political muscles and consolidated a towering political organization, there was a backlash. The radical left was initially squeezed by the center left, but these groups received an opportunity to win back power. For Dussán, using clientelism and corruption to mobilize voters was a double-edged sword. While clientelism was effective in scaling up mobilization, it created a rallying point for rival factions. In 1997, an investigative reporter at *Alternativa*, a respected independent news magazine, uncovered kickbacks to Dussán's allies from contracts to provide health care and affordable housing.[4] This revelation galvanized radical groups, which rallied against the center left for colluding with the Liberal government of Ernesto Samper and embezzling union funds. In other words, the instrumental negotiations of Dussán with the government and particularistic modes of exchange engendered a backlash. In the 1998 internal union election, the Alternative Bloc, a coalition of left union leaders, won ten of fifteen seats in the national executive committee.[5] Despite his best efforts, Dussán failed to consolidate control over the national executive committee.

Clientelism was not the modus operandi for the radical left. If Dussán and his adherents embraced clientelistic modes of exchange with departmental union leaders and rank and file teachers, then the more radical left relied more on ideological and programmatic appeals *against*

---

[4] Dussán allegedly used his influence over the Fondo de Prestaciones del Magisterio for campaign finance and as a means to direct resources to political allies. See "El Fondo Prestacional Del Magisterio," *El Tiempo* October 6, 1992.

[5] See "Las elecciones de fecode: Derrotado el Samperismo," *Tribuna Roja* January 26, 1998.

clientelism. The communists, Maoists, and other radical groups did not have a vast store of patronage resources to mobilize teachers; instead, they relied mainly on party discipline and programmatic appeals. Left factions engaged in political outreach and appealed to teachers by touting their economic program, which was aligned with teacher demands for better pay. Left parties claimed credit for advancing teacher interests through protests and hardline tactics, pointing to how they negotiated the 1979 Teacher Statute. Leaders from the Communist and Maoist parties also recruited charismatic union leaders with broad appeal among teachers. Finally, left parties had already established hierarchical national organizations, headed by cadres of party leaders. These structures served as a blueprint for building union factions.

Radical groups in FECODE were initially reluctant to redirect their energy from competing in internal union elections to broader participation in politics. With fresh memories of the political genocide of the 1980s against leftist activists, some groups were understandably hesitant. But union factions with political connections and resources were more likely to win seats in internal union elections; factions that lacked political connections and resources could be crowded out. Seeing the success of the center-left groups, more radical union leaders pursued public office. By the early 2000s, the radical left – namely the Maoist and Communist parties – began to use the union to seek public office as well. They rallied behind charismatic leaders. Jorge Robledo had a strong base in FECODE and was elected to the Senate in 2002 by the Maoist party; FECODE President Gloria Inés Ramírez was elected to the Senate in 2006 by the Communist Party. By gaining representation in public office, these radical factions secured their beachhead in FECODE.

Overall, it was competitive dynamics among factions that produced a robust teacher voting bloc. Electoral mobilization was rooted in allegiance to specific small parties on the left. FECODE and left parties became deeply interpenetrated. Various left parties established themselves, and the union maintained an ideological allegiance to these parties. In Colombia's fluid party system, left parties frequently changed names and rebranded themselves, but these parties recruited FECODE leaders as political candidates because they had a strong following among teachers. Union leaders claimed credit for delivering policy benefits during their tenure and for protesting neoliberal education policies. In other words, they were positioned to win seats in the national legislature, based primarily on their standing with teachers. According to the database Congresovisible, union leaders who became political candidates – Jaime Dussán, Jorge Guevara, Tarsicio Mora, and Gloria Inés Ramírez – mentioned their tenures in FECODE in their political biographies; they claimed credit for representing teacher interests and defending public education.[6]

Union leaders had access to various resources. FECODE was itself one obvious source of resources for political campaigns; union presidents traveled throughout Colombia and met with departmental union leaders and teachers. This enabled them to build national networks.

There were also resources in teachers' financial cooperatives. These financial cooperatives were originally organized in the 1960s as self-help organizations, so teachers could deposit savings and get access to lines of credit when governments did not pay salaries on time. But by the 1990s and 2000s, they had evolved and accumulated significant assets – the Cooperative of Teachers (CODEMA) in Bogotá, which organized 25,500 teachers, managed assets that were valued at $US20 million.[7] The cooperatives operated like banks even while they operated outside the financial regulatory framework. Union factions aggressively competed for representation on their boards: These cooperatives enabled them to gain financial resources for political activities. For example, Tarsicio Mora, who was president of FECODE, founded new financial cooperatives in regions of influence, such as Cootradecun in Cundinamarca, strengthening his faction.[8] As teacher salaries improved, and as teachers put their savings in them and took out loans, these cooperatives became flush with cash; they became large financial institutions that provided valuable services to teachers.

In addition to rivalries between the center and radical left, there were also personal rivalries. Union leaders split from existing factions and formed rival groupings. In 2002, Luis Carlos Avellaneda, a labor lawyer, founded a group called Democratic Unity. In 2006, Jorge Guevara, Jaime Dussán's campaign manager, split the center-left Social Democrats in two. This was because Dussán did not want to share power, and the only way to pursue public office was to form a new faction (Jorge Guevara, interview, June 26, 2012). Moreover, a regional leader and former militant of the M-19, Luis Alberto Gil, formed the party Citizen's Convergence; the teachers' union in the department of Santander was a

---

[6] Congresovisible database, accessed October 3, 2023, via https://congresovisible.uniandes.edu.co.
[7] "Codema tiene represados unos 40.000 millones para créditos a los maestros," *El Pais* December 5, 2010.
[8] "Tarsicio Mora Godoy." *La Silla Vacia* February 12, 2021.

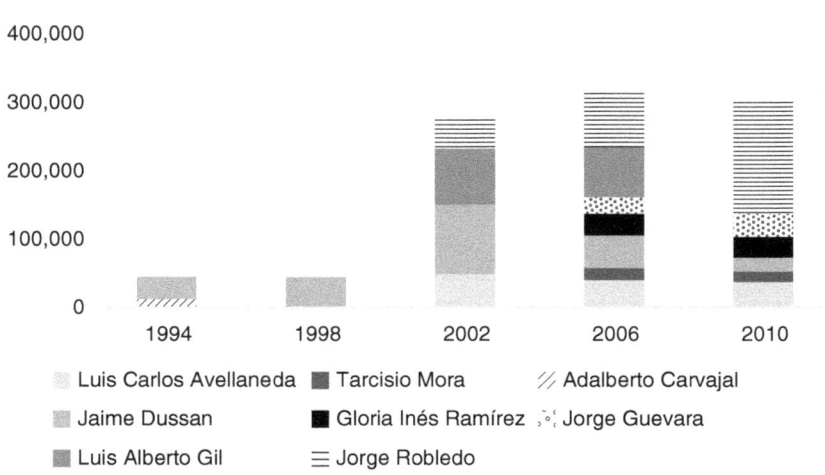

FIGURE 9.1 Vote share of Colombian Senate candidates, linked to teachers, 1994–2010
Source: www.registraduria.gov.co

crucial base of support. Regional leaders of FECODE were also elected to governorships, such as Raúl Delgado in Nariño. There was a tendency for union factions to split apart as union leaders pursued pathways into politics and built their own personalized groupings to do so.

The scale of electoral mobilization through FECODE was remarkable. Electoral mobilization did not take place exclusively in the Senate, although the Senate clearly demonstrates the scale of mobilization. Figure 9.1 shows the vote share of senators who had strong ties to the union, illustrating the tremendous capacity of the union for electoral mobilization. While the electoral experiment began in 1994 and accelerated in 1998, the year 2002 marks a sharp discontinuity when there was a jump in the vote share of candidates with links to teachers. By 2006, the combined vote share of these candidates exceeded 300,000 votes – recall that FECODE had 270,000 members. Teachers were a core constituency for these Senate candidates.[9] The teacher voting bloc was large since it included retired teachers (who retired at the age of fifty-five, and thereafter were no longer eligible to be union members), teachers in training (who were also not yet eligible to join the union), and the family members of teachers.

---

[9] In addition to teachers, various small labor groups, leftist militants, regional voters, and social movements accounted for other voters that supported these senators. These groups were smaller and more heterogeneous than teachers. Teachers were the largest group that supported the left.

In line with my organizational argument, electoral mobilization in Colombia ramped up due to the hierarchical structure of union factions and the competition among them. The national executive committee involved a power-sharing arrangement, and there was turnover in the faction that held the union presidency. Factions constructed robust organizations, acquired resources, and obtained campaign experience before launching competitive electoral bids. Voter mobilization ratcheted up over time, as rival factions consolidated hierarchical organizations. The Senate was a focal point of mobilization, since the barriers to entry were low, but it was by no means the only public office where teachers gained representation. With electoral reforms and state resources, union factions launched campaigns from the union. They targeted teachers as voters, forming a voting bloc for left parties – a bloc that had not existed as such before 1991.

MANAGEABLE PROTESTS

Teacher protests by FECODE in Colombia differed from those of CTERA in Argentina. Recall that in Argentina, teacher protests were highly disruptive, drawing political attention and having dramatic effects on policy. By contrast, in Colombia, during the 1990s, 2000s, and 2010s, protests were not the main part of the union's political repertoire. Murillo (2001) argues that leadership competition, or factionalism, can lead to greater union militancy. However, fierce leadership competition in FECODE produced more muted militancy – at least if militancy is defined as disruptive protests. This section argues that the more hierarchical organization of FECODE, which stood in stark contrast to the weaker organization of CTERA, helps to explain this lower level of protest activity. While left factions had a militant ideology and sought to discredit each other for selling out the union, these factions had political objectives and hierarchical organizations. They were more oriented toward political rallies, party-building activities, and fundraising, and less toward mobilizing strikes. In other words, the hierarchical organization and office-seeking objectives of factions reshaped their political behavior and diminished the significance of protest.

My argument stresses that teacher protests in Colombia were more manageable than their Argentine counterparts. They were less disruptive and they were usually taken less seriously by officials. Data comparing protest activities in these two countries, collected by the Argentine Ministry of Labor and the Center for National Investigation and Popular

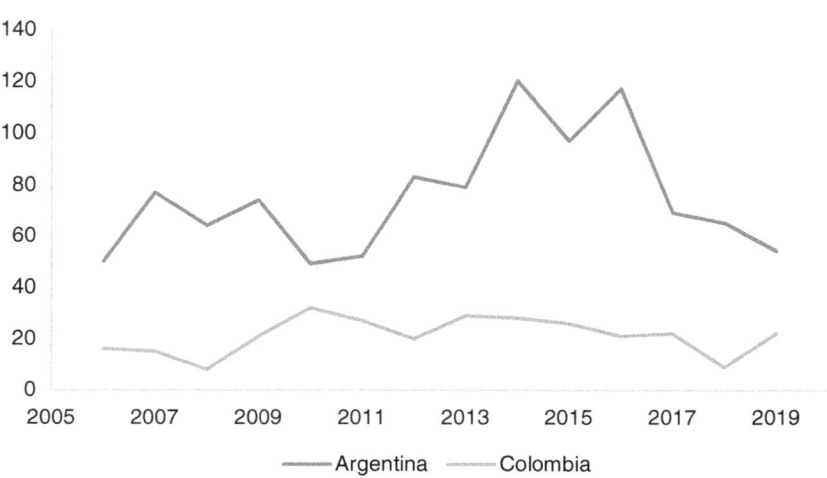

FIGURE 9.2 Number of teacher protest events, Argentina versus Colombia
Sources: Labor Conflict Database, Ministry of Labor, Argentina, CINEP

Education (CINEP) for the period 2006–19, shows that the number of protest events were fewer in Colombia each year than in Argentina (see Figure 9.2). Few analysts would dispute the claim that Argentine teachers protested more frequently than their Colombian counterparts. Indeed, Figure 9.2 shows that after 2013, there were more than double the number of protests in Argentina.

In Colombia, teacher protests were taken less seriously by officials. In interviews, union leaders reported that the government dismissed them and ignored the lists of demands (*pliegos de peticiones*) that they made (Union leader, interview, July 11, 2013). In response to this slight, FECODE would protest, but governments usually continued to ignore the union's demands. Protests by FECODE were more of an annoyance or inconvenience than a threat to public order. While protests did occur, they were less likely to be disruptive and sustained over time. Protests in Argentina were impossible for governments to control or ignore. But in Colombia, with the Constitution of 1991 and the ensuing shift in teacher–state relations, FECODE developed a more institutionalized and bureaucratic organizational structure. This is central to understanding the differences in the character of teacher protests. Whereas militancy is strongest when organized by an activist base, union leaders in Colombia were more interested in organization building, securing resources, and burnishing their political credentials.

Despite the ideological tendencies and oppositional positions of FECODE leaders, protests were not a central part of the political repertoire. The union's hierarchical organization did not sustain protests. While FECODE opposed the government, the subsidies and representation in state institutions that it received undermined the basis for disruptive strikes. Union leaders embraced oppositional rhetoric, harshly criticizing the government, but they ultimately abided by labor law and organized strikes that complied with the law. The inclusion of FECODE in politics with the Constitution of 1991 and its role in the managing of the teacher pension fund domesticated the union. By contrast, in Argentina, the union had more of an arm's-length relationship with the government.

Protests were a secondary mode of interest representation in Colombia. Large strikes occurred only in response to certain policy proposals and after long periods of salary stagnation. In Colombia, there was no analog to the dissident activist groups that mobilized large numbers of teachers in Argentina and Mexico (i.e., CNTE). This meant that wildcat strikes, organized against the wishes of the national executive committee, rarely occurred. The bureaucratic structure of FECODE and the dearth of grassroots activists reduced the propensity for spontaneous protests. Power was in the national executive committee and in leaders who had entered the senate, not in the grassroots.

Because of the union's organizational structure, governments were relatively effective in managing teacher protests. The government created conditions that made strikes difficult to organize. During the presidency of Álvaro Uribe (2002–10), the minister of education María Cecilia Vélez White made sure that teachers were paid on time, to avoid the labor grievances that had fueled unrest in the past. At the same time, she did not cede to union demands for higher pay, so salaries were stagnant. Meanwhile, when teachers threatened to go on strike, she took a hardline stance and adopted a policy of deducting pay for each day teachers spent on strike.[10] This strategy worked. Even when new policies, such as merit-based evaluations for teachers, were adopted in 2004, and teachers organized protests to disrupt them, the protests failed to change policy. Throughout Uribe's presidency, there were few protests. Unlike their

---

[10] Grievances were also managed by maintaining the status quo for already hired teachers, while changing policies for newly hired teachers. The new teacher labor code, which imposed stricter evaluations and slowed advancement up the salary scale, only affected teachers hired after 2005.

Argentine counterparts, Colombia teachers were afraid of losing pay for participating in strikes. Most Colombian teacher strikes were twenty-four or forty-eight hours long. Teachers participated by teaching half days and asking the principal for permission to take a few hours off work. This reduced strike participation.

In contrast to CTERA in Argentina, where teacher protests strongly shaped political life, teacher protests in Colombia were less significant. Two factors help to explain this contrast. With the teacher statute of 1979 in Colombia, there were fewer labor grievances to spark teacher unrest. Whereas teachers in Argentina experienced more economic volatility and saw a sharper erosion in salaries, teachers in Colombia saw more stability. Moreover, in a political context in which conservative politicians, such as President Uribe, held power, and where there was ongoing violence against labor and social leaders, there were risks to protesting and limited opportunities to shift policy. By contrast, Argentina had a political climate that was more supportive of movementism – with frequent protests and mobilization by various labor and popular sector groups. These factors – labor grievances and political opportunities – were undeniably important. However, my organizational argument highlights the ways in which changes in teacher–state relations and the increasingly hierarchical and politically oriented character of union factions contributed to a shift away from contentious politics. Since the union received subsidies from the state, this served as a constraint on demand making (Collier and Collier 1979). Moreover, because factions were electoral vehicles that sought representation in the national legislature, they were less combative than grassroots activists. The government had leverage over the union, a result of the subsidies and representation in state institutions. Even though union factions had a radical ideology, they followed the law and did not organize wildcat strikes. Union leaders made fiery ideological speeches that were directed at copartisans, but large-scale protests were not the central part of the union's political repertoire.

A MARGINAL ROLE IN THE POLICY PROCESS

In Mexico, instrumentalism shed light on a tendency for the union and government to negotiate pacts and new political alliances. By contrast, in Argentina, ongoing protests ultimately produced a major new institution of collective bargaining. For Colombia, then, leftism relegated the union to the margins of the policy process. Factionalism there did not lead to the sort of pact-making that took place in Mexico, nor did it produce an institution of collective bargaining like the one that was founded in Argentina.

Unlike instrumentalism, which proved relatively effective in gaining access to the government and negotiating concessions for teachers, leftism produced few concessions for teachers. Inside FECODE, infighting between moderate and radical factions resulted in dissonant strategies that relegated the union to the margins of policy decisions. Center-left leaders who sought to moderate demands and open negotiations with presidents from conservative parties had limited leeway for their negotiations because rivals on the radical left subjected them to constant criticism. At the same time, the hardline positions of the radical left isolated the union politically, and the political outreach of the center left undercut the radical parties. For teachers, the inability of the national executive committee to coordinate on a negotiating strategy contributed to the union's marginalization. While FECODE enjoyed strong influence on policy in the early 1990s, when many new societal groups were included in politics, the union's influence diminished as leftism took root. Leftism in Colombia meant that teachers had less influence on education policy, at least under governments of the right. This strategy was more expressive, rather than one that sought to maximize the union's influence on policy decisions.

If the Pedagogical Movement bolstered FECODE's capacity to negotiate, leftism undermined the union's bargaining leverage. In Mexico, the dominant faction was ideologically flexible and could redirect political support. By contrast, in Colombia, rival factions were ideologically rigid. They prevented the union from aligning with the president and joining broad-based coalitions. Infighting weakened FECODE's ability to coordinate on one negotiating position, while hardline positions isolated the union politically. A recurring problem with a divided leadership was that different factions pulled in different directions. With factions jockeying for position, the dissonance from multiple bargaining positions prevented the union from speaking with one voice. There was little coordination in the fifteen-member national executive committee. For Abel Rodríguez (Interview, October 4, 2012), different factions were "so politicized" that they fell back on their "partisan positions" rather than the collective interests of teachers. In other words, union leaders prioritized scoring political points with party activists rather than coordination with political rivals.

The center and radical left were both deeply rooted. Yet the center left sought pragmatic negotiations and the radical left pursued a hardline strategy. These strategies undercut each other. Policy episodes during the presidency of Andrés Pastrana (1998–2002) illustrate this dynamic. In the late 1990s, education spending increased due to Law 60 of 1993 along with the teacher raises and pension liabilities of the Samper administration. While education spending was 3.1 percent of gross domestic product (GDP) in 1991, it increased to 4.4 percent of GDP by 1997 (Borjas and Acosta 2000). There were growing concerns from the finance ministry about the rapidly increasing cost of education.

With growing factionalism, the union proved ineffective in policy negotiations in the early 2000s. This stems partly from the economic crisis and problems with the education policies of the early 1990s, which galvanized a conservative coalition (Díaz Ríos 2016). In 2001 President Pastrana, with the support of finance minister Juan Manuel Santos and education minister Francisco José Lloreda, pushed through a constitutional amendment, Legislative Act 01, which changed the formula governing education funding, setting the stage for cost-control measures (Cárdenas et al. 2006). Then Law 715 of 2002 imposed a freeze on increases in education spending. These reforms also forcibly transferred teachers to less desirable, understaffed schools and eliminated redundant teaching positions (López 2008, 35). The new formula for staffing schools was based on a fixed teacher–student ratio (López 2008, 39).

Factional divisions are crucial for understanding why President Pastrana did not negotiate with FECODE. First, in 1999, FECODE president Tarsicio Mora, who was a former communist, was blamed by other factions for pursuing his own negotiating strategy. More radical groups criticized him for trying to sell out the union and cut his own deal. At the same time, there were conflicts of interest involving Mora's use of the union for the headquarters of his senate campaign (Jorge Guevara, Interview, June 26, 2012). In 2000, the national executive committee unanimously forced Mora to step down from the union presidency.[11] Factionalism contributed to union leaders taking a go-it-alone approach, which prompted rival factions to take extraordinary steps to block their strategies.

While the center left pursued moderation and negotiation, radical factions pursued confrontation. In 2000, Gloria Inés Ramírez of the Communist Party became the next union president. She pursued a hardline strategy, organizing a large strike against the proposed cuts to education and railing against neoliberalism.[12] At the same time, the former FECODE president Jaime Dussán – who was in the Senate – pursued a strategy of

---

[11] See "Tumban a Tarcisio Mora de la presidencia de Fecode," *El Tiempo* May 30, 2000.
[12] Gloria Inés Ramírez, "Educación vs lógica de mercado," *Semana* June 29, 2002.

negotiation. Dussán voted "yes" for Law 715 of 2002, in exchange for minor modifications to the bill. He was criticized by left factions for his "conciliatory attitude" and "parliamentary wanderings" (Benavides 2002, 11). According to Gloria Inés Ramírez (interview, October 17, 2012): "The government divided FECODE by making a negotiating proposal behind the union's back. I told the national executive committee that they made an agreement with Senator Jaime Dussán that did not represent FECODE... This agreement was not endorsed by FECODE because we knew the great damage it would do to the financing of education."

Another member of the executive committee (Interview, July 26, 2010) confirmed that factionalism did indeed undermine policy influence.

The political orientation of the union was to negotiate ... and the union organized a strike lasting twenty days that paralyzed the school system. Jaime Dussán was a senator and without taking into account the will of the teachers, he proposed legislation that changed the articles of the constitution and Law 715, which the union was against. Members of the national executive committee, Jorge Eliecer Guevara, Boris Montes, and Rafael Cuello, supported the proposals of Dussán, while twelve members of the national executive committee were against them.

This was a major setback and a turning point in the union's capacity to shape policy. Competing negotiating strategies weakened the union's bargaining position.

Moreover, factional competition hardened the ideological rigidity of the far left. The presence of radical factions undermined the basis for the types of negotiations that took place in Mexico. The established factions, specifically the Communist and Maoist parties, remained recalcitrant and confrontational. Ultimately, these more radical forces anchored the union on the left, maintaining a hardline, ideological program for a core group of militant partisans. The association with extreme ideologies prevented the union from building broad coalitions. Unlike the MP during the 1980s, FECODE in the 1990s and 2000s became stigmatized for its association with groups that were equivocal about their support for the FARC and other rebel groups involved in the armed struggle. In Interviews, Abel Rodríguez (Interview, June 28, 2012) repeatedly mentioned the problem of radicalism: "Of course, there are problems ... with the radical policy proposals. There are some union leaders who believe that education policies depend on radicalism and have positions far on the left ... and I believe that the union could have better representation if leaders were more measured in their policy positions."

Former FECODE president and senator, Jorge Guevara (Interview, June 22, 2012) described how the fragmentation of the left prevented a broad coalition from forming, which bolstered conservative politicians. The political power of teachers was not fully realized because of ideological divisions among union leaders.

Leftism was not an effective strategy for dealing with right-wing governments. The window for negotiating with these governments was narrow, and leftism made the union a pariah. President Uribe established a flexible labor code for teachers hired after 2005, in which teacher entrance exams were open to all professionals and promotions were based on merit-based performance rather than seniority. This law created a division between the teachers hired under the "old" teacher statute of 1979 and the "new" statute of 2005. Uribe also controlled the cost of education by limiting the number of promotions that were available to teachers.

Union leaders railed against these policies but were unable to mobilize support for alternatives. The union launched an ambitious project to unify the teacher labor code, under the banner of a Unitary Teacher Labor Code. After teachers were divided between the "old" teacher statute of 1979 and the "new" teacher statute of 2005, the union demanded that all teachers be restored to a single labor code. However, there was little progress on this front, and much pessimism – a consequence of the ideological discord, as well as the distance separating the union and the government, especially regarding teacher evaluation.

During the presidency of Juan Manuel Santos (2010–18), FECODE continued to embrace its strategy of leftism. President Santos moved away from the right-wing populism of Álvaro Uribe and adopted a more centrist position. He supported a negotiated settlement with the FARC, despite the political risks associated with his more conciliatory stance toward this guerrilla group. However, relations between FECODE and the government remained marked with tension. Although in 2014 some teachers and union leaders supported Santos against his right-wing challenger Oscar Iván Zuluaga, to demonstrate their support for the peace process, teachers were split, and many refused to support the president's reelection bid. During Santos' second term, FECODE organized protests for better pay and more education funding. Union leaders claimed credit for organizing a major strike in 2017 and securing an 8.75 percent increase in salaries from the government, although this represented a modest gain since the union had been excluded from policy decisions since the late 1990s.[13] There were ongoing tensions between the government and

---

[13] See "Gobierno anuncia aumento salarial de 8,75 percent a maestros, pero Fecode dice que el paro sigue" *El Heraldo*, June 7 2017.

the union owing to ideological differences. Overall, the union remained aligned with the left and organized strikes from the opposition but had only limited influence on education policy.

Factionalism helps to explain the policy setbacks suffered by teachers in the 2000s and the limited capacity to advance FECODE's agenda in the 2010s. Hardline demands, stemming from the radical left, along with the dynamics of factionalism – and competing negotiating strategies – weakened opposition. Centrists showed some willingness to moderate demands and negotiate with the government. These union leaders faulted the radicals for isolating the union politically and undermining broad-based coalitions. By contrast, the radicals accused the centrists of corruption, clientelism, and being out of touch with the rank and file because of their lack of principles and desire to cut a deal with the government.[14] The leftist repertoire undermined the union's capacity to articulate and defend teacher interests.

ONGOING MOBILIZATION FOR LEFT PARTIES

There were no fundamental changes to FECODE's organizational structure in the aftermath of the political opening in the 1990s. In the 2000s and 2010s, factionalism persisted and strong ties remained between teachers and left parties. The political repertoire remained unchanged.

The ongoing leftism of teachers was reflected in the political cleavages over education policy in the party system. As Colombia's party system became deinstitutionalized, with a breakdown in party cohesion and discipline (Dargent and Muñoz 2011), the alignment of teachers with the left created a programmatic cleavage on education policy. The traditional parties mostly embraced a technocratic model for education that was in line with the interests of probusiness allies. Teachers sharply opposed this model and embraced a vision of education reform that emphasized inclusion, asserting the role of the state in providing public education and improving teacher compensation and opportunities for continuing education. As the cleavage between teachers and the right grew, left party programs closely resembled the demands of the union. This cleavage helped to cement the ties between teachers and the left.

---

[14] A former union leader from the Communist Party (Interview, June 20, 2012) mentioned how Jaime Dussán was known to be corrupt.

The left gained strength in 2005, but it remained a small and heterogeneous coalition composed of a variety of middle-class and labor groups. These groups founded PDA, which was the main opposition against President Álvaro Uribe. While PDA was a small and loose leftist coalition, within the party FECODE was the largest labor organization, and FECODE leaders held high-ranking positions in this party. The national executive committee of FECODE changed its partisan identity. Instead of referencing their particular union faction, fourteen of the fifteen members of the committee declared their allegiance to this party (López 2008). To be sure, there were underlying factional currents within the party, and ultimately factions moved away from the party because the left reconstituted itself in an alliance with the Green Party. PDA made a strong push to win teacher support and to include the union's demands in its statement of principles: "Public education should be universal, high quality, free, and compulsory for preschool, elementary, and high school, as well as for technical and higher education. We will reestablish the labor rights, salaries, and professional development of teachers."[15]

Although at the national level leftism was not effective in shaping policy, left parties advanced proteacher education policy in departments and municipalities. For example, in progressive cities, such as Bogotá, left parties won power and governed – they did not have to negotiate with centrist or right-wing parties. As a result, education policy reflected the interests of teachers. In Bogotá, the teachers' union helped elect leftist mayors in 2003, 2007, and 2011, bringing about a subnational "left turn." Also in Bogotá, union leaders were promoted and took high-ranking positions in the education bureaucracy. Abel Rodríguez, one of FECODE's most prominent leaders, was named the Secretary of Education in 2003 and again in 2007. Union leaders embraced a "social investment" model of education in Bogotá, and spending on education ramped up dramatically. Under Lucho Garzon and Samuel Moreno, two leftist mayors of the city, the budget increased from 6 to 12 percent, and under Gustavo Petro it reached 17 percent. In Bogotá, a number of proteacher policies were adopted: improvements in teacher training; new scholarships for continuing teacher education; the construction of

---

[15] See "Ideario de Unidad" – created by Independent Democratic Pole and Democratic Alternative at the moment of inception of the Democratic Alternative Pole, accessed October 3, 2023, via www.polodemocratico.net/wp-content/uploads/2023/07/IDEARIO-DE-UNIDAD.pdf.

modern public schools (*mega-colegios*) in poor neighborhoods; and an expansion of social policy through schools, for instance by offering free breakfast and lunch to all children (Interview, Bogotá, June 5, 2012). Thus, when left parties were large enough to govern (at the subnational level), they enacted important changes to teacher policy.

While teachers continued to support left parties, the character of teacher representation changed because of electoral reforms introduced in 2003. There were efforts to fix some of the institutional problems in Colombia that were caused by the electoral system that was established with the Constitution of 1991. Until 2002, the electoral rules set a very low bar to launch a successful bid through a personalistic electoral vehicle, which resulted in a highly fragmented political system. New rules were adopted in 2003, which required that political parties submit only one list of candidates, with the aim of producing broader-based political parties that were more unified. The new rules increased the threshold of votes needed to obtain representation in the legislature from 2 to 3 percent (Pachón and Shugart 2010).

This change made it more difficult for FECODE presidents to enter the Senate. Senate candidates had to broaden their appeal since votes were aggregated to a party list, but they did not break the teacher–left party alliance that had been put in place. Consequently, in elections in 2014 and 2018, union leaders continued to run for the Senate, but fewer were elected. In 2014, members of FECODE's national executive committee, Senen Nino, Tarsicio Mora, Witney Chavez, and Jorge Guevara, ran for Senate, but none was elected. In 2018, Tarcisio Mora and Libardo Ballesteros ran for Senate but lost, although Jorge Guevara was reelected on the list of the center-left party Green Alliance. Teacher support seemed to shift to Jorge Robledo, who in 2014 won 191,910 votes – the largest vote share of any senator. Moreover, in 2014, as a Senate candidate, teachers backed Claudia López, who ran with the Green Alliance. Alexander López, a lawyer whose career was in PDA, also represented teacher interests.[16] Even if it was more difficult for FECODE leaders to pursue senate seats by narrowly appealing to teachers, teachers remained an important voting bloc. By the 2010s, the left parties that teachers supported were in a stronger position than they had been in the 2000s, but remained divided between centrist and radical factions.

---

[16] "El senador Alexander López le exigió al Gobierno Nacional solucionar el paro de Fecode y buscar los recursos necesarios," Polo Democratico June 8, 2017.

Teachers have remained core constituents and political backers for left parties. In 2016, with the peace process ratified by the legislature (even if it remained divisive and the referendum on it failed), the left was gaining strength. In the first round of the 2018 presidential election, teachers were divided between support for Sergio Fajardo (Alianza Verde), who represented a center-left position, and Gustavo Petro (Colombia Humana) who represented a more populist expression. In the second round, Petro won the largest vote share of any leftist presidential candidate in the history of Colombia, although he ultimately lost to Iván Duque. In the context of a strengthening left, former union leaders, such as Jaime Dussán, continued to hold high-ranking positions in left parties and teachers remained core constituents for center- and radical-left parties. In sum, the organizational structure of the union did not change much during the 2000s or 2010s, nor did the union's political repertoire. The partisan identities of teachers were sticky. Once the organizational structure of the union was locked in by the 1990s, the pattern of mobilization was cemented. Teachers were aligned with left parties. The leftist coalition remained fractured, but it became stronger by the late 2010s.

CONCLUSION

This chapter has demonstrated how a union structure that was hierarchical and grounded in factional competition shaped the tendency toward electoral mobilization for political parties of the ideological left. The hierarchical organization resulted in electoral mobilization. Competition among factions cemented strong ties to left parties. Political inclusion in the 1990s demobilized the Pedagogical Movement and generated rival factions in FECODE, which were the driving force behind teacher mobilization and demand making. While the political opening engendered conflicts among union leaders related to whether and how to pursue political power, these conflicts were eventually overcome – all major union factions pursued political power. The union developed strong ties to left parties and mobilized teachers as a voting bloc. Over time, protests by teachers became sporadic, owing to suppression by conservative governments but also constraints from the union's hierarchical organization.

Electoral mobilization through the union began when union leaders claimed credit for policy victories and gained access to state subsidies. The partisanship of teachers was expressed in a programmatic cleavage: The left opposed neoliberal education policies, while the other parties increasingly supported them. With this cleavage, union leaders became political candidates who made targeted appeals to teachers. Left parties adopted FECODE demands into their party platforms. While left parties in Colombia were weak in the 1980s and 1990s, they made gains with the organizational backing of the teachers' union. FECODE's electoral mobilization played a crucial role in the construction – and contradictions – of Colombia's parties of the left.

However, the jockeying of factions undercut the union's capacity to negotiate. Center-left leaders pursued strategic negotiations, showing a willingness to approach political leaders from any party that was in power. But the center left was unable to convince the radical left to moderate its demands and make itself more palatable to mainstream parties. The radical left undercut pragmatic negotiations and made demands that isolated the union politically. Policymakers dismissed the demands of the union as a whole for being "out of date" and "unrealistic" (Montenegro 1995), even when these demands were voiced by only some union factions. Leftism and ideological rigidity ultimately undermined the union's capacity to stick to one negotiating position. The center left could not speak over the oppositional rhetoric of the far left, which undercut the ability of union leaders to negotiate and compromise.

10

Teacher Politics in Comparative Perspective

This book has analyzed the organizational development and political strategies of teachers' unions. Overall, labor in Latin America is weaker now than during the 1940s and 1950s, but in nearly every Latin American country (and in many countries in other world regions) teachers have strong labor organizations. By the 2000s, most countries had consolidated systems of mass public education. These gains in public school enrollment went hand in hand with the hiring of more teachers, which made teachers' unions powerful. Teachers' unions can serve as vital coalition partners to political parties or they can reside in the opposition; either way, they can play a prominent role in the policy process (Nelson 2007; Moe and Wiborg 2017). The strategies of teachers point to a new pattern of labor politics in which unions have more opportunities to participate in politics and to do so with greater independence from political parties.

This chapter takes stock of the main argument. I have shown that deeply rooted organizational structures are the best explanation for the strategies of teachers' unions. I then extend the organizational argument to three shadow cases, teachers' unions in Chile, Peru, and Indonesia, to demonstrate that my framework can indeed travel – within Latin America and also to developing democracies in other world regions. These shadow cases also address concerns about features of the political environment (rather than organizational structures) shaping union strategies, since the electoral rules and party systems in the paired cases (Chile–Colombia, Peru–Argentina, and Indonesia–Mexico) differ quite significantly. The chapter then examines how the organizational argument opens avenues for research on education policymaking, interest representation, and labor politics.

SUMMARY OF THE ARGUMENT

Teachers serve as a useful laboratory to explore the foundations for different political repertoires. They have employed a variety of forms of collective action across countries, and these differences have become pronounced in the wake of regime openings. While teacher protests occurred throughout the twentieth century, with mobilization for better salaries followed by harsh crackdowns, the tempo of teacher protests accelerated in the 1980s, as teachers endured hardship during the debt crisis and as political openings (i.e., democratization and steps toward greater political inclusion) created opportunities to voice demands. In the 1990s, teachers made inroads into the electoral arena, as they experimented with voter mobilization.

However, these inroads proved uneven across countries. By the 1990s and 2000s, protests became more intermittent and relegated to regional enclaves in Colombia and Mexico. By contrast, teacher protests became a recurrent feature of politics in Argentina, whereas participation in electoral politics was limited. This book has developed the concepts of movementism, leftism, and instrumentalism to highlight crucial differences in the ways teachers engaged in politics. Unions can establish strategic alliances (i.e., instrumentalism), double down on support for left parties (i.e., leftism), or adopt an antiparty stance (i.e., movementism). While some have noted how social movement activity can transform into party activity (McAdam and Tarrow 2010), I question the interchangeability of protest and electoral mobilization, highlighting instead distinctive organizational logics.

I argue that for teachers, scholars should focus on key features of organizations. Indeed, labor union and social movements can be defined by the organizational traits that reveal where power is located among leaders. These traits generate expectations about the capabilities of labor and movement leaders to orchestrate different types of collective action. They shed light on union democracy (i.e., the procedures for selecting leaders) and union bureaucracy (i.e., the staff on the union payroll that extend the reach of the union leadership). Ultimately, both union democracy and bureaucracy shape the political actions that are available and unavailable to union leaders, depending on the backlash they can expect from the base or rival factions. An organizational approach explains a range of strategies and the logics that account for each one. Hierarchical relations shape the balance of electoral mobilization and protest, and dynamics of factionalism shape the character of partisan alliances.

A comparative-historical analysis of teachers' unions reveals that certain organizational features became deeply rooted, and these shaped political strategies. I have analyzed the political development of three teachers' unions in Mexico, Argentina, and Colombia. Early in the twentieth century, when Latin American countries were industrializing, public school systems were embryonic, especially in rural communities (Cabal 2021). In this context, teacher organizations were fragmented and weak. Early teacher movements struggled to form encompassing national teacher organizations. Across countries, there was a crowded field of rival organizations, but in no country was there a dominant, permanent organization.

In the mid-twentieth century, national teacher organizations were founded, and there was divergence in what these unions looked like. By the 1970s, teachers' unions were on different paths, having established different relations to the state. Teachers consolidated strong and hierarchical organizations when labor laws strengthened national union leaders and the national government engaged in ongoing political exchanges with unions. Teachers were more like social movements organized around diffuse networks and they became associated with parties in the opposition when they endured harsh crackdowns by military regimes, ongoing labor grievances, and initiatives to decentralize education. Such conditions prevented robust organizations from being established – they gave unions more movement-like qualities.

Mexico is a case of instrumentalism because of the union's hierarchical organization and the presence of a dominant faction in the national executive committee. In 1944, SNTE became one of the most centralized and bureaucratic labor organizations in Latin America. However, in the 1980s, the debt crisis, democratization, and the dissident teacher movement challenged SNTE's authoritarian character. But as Mexico's ruling party struggled to remain in power, President Carlos Salinas shored up SNTE, making the fateful decision to bolster national union leaders by distributing subsidies and policy concessions to them as part of a broader education reform package. As a result, Elba Esther Gordillo, the secretary general of SNTE, had the resources to rebuild the union's hierarchical organization and establish a new dominant faction. Union leaders had the capacity to orchestrate a national electoral operation. Ironically, while the original aim was to strengthen a labor union that would remain loyal to the party, the outcome was disloyalty, or instrumentalism. A dominant faction split from its long-standing partisan ally, the PRI, launched its own teacher-based party, and negotiated new alliances.

Argentina is a case of movementism brought about by the weakness of hierarchical relations in CTERA. This union was founded in 1973, later than many other labor organizations in that country. But after its founding, it was beset by military rule and a decentralization reform that undermined national union leaders and exacerbated labor grievances. The 1982 transition from military rule to free elections did not produce a government that increased spending on education to address teacher grievances, nor did the government assist the union in consolidating a hierarchical organization. Elected leaders ignored teacher demands and the union received little support from the national government. For CTERA, power resided in the provincial organizations and in the base. The national union leadership was comparatively weak. Thus, CTERA's political strategy centered on recurrent protests.

In 2003, the election of a prolabor government that improved teacher compensation by establishing an institution of national collective bargaining empowered a leadership cadre that was aligned with the Kirchner faction of the Peronist party. Still, my argument highlights ongoing teacher militancy, even with presidents who were friendly to labor, because hierarchical relations remained weak. CTERA had a limited capacity for electoral mobilization, and local protests and demand-making continued apace. While CTERA was a big and strong union, it had few mechanisms of internal control. National union leaders were not really in charge. Rather, this confederation provided a structure to build networks of teacher activists that operated informally and alongside the union, but did not abide by the national union leadership.

Colombia is a case of leftism due to a hierarchical organization combined with factional divisions. In the 1960s and 1970s, Colombian union leaders built a centralized organization through their own organizing initiatives. The 1991 Constitution included FECODE in a more open political regime. In the wake of this constitution, an education decentralization reform did not touch the national teacher labor code and continued to afford FECODE a hierarchical structure, where the national executive committee was supreme. At the same time, longstanding factional dynamics were reinforced. New union leaders emerged with ties to the center-left, which divided the union leadership into rival factions. The competitive relationship between factions anchored the union on the left end of the ideological spectrum, since any faction that pursued instrumental negotiations was undercut by rivals.

SHADOW CASES

Can this organizational argument travel to other contexts? The scope of this argument is broad; an organizational approach is relevant for any labor union or social movement that has a large membership and must decide between protest and electoral participation. To illustrate how this argument could be extended, I present shadow cases relating to teachers' unions in Chile, Peru, and Indonesia. It makes sense to maintain the focus on teachers because they operate in the same policy arena and share similarities with the primary cases. These shadow cases can be paired with the primary cases, and in so doing they demonstrate the centrality of organizational mechanisms against the backdrop of different political environments for the paired cases (Chile–Colombia, Peru–Argentina, Indonesia–Mexico). Without field research, it is hard to get a full picture of the inner life of these unions. Still, a review of secondary literature, online newspapers, and union documents indicates that these three cases seem to corroborate the argument.

Leftism in Chile

The Colegio de Profesores's strategy closely resembles leftism. Union leaders either ran as political candidates or mobilized electoral support for institutionalized left parties. Like FECODE in Colombia, left parties used their influence in the teachers' union to gain power in the national labor central (the CUT) and elevate their political profile. High-ranking leaders, such as Bárbara Figueroa, ran as a candidate for the national legislature with the Communist Party in 2009 and became the president of the CUT. Strong ties to the center-left coalition, Concertación, hindered the ability of union leaders to mobilize independently (Burton 2012, 38). The union supported left parties. Indeed, when President Gabriel Boric, a former leader of the Chilean student movement, ran for president in 2021, the Colegio endorsed his candidacy.[1]

Chilean teachers were more restrained than their Argentine counterparts. While, the Colegio did call strikes, these only occurred episodically. Rather, militant Chilean students mobilizing around issues of unequal access to good schools became the driving force behind contentious mobilization. In 2006, the "*pingüino* revolution" of high school students

---

[1] "Las profesoras y profesores no seremos neutrales: Apoyamos a Gabriel Boric," Colegio de Profesores November 29, 2021.

launched large protests. In 2011, university students (who had been in high school in 2006) organized a large movement, without a formal organization, that demanded access to public universities and an end to for-profit education (Somma 2012; Donoso 2016). The Chilean student movement has few parallels because it mobilized against the country's unique experiment in education privatization. While the Colegio expressed solidarity with these protests, the union did not lead them – nor did Chilean teachers routinely protest. According to Pérez and Sandoval (2008, 28), only twenty-six days of teacher work stoppages were recorded between 1990 and 2001, a far cry from Argentina. If Chilean students were political outsiders demanding systemic changes, teachers had stronger ties to the establishment (Villalobos Dintrans 2019).

My argument helps to explain this outcome of partisan ties and relative restraint. The Colegio became more hierarchical because policies enacted in the aftermath of democratization recognized the union, included union leaders in policy decisions, and subsidized the national executive committee. Competition among rival factions reinforced the union's ties to left parties.

Before the democratic transition, the union suffered organizational setbacks from military rule. In 1972, disparate teacher organizations aligned with the Popular Unity government of Salvador Allende. This government unified the teaching profession, by supporting the Unitary Union of Education Workers (SUTE). In 1973, a military coup orchestrated by General Augusto Pinochet toppled the Allende government; and the military junta immediately dissolved SUTE and cracked down on teachers as part of its efforts to repress labor and leftist activists. The legal registry of SUTE was canceled, its buildings and properties confiscated, and its leaders were persecuted (Reyes Aliaga n.d., 6): At least 103 teachers were disappeared during the dictatorship.[2]

Military rule weakened the teachers' union. On October 16, 1974, the junta founded a new, depoliticized teachers' organization, the Colegio de Profesores, which henceforth has been the primary organization for teachers (Pérez and Sandoval 2008, 15). As in Argentina, the Chilean dictatorship's persecution of the left created a climate of fear and forced many into exile. Moreover, in 1979, the junta decentralized education to municipal level and established a voucher program for students to attend private schools. These reforms meant that public school enrollment was

---

[2] Gabriel Muñoz, "A 45 años del golpe militar. El golpe contra los profesores: Cifras de la represión en dictadura," *La Izquierda Diario* September 9, 2017.

lower in Chile than in other Latin American countries, with fewer teachers in public schools to unionize. Therefore, the Colegio had a comparatively smaller member base. Only about 50 percent of teachers were union members, for a total membership of 100,000, and the smaller membership reduced the union's political clout.

To survive the dictatorship, the Colegio was officially supportive of military rule throughout the 1970s. It began to drift toward the left as activists repopulated it in the 1980s. Facing unfavorable policies and repression, leftist teachers formed the Chilean Educators' Association (AGECH), a dissident union that organized against the Colegio. Teachers aligned with AGECH protested limited access to education and a lack of professional recognition (Pérez and Sandoval 2008). The dissidents also protested arbitrary layoffs that took place with the imposed decentralization of education to municipal governments. In 1986, AGECH supported a general strike, the Assembly of Civility, which protested austerity policies implemented by the authoritarian regime.

The Colegio demonstrated its support for Chilean democracy by instituting union democracy, which produced a factionalized leadership. In 1985, the union called direct elections for leadership positions. Various centrist (i.e., Christian Democrats and Radicals) and left parties (i.e., Socialists) competed for power. Osvaldo Verdugo, a twenty-nine-year-old militant of the Christian Democratic party was elected president of Colegio (Reyes Aliaga n.d., 7). The leftward tilt accelerated in 1987, when leaders of AGECH were integrated into the Colegio, and the Colegio gained 4,000 new members (Pérez and Sandoval 2008, 17). The national executive committee was expanded from five positions to fifteen. Osvaldo Verdugo and five of his comrades from the Christian Democratic party remained in power, but leaders from left parties entered the leadership (Reyes Aliaga n.d., 9).

As Chile moved toward democracy, the union began to experiment with electoral participation. In 1988, the military regime, confident in its support, held a national plebiscite to determine whether to extend military rule for eight more years or not. The "no" vote prevailed, paving the way for free elections in 1989. Osvaldo Verdugo and leftist leaders of the Colegio came together and vigorously campaigned against the junta (Reyes Aliaga n.d., 11). After this election, the union remained a staunch supporter of democracy and participated in elections. In 1989, Verdugo was again reelected as the president of the Colegio, and the union supported the center-left Concertación. "The electoral triumph of the Christian Democratic leaders reinforced their position and its tactics, such that they repeated their call to vote in presidential and parliamentary elections, and they used the national infrastructure of the Colegio to get out the votes for the candidate of the Concertación, Patricio Aylwin" (Reyes Aliaga n.d., 12). During the campaign, Patricio Alywin and Concertación legislative candidates met with leaders of the Colegio. Democracy launched the teachers' union into the electoral arena, and the union established strong ties to centrist and leftist parties.

The return to democracy coincided with policy and organizational gains, which strengthened hierarchical relations. To be sure, democracy did not radically change the core features of the privatized model of education (Bellei and Vanni 2015). In the final days of the dictatorship, the Organic Constitutional Law of Teaching was decreed, which institutionalized the municipal government management of public schools, subsidies for private schools, and the subsidiary role of the state in education (Reyes Aliaga n.d., 13).

Still, the union was included in policy negotiations because it gained popular support for opposing the dictatorship and because elected governments sought to avoid strikes. Teacher salaries had eroded during military rule, which created an opportunity to improve them (Mizala and Schneider 2014, 90). Teachers also demanded redress for pension payments that the military junta refused to make, the so-called "historic debt." Union leaders such as Gastón Gilbert were appointed to high-ranking positions in the Ministry of Education, which helped to coopt militant groups of teachers (Reyes Aliaga n.d., 14).

Important steps were taken toward building a strong, hierarchical teachers' union. On October 15, 1990, a day before Teachers Day in Chile, President Aylwin proposed a teacher labor code (Reyes Aliaga n.d., 15–17). This bill was signed into law in 1991 (Law 19,070), and it established working conditions, teaching schedules, vacations, tenure, teacher transfers, salaries, and benefits. During the early 1990s, the teaching profession grew by 10 percent, along with increases in student enrollment (Pérez and Sandoval 2008, 28). In 1995, there were reforms to the teacher statute that modified bonuses and deemphasized seniority. Although these reforms did not undo the policies adopted by Pinochet, they strengthened union hierarchies, since national union leaders negotiated better working conditions for teachers.

In both Chile and Colombia, the national executive committee negotiated new policies that favored teachers in the 1990s. In Chile, between 1990 and 2009, teacher salaries increased 300 percent, dramatically outperforming average real wages, which increased only 170 percent (Mizala and Schneider 2014, 94–5). Democratization brought about greater state involvement and investment in education. These policies strengthened hierarchical relations, since the national executive committee benefited from the influx of union dues and was the primary entity that negotiated salary increases. This marks a contrast to the Argentine case, where policymakers delayed a response to teacher demands. In Chile, newly elected leaders benefited from strong economic growth and were in a better position to make concessions to teachers.

Like FECODE, the Colegio held internal union elections starting in 1985; these cemented well-defined factions. The union had included rival factions since its founding, with Christian Democrats, socialists, communists, as well as a tiny faction linked to the conservative party. There was ongoing friction between the more centrist or center-left Christian Democrats, socialists, and communists on the one hand, and the more radical leaders on the other. The union selected its leaders through internal elections that were open and contested, with multiple factions given representation based on the proportion of the vote they secured, in parallel with FECODE.

The national executive committee has been characterized by intense competition among factions. Beginning in 1992, there was a backlash by left leaders against the Christian Democratic leadership for allegedly making deals with the government that did not benefit teachers and using the union to mobilize votes (Reyes Aliaga n.d., 20). While Osvaldo Verdugo prevailed and remained president of the Colegio until 1995, Communist Party leader Jorge Pavez was elected president from 1995 to 2007. Pavez was from a faction of the Communist Party, Social and Democratic Force, and he took a more radical approach to negotiating with the government. There were ongoing tensions between center-left union leaders and those who were more radical. In 2007, Pavez was succeeded by Jaime Gajardo (2007–16), who was from the Communist Party but supported the New Majority coalitions.[3] The dynamic of competition between a center and radical-left constrained the union's capacity to reach out to conservative political parties.

---

[3] In this internal union election, New Majority received 9,302 votes (five seats), Concertación received 9,141 (four seats), Social Force (which is also aligned with the Concertación) received 7,370 votes (three seats), a conservative faction, National Renovation, received only 4,941 (two seats), and an anarchist faction received 1,949 (one seat) (Pérez and Sandoval 2008, 20).

In 2017, Mario Aguilar (2017–21) became president of the Colegio; he was from an even more radical left group, the Humanistic Party, which had been consigned to the opposition. Jaime Gajardo was accused of deferring to the party and seeking to accommodate Michele Bachelet's New Majority Coalition, while the dissident group sought more militancy.[4] In a scandal, Gajardo was recorded on a telephone call with officials in the Ministry of Education in an attempt to restrain teachers who wanted to protest.[5] This leadership turnover resembles the pattern described in FECODE in which factions competed for power, mobilized votes for their respective parties, and were less willing to use protests.

While Chile resembles leftism in Colombia in several ways, it is important to note differences in the political context. In contrast with Colombia, the electoral rules in Chile, known as the binomial system (in place from 1990 to 2015), were less supportive of teacher representation. In Chile, key institutions were holdovers from military rule; specifically, the binomial electoral formula meant that each district had two seats. This formula created incentives for parties to group themselves into two large coalitions and they gave power to party leaders. The binomial system skewed representation toward right-wing parties, which were the second-largest bloc after the Concertación, while underrepresenting centrist and left-wing parties (Scully 2017). The electoral rules limited the opportunities for small left parties to enter politics relying on teachers as a voting bloc. If Colombia's electoral rules amplified electoral mobilization by FECODE, the binomial system in Chile muted teacher mobilization. Few Chilean union leaders ran for public office, and fewer still won. And yet Chilean union leaders maintained strong ties to left parties and mobilized steadfast support for them in elections.

In Colombia, left parties were small and relegated to the opposition; by contrast, in Chile, the center-left Concertación was strong, and Socialist leaders Ricardo Lagos (2000–6) and Michele Bachelet (2006–10; 2014–18) both served as president. With leftist governments in power, Chilean union leaders had more opportunities to negotiate policy concessions (Weinstein 2006; Mizala and Schneider 2014). The Colegio negotiated with the Concertación to improve teacher compensation, while accepting a merit-pay scheme and teacher evaluations. Such negotiations only took

---

[4] Natacha Ramírez, "Cuáles son las fuerzas políticas que predominan al interior del Colegio de Profesores," July 3, 2019.
[5] See "La caida de Jaime Gajardo, el profesore de Historia que lidero su gremio por casi 10 anos," Emol November 24, 2016.

place between parties of the left and union leaders. Negotiations with conservative presidents did not take place, and the union did not exhibit tendencies for instrumentalism.

In sum, the Chilean case supports the organizational argument. Policy changes after the democratic transition strengthened hierarchical relations, which enabled the union to become an institutionalized base of support for left parties. At the same time, factionalism, inherited from divisions among union leaders at the union's founding and during internal union elections, has been an ongoing feature. As a result, the union has resided on the left side of the ideological spectrum, and it has mobilized teachers to support partisan allies. It has been restrained in its propensity to mobilize strikes.

Movementism in Peru

The Peruvian teachers' union, the Unitary Union of Education Workers of Peru (SUTEP), resembles movementism because disruptive, long-lasting protests were a routine occurrence. There were major protests in 2003–4, 2006–7, 2012, and 2017–18. Teachers are a leading sector of labor that has mobilized against neoliberal policies (Arce 2008). Some protests were disruptive but peaceful, but others devolved into violence, with teachers occupying public buildings, blocking highways, and clashing with police. In departments such as Junín, strikers broke into schools and assaulted teachers who refused to participate in protests (Quinto de la Cruz 2007, 38). Such protests were often declared illegal and prompted the national government to declare a state of emergency. These harsh responses, however, did little to deter subsequent demonstrations. Teachers routinely negotiated by confronting the national government and making radical demands, although this strategy generated mixed results in terms of improving teacher pay.

Since its founding in 1972, SUTEP's national executive committee was headed by the Peruvian Communist Party. Unlike the Chilean Communist Party, which routinely participated in elections and formed alliances with center-left parties, the Peruvian Communist Party was ultraradical and did not have serious electoral ambitions. SUTEP's role in electoral politics was limited.[6] Moreover, this party had weak ties to

---

[6] While a handful of union leaders campaigned for the presidency of Ollanta Humala in 2011 and a few won seats on his coattails in the national legislature, as in Argentina these union leaders did not have the strong backing of teachers. Humala's 2012 education reform generated teacher opposition.

the rank and file and lacked control over local union leaders. The teachers' union has been fragmented, undisciplined, and it has not sustained a voting bloc. In Peru, the union has a bottom-up structure, and the energy comes more from local union leaders than the national executive committee. Therefore, teacher mobilization in Peru fits better with movementism rather than leftism.

Analyzing policy decisions and organizational development is crucial for understanding persistent protests and limited electoral mobilization. While from 1930–56 most Peruvian teachers aligned with the populist Popular Revolutionary Alliance, over time they drifted toward the revolutionary left. The teacher labor struggle ramped up in 1968, under the modernizing reforms of the military regime (vom Hau 2009). In 1970, the Teacher Committee for Unification and Struggle (COMUL) unified disparate teacher movements that organized primary and secondary school teachers. Like CTERA in Argentina, SUTEP developed late. It was founded in 1972, during the height of military rule, and legally recognized in 1984 after democracy was restored (Vargas Castro 2005, 3; Quinto de la Cruz 2007, 13). Throughout the 1970s, the Communist Party leader Horacio Zevallos headed SUTEP and challenged the military dictatorship. Although teachers during this period were referred to as "classroom Maoists" for their radical politics (Angell 1982), they also gained some legitimacy among ordinary Peruvians because of their opposition to military rule. A teacher strike in 1978 that lasted 81 days and another in 1979 that lasted 118 days crippled the military regime.[7]

The democratic transition benefited the teachers' union in terms of institutional recognition, but it did not improve teacher salaries. Under democracy, the union received a legal registry from President Fernando Belaunde Terry in 1984. That same year, teachers won the teacher law (Law 24,029), which established national labor standards, and SUTEP began to manage the teacher pension fund (Quinto de la Cruz 2007, 16). And yet there were volatile swings in policy, with shocks to teacher pay (Bruns and Luque 2014, 83). There were limited organizational gains for SUTEP. With the democratic transition in 1980, teachers were aligned with a coalition of movements and left parties, and excluded from the policymaking process. The alignment of teachers with left parties was not institutionalized, and teachers became politically independent (Quinto de la Cruz 2007, 16).

---

[7] SUTEP, "Huelgas Historicas," accessed January 13, 2022 via https://sutep.org/organizacion/huelgas-historicas/.

As part of the opposition, SUTEP was not in a strong position to demand favorable policies for teachers. Moreover, Peru experienced hyperinflation in the late 1980s and early 1990s, and President Alan García (1985–90), unable to achieve macroeconomic stability, could not address teacher grievances. In 1990, teachers mounted a strike to pressure the government to amend the teacher statute (Law 25,212), but there was a simultaneous sharp decline in education spending and teacher pay (Vargas Castro 2005, 11). During the economic crisis, there was little investment in education; public schools were largely abandoned by the state.

In 1992, the self-coup by President Alberto Fujimori (1990–2000) marked another interlude of authoritarian rule. Neoliberal and hard-line security policies put teachers on the defensive. Teachers were stigmatized for their association with the Shining Path, which engaged in terrorism and guerrilla warfare. Fujimori played up this association to justify his crackdown on protests and ignoring of teacher grievances. The government only invested about 2 percent of GDP in education throughout the 1990s, a pittance compared with other countries in the region. Real teacher salaries in Peru declined from 1960 to 2010 (Bruns and Luque 2014, 83; Cuenca and Castro 2018). Teacher pay has been very poor in Peru; in 2014–15, Peruvian teachers earned just 55 percent of the wages earned by other professionals, compared with 83 percent in Mexico (Elacqua et al. 2018, 20). When Fujimori was in power, SUTEP leaders were excluded from policy decisions and the union made no organizational gains.

When Fujimori fled to Japan in 2000 to avoid prosecution related to a bribery scandal, Peru redemocratized. But policies to address teacher grievances were limited. President Alejandro Toledo's (2001–6) signature education policy was the General Law of Education in 2003, which created a more decentralized and participatory public school system (Balarin 2021, 39). The president advanced a decentralization reform, in which regional presidents were directly elected and the payroll of teachers was handed over to departmental governments. To address salary erosion, the president promised to double teacher pay, but only raised compensation by 45 percent (Chiroque Chunga 2005). In response to these policies, teachers mobilized a strike in 2003.

In his second term, President Alan García (2006–11), sought to introduce reforms to teacher career structures, with mandatory competency exams for new teachers, opening the teaching profession to professionals trained in other fields, and promotions based on measures of performance (Balarin 2021, 46). The union staunchly opposed these policies and organized massive strikes. There were also changes to the governance structure of the teacher pension fund that weakened SUTEP's power over it. Education policies angered teachers, and an aggrieved base lost confidence in the national union leadership. In 2012, President Ollanta Humala (2011–16) adopted a new teachers' career reform law (Law 29,944), which placed all teachers under the same rules: They had mandatory evaluations, and teachers who failed were required to undergo retraining (Balarin 2021, 50–1). SUTEP fell back on its repertoire of organizing a strike against this law.

The internal structure of SUTEP is organized around weak hierarchical relations. At the national level, cadres were aligned with the Communist Party. This faction controlled the national executive committee and the pension fund. However, it did not have control over the base. Quinto de la Cruz (2007, 20–1) describes SUTEP as being composed of various factions with regional identities and ties to charismatic regional leaders. The dominant faction had a strong presence in Lima, the capital, and had support among an older generation of teachers. But outside the capital, there were other factions, some of which were aligned with the political arm of the Shining Path, others with small leftist currents.

The procedures for selecting union leaders created a dynamic in which the national executive committee held little sway over union locals or rank-and-file teachers. Unlike in Chile and Colombia, in Peru the union convened a national labor congress to select the national executive committee. Five hundred delegates from across the country met to decide what leaders would head the union. These congresses never produced turnover in the faction that controlled the national leadership, and they were widely perceived as undemocratic. According to Quinto de la Cruz (2007), union locals held direct elections erratically, and when they did opposition factions tended to win. The procedures used to select union leaders reinforced the disarticulation between national and local leaders.

The weakness of the national union leadership, along with its inability to control union locals, can also be interpreted as reflecting the weakness of the Peruvian state itself, which suffered from pronounced capacity deficits (Eaton 2010). The national executive committee of SUTEP was not able to deliver benefits to the base; it had weak ties to union locals. Power was instead rooted in the departmental base organizations. When deciding whether to call a national strike, the national executive committee of SUTEP conducted a "consultation with the bases" to see if there was sufficient enthusiasm, because regional organizations were the driving force behind mobilization (Vargas Castro 2005, 24).

National union leaders were undercut by local union leaders, a dynamic with strong echoes of Argentina. The unit of mobilization is the departmental unions. There is a strong dissident group that resents the national union leaders because of their control over the teacher pension fund (Vargas Castro 2005, 11). In 2007, protests were driven by regional union leaders such as Robert Huaynalaya from the city of Huancayo in the department of Junín, who organized protests across departments. Ten years later, in 2017, another regional leader, Pedro Castillo of the department of Cajamarca, led a wave of protests. In 2021, Castillo was elected president of Peru, after gaining political visibility by leading teacher strikes. When Castillo was removed from the presidency for trying to dissolve Congress, teachers displayed their movementist tendencies by mobilizing massive and disruptive protests.[8]

Organizational hierarchies were weak in Peru. Local leaders and activists were the driving force behind teacher protests, in line with my argument. This is a case where teachers articulate interests through bottom-up protests. There are strong parallels between Argentina and Peru, in terms of the frequency of teacher protests and the limited electoral footprint. To be sure, the political context of Peru might also be helpful for understanding the phenomenon of regional teacher protests. The country's inchoate party system, a system in which parties are unstable, personalistic vehicles with weak roots in society, has prompted many groups to turn to protest. Indeed, various local actors in Peru, with mayors taking a lead role, have challenged mining projects by transnational corporations (Eaton 2010, 2015). Still, the weakness of hierarchical relations in SUTEP is central to understanding the pattern of recurrent protests.

Instrumentalism in Indonesia

For the dominant teachers' union in Indonesia, Persatuan Guru Republik Indonesia (Teachers Association of the Republic of Indonesia, PGRI), instrumentalism most closely approximates the political repertoire. This case demonstrates how the framework can travel to developing democracies outside Latin America, which differ in terms of culture, economic development, and institutional design. In Indonesia, the teachers' union is large, with about 1.9 million members, or two in three teachers (Rosser

---

[8] Castillo was removed from office in 2022 and discredited owing to corruption allegations and an attempted self-coup. Following his ouster, teacher protests – and police crackdowns – resulted in at least fifty deaths.

and Fahmi 2016, 20). PGRI engages in negotiations with presidents from different political parties. In a political system characterized by "promiscuous powersharing," with political elites routinely bringing every major party into the government (Slater and Simmons 2013), PGRI has developed a strategy of cultivating friendly relations with presidents from different parties, from B. J. Habibie (1998–9), the first democratically elected president, to Joko Widodo, popularly known as Jokowi (2014–24). PGRI was affiliated to the Confederation of Indonesian Trade Unions (KSPI) until 2019, but when KSPI backed Prabowo Subianto for president in 2019, PGRI separated from KSPI to maintain ties to Jokowi, the incumbent president. Thus, teachers developed relationships to political parties based on strategic maneuvering.

Like the union in Mexico, the Indonesian union seeks to accommodate various political leaders to maintain avenues for negotiation. Indonesian teachers regularly meet with presidents on national teacher day (November 25 in Indonesia) and present joint proposals for education reform. Unlike leftist and movementist unions that have an adversarial relationship with political elites, teacher labor relations in Indonesia are amicable – at least in public. One union leader described PGRI as the government's "strategic partner," meaning the union seeks to support whoever is in power (Interview, January 15, 2021).

Moreover, PGRI avoids protests; strikes are mostly carried out by contract teachers and newly formed unions that are smaller and weaker than PGRI. As in Mexico, democratization meant that new dissident teachers' unions emerged to challenge the dominance of PGRI, the primary teachers' union that was founded by an authoritarian regime. These dissident unions never became large, and PGRI has remained the primary representative of teachers. Teacher protests are a relatively infrequent occurrence in Indonesia, and protests are not the main strategy used to represent interests.

The organizational argument helps to explain key features of PGRI's political strategy. The internal structure of the Indonesia teachers' union is like that of its Mexican counterpart in several ways. Both unions were founded by authoritarian regimes, SNTE in 1944 and PGRI a year later in 1945. Both were corporatist entities that were the only unions legally authorized to represent teachers. In both countries, union leaders claimed a monopoly on the representation of teachers and had discretionary control over the funds in union coffers (Rosser and Fahmi 2016, 23). As a result, both unions developed hierarchical organizations that were headed by dominant factions. Moreover, both supported ruling parties;

in Indonesia, during "the New Order" when Indonesia was ruled by the Suharto dictatorship, PGRI followed the directives of and mobilized electoral support for Golkar, the ruling party. Rosser and Fahmi (2016, 14) note: "[T]eachers and lecturers who had civil servant status were required to support the ruling Golkar Party, and both take and teach compulsory courses in the state ideology." With democracy, PGRI and SNTE had the resources to gain autonomy from the party that they had supported in the past (Rosser and Fahmi 2016, 27).

The collapse of the authoritarian regime in 1998 endowed PGRI with more resources and made the organization more hierarchical. Democratization coincided with decentralization and an uptick in education spending. Indonesia is a vast archipelago of 6,000 inhabited islands. The regime transition set in motion a decentralized system of governance, a departure from the centralized system that the dictatorship had established. Nevertheless, PGRI remained hierarchical with top-down influence over union locals because the national executive committee continued to play a major role in policy negotiations and improved teacher pay.

During the late 1990s, the economic contraction from the Asian financial crisis resulted in a decline in social spending and lower teacher salaries. In 2005, as the economic recovery was underway, the national government responded to the demands of teachers to improve salaries. In 2005, six years after the country held its first free and fair elections, PGRI negotiated and drafted a bill that became the Teacher Law. This required that teachers become certified and set standards for certification that made it relatively easy for most civil servant teachers to get certified; it also established that certified teachers received a professional allowance that effectively doubled their salaries (Chang et al. 2014; de Ree et al. 2018). In contrast to Mexico, in Indonesia there was no institution for collective bargaining of teacher salaries: PGRI leaders pressured policymakers to enact legislation that benefited teachers by improving take-home pay. The inclusion of national union leaders in policy decisions cemented the power of PGRI's national leadership.

During the period of brutal authoritarian rule, PGRI was headed by a group of union leaders who were aligned with the regime. Since democratization, the union has remained largely unchanged. As in Mexico, the procedure for selecting union leaders is a national labor congress, and this has prevented rival factions from taking power. PGRI is not characterized by factionalism. Rather, with democratization, teachers who were unhappy left PGRI and formed rival teachers' unions. However, these new unions are comparatively small and weak. The chair of PGRI has been selected from the same cadre of leaders: Mohamad Surya (1998–2008); Sulistiyo (2008–16); and Unifah Rosyidi (2016–20) were all from the same group. The fact that union leaders garner nearly unanimous support in labor congresses suggests the presence of a dominant faction that is internally cohesive.[9] Such a faction facilitates negotiations with presidents, since union leaders purport to speak for the whole union.

Multiparty competition in Indonesia afforded PGRI opportunities to conduct outreach to new political leaders. Rosser and Fahmi (2016, 46), comparing two municipalities and two districts. argue that "political and bureaucratic elites have for decades used the school system to accumulate resources, distribute patronage, mobilize political support, and exercise political control." Within this context of political competition and patronage politics, there is evidence that the leaders of PGRI have been appointed to high-ranking positions in government as a political concession to the union. For example, a leader of PGRI, Unifah Rosyidi, served as a subdirector at the Ministry of Education from 2011 to 2015; in 2017, she assumed the top leadership position at PGRI, becoming the first chairwoman. This suggests another interesting parallel with Mexico, where in both cases negotiations behind closed doors resulted in union leaders gaining high-ranking positions in the Ministry of Education.

The Indonesian teachers' union deserves more attention from scholars. Still, available evidence suggests that the consolidation of power in a single faction has enabled union leaders to conduct outreach to different political parties, even parties that are not particularly friendly to workers. As with SNTE, PGRI is not ideological. It seems to have been successful in forming alliances with politicians in various parts of the government. While some of these alliances do not seem to result in many benefits to teachers, the union has used its political clout to get policy concessions, as is evidenced by the 2005 Teacher Law. Competitive elections in Indonesia created an opportunity for the teachers' union to reach out to various parties.

It is important to highlight key differences between PGRI and SNTE. The Mexican teachers' union had a vast union bureaucracy and a very high capacity to mobilize its base because the PRI created strong and encompassing mass organizations for the popular sectors (Collier and Collier 1991). By contrast, exclusionary corporatism in Indonesia afforded PGRI fewer resources, and after democratization, PGRI had a comparatively weaker organization (Caraway 2012). Moreover, whereas

---

[9] See PGRI "PGRI New Direction with the Power of Woman 'Srikandi,'" PGRI January 2, 2017.

in Mexico the electoral rules created an opportunity for SNTE to form a new teacher-based party, by contrast electoral rules hindered unions from participating in politics in Indonesia (Caraway and Ford 2020, 13). Indeed, the electoral system makes it difficult to assess the scale of PGRI's electoral footprint, given that union leaders were less likely to become political candidates.

Although they are by no means identical, PGRI has several important similarities with SNTE, stemming from common organizational characteristics. The Indonesian case reaffirms the analytic utility of the organizational argument and does so in a political context that is quite different from the Latin American cases. Authoritarian regimes endowed both these unions with dominant factions and top-down mobilizing structures. As in Mexico, the transition to democracy in Indonesia consolidated PGRI's organizational structure. It was in this period that the union became an important ally for presidents of various political parties.

AVENUES FOR FUTURE RESEARCH

The fields of education and labor politics are rapidly evolving and there are many avenues for future research. This section identifies some ways in which the organizational framework could be used to advance scholarly debates about the politics of education, interest representation through protests, and contemporary labor politics.

Teacher Strategies and Education Politics

An influential literature in political science has focused on teachers' unions as vested interests. The idea is that they have the capacity to derail policies that might improve the quality of education. While it is relatively popular, in political terms, to spend more money on education and increase school enrollment, policies that aim to enhance the quality of education, such as reforms to teacher career structures, evaluations, and efforts to make public school systems more accountable, generate strong opposition from teachers' unions (Corrales 1999). These quality-enhancing reforms are thought to impose concentrated costs on organized groups (i.e., teachers' unions) while delivering diffuse benefits to larger, less organized ones (i.e., parents, students, and businesses seeking skilled workers).

Terry Moe (2015), Ben Ross Schneider (2022), and Sarah Anzia (2014) have emerged as intellectual leaders when considering how teachers' unions exert strong influence on the policy process. Moe (2015) has proposed a compelling framework for analyzing teachers' unions as "vested interests," or groups with incentives to defend the institutional status quo even when there is systemic failure.[10] Schneider (2022) argues that teacher opposition to reforms to career structures depends in part on whether reform will undermine the power of the union to mobilize in politics. Anzia (2014) makes an inference from the influence that teachers exert as a voting bloc by looking at off-cycle school board elections, when teachers are more likely to vote but other voters stay home. Where school board elections take place off-cycle, teacher pay tends to be higher, because unions have secured greater representation on school boards.

My research agrees with this literature on several points. In Argentina, Colombia, and Mexico, teachers' unions prioritize material interests related to salaries and job security; they oppose school choice and accountability policies. It is less clear that teachers' unions place much emphasis on upgrading pedagogy and improving student welfare; these initiatives are at best inconsistent. Teachers' unions in Latin America tend to operate more like labor organizations and less like professional associations, and so issues of pedagogy, professional development, and high standards for entering the profession are usually a secondary priority.[11] In interviews, some activists (who sympathized with teachers and labor organizations) confided that they were frustrated with unions for ignoring pedagogy and classroom learning and setting low professional standards for teachers. Teachers' unions mainly focus on their economic interests, a point that fits well with the concept of vested interests.

However, I point to a different way to analyze the roles that teachers play in the policy process. Rather than looking at teachers' unions as blocking reforms, my research points to the ways in which the strategies of teachers can put different issues on the education agenda and trigger different reactions.

Union strategies can shape policy by putting certain issues on the agenda. In Argentina, movementism seemed to put teacher salaries and

---

[10] Moe (2015, 304) argues that "vested interests ... are well organized and politically powerful ... teachers unions are pivotal to an explanation of why American education reform has proved so difficult."
[11] Teachers in Latin America organized around labor issues because they have contended with patronage politics and precarious salaries. Professional associations, by contrast, prioritize the quality of education, improving teacher training and professionalization, and setting high standards for teaching practice.

education spending front and center, crowding out other issues. Ongoing protests established an institution of national collective bargaining to address teacher grievances. Conservative governments such as that of President Mauricio Macri sought to control the costs of education and weaken collective bargaining. However, education policy debates revolve around questions of teacher salary and education spending; discussions about the quality of education are crowded out by labor issues. Movementism and the national institution of collective bargaining have proven to be sticky. While this institution has been contested, teacher labor issues seem to be a key point of dispute.

For Colombia, the union's strategy of leftism seemed to have a weaker influence on education and labor policy. And yet mobilization for left parties created a partisan cleavage on education issues. Conservative governments held down the costs of education and sometimes supported reforms to improve the quality of education by changing the rules governing teacher hiring and promotion. Left parties in the opposition prioritized increased spending on education to address labor issues and to enact social policies through schools (i.e., school nutrition programs) that benefited low-income students. In other words, left parties sought to use education to cobble together a popular sector coalition. With leftism, the education policy agenda is more contested, with a more conservative, technocratic position on education reform contending with a more progressive, social investment one.

The strategies of teachers' unions can trigger different policy responses. The Mexican teachers' union's strategy of instrumentalism at first seemed to create a tendency for the union and government to negotiate pacts and alliances. Ultimately, however, instrumentalism triggered a reform backlash in 2013. When teachers negotiated instrumental alliances with the ruling parties, they gained ongoing access to policymakers, they delayed the roll out of new education policies, and demanded concessions from policymakers in the form of side payments. However, while SNTE had power to pressure governments through its political machinery, it lost control over the education agenda and became stigmatized and politically isolated owing to its association with corruption. This strategy set off a major policy shift in a direction that the union opposed.

Instrumentalism became a focal point for countermobilization by political elites and the business community, making SNTE a political target. In response to instrumentalism, President Enrique Peña Nieto adopted reforms in 2013 that stripped the union's national executive committee of some of its power to mobilize teachers as a voting bloc. Teacher influence over education policy may be contingent and policy gains by teachers can engender policy responses against them. In line with Collier and Collier (1991), education and labor politics may be characterized by reactions and counterreactions. Rather than studying the politics of policy capture, reform blocking, and vested interests, it may make sense to study education politics in a more dynamic way, focusing on the responses to different political strategies.

If the vested interest framework highlights the similar core interests of teachers' unions and their opposition to certain reforms, my research points to the various ways teachers' unions are involved in the policy process. It can be analytically helpful to split cases apart (Hexter 1979). Specifically, my research has highlighted the value of examining cross-national divergence in education policymaking dynamics based on distinctive strategies. Instrumentalism, movementism, and leftism set the political agenda in different ways, and generated different reactions. If the vested interest framework highlights how union organizations have a sort of structural power, my research highlights teacher influence based on the strategies that are employed, which produce more reactive and contingent dynamics of education politics.

Contentious Politics and Interest Representation

This book also speaks to a literature on large-scale protests and their capacity to shape public policy. Many scholars argue that political elites are largely unmoved by popular sector demands when electoral competition is the primary mechanism of responsiveness. Garay (2017) has argued that social policy expansion was more inclusive when it was triggered by mobilization from below. Anria (2018) has argued that left parties are more responsive to their base when they become movement-based parties, and when movements maintain pressure on elites. Rich (2019) has argued that state-sponsored activism, or bureaucrats who provide resources to activists, can make progress in health policy. Levy (2023) shows that in France, large-scale protests have stalled unpopular liberalizing reforms by technocratic elites. The claim is that popular sector demands are articulated more forcefully through protests in the streets and mobilization from below engenders policy responsiveness.

This book has focused on how teachers' unions articulate interests both inside and outside the electoral arena. The story I have told is partially compatible with the claim that protests are a better vehicle for representation than electoral participation. First, a preliminary survey of landmark education and labor laws for teachers in Latin America suggest that large-scale protests by teacher movements were significant.[12] Across many countries, teacher protests seemed to deliver policy packages that were largely aligned with teacher interests. Building on the social movement literature, a groundswell of grassroots mobilization by militant teacher movements can strongly shape the education agenda. Teacher salaries vary considerably across countries, but when teacher work is precarious due to low salaries and public schools that are chronically underfunded, teachers can articulate demands as reformist labor movements. They can win public sympathy and transform teacher labor policy. Broad-based teacher movements have had success in advancing landmark education laws and major institutional innovations throughout the region, especially during the 1990s.

Second, electoral representation, as analyzed in this book, provides a flawed vehicle for interest representation. The most prominent union leaders who became politicians – from Elba Esther Gordillo in Mexico to Jaime Dussán in Colombia – were criticized for being political bosses, for engaging in corruption and clientelism, and for advancing their own interests. When union leaders pursue an instrumental strategy or align themselves with left parties, they may improve teacher salaries in the short term, but they have been less successful in enacting landmark education laws or setting the policy agenda. If in developing democracies patron–client relations permeate party organizations, neighborhood associations, and labor organizations, then teacher organizations are also susceptible to machine politics, which distort the representation of teacher interests.

Union leaders who have taken public office and have been committed to programmatic principles – such as Marta Maffei in Argentina or Gloria Inés Ramírez in Colombia – were relegated to the margins and unable to claim credit for major legislation that benefited teachers. A small cadre of union leaders in government has had little capacity to influence policy. In other words, electoral representation did not benefit rank-and-file teachers; the story across countries is that union leaders who became politicians and political brokers responded to their own

---

[12] For example, major legislation and policy shifts that took place in Mexico (Acuerdo Nacional para la Modernización de la Educación Básica, 1992), Colombia (Ley General de Educación, 1994), Argentina (Fondo Nacional Incentivo Docente, 1998; Ley de Educación Nacional, 2006), Chile (Estatuto de los Profesionales de la Educación, 1991), and Peru (Ley del Profesorado, 1984) came in the wake of major teacher protest movements, and some of these laws were written by union leaders themselves.

interests or were unable to do much for teachers. Elected leaders provide more symbolic rather than substantive representation. Over time, there are indications that rank-and-file teachers across countries grow frustrated with the union leaders that represent them and there are questions about the sustainability of teacher-based electoral vehicles and parties.

But it is also important to add a note of caution. The relationship between contentious politics and policy responsiveness is complex. Political repertoires centered on recurrent protests, movementism, can be deeply rooted in organizations. For each case, there was a lag, sometimes as long as a decade or more, between the onset of protest movements and the policy response; in other words, it takes a lot of sustained disruption for teachers to get the attention of policymakers. There are also clear limits to the extent to which teacher protests can achieve policy responsiveness. The success of teacher movements depends on their capacity to generate public sympathy, overcome internal divisions, and draw attention to specific issues.

There are conditions when teacher protests are unlikely to generate much of a response. They may have diminishing returns. Since the turn of the century, there have been few cases of robust teacher mobilization achieving landmark labor or education laws. If social mobilization around certain issues can get them on the political agenda, ongoing mobilization around those same issues can result in unresponsiveness. Movementism in Argentina is a story about protests being sometimes effective, at least in improving salaries; but sometimes these protests fell on deaf ears. By contrast, movementism in Peru is a story of ongoing exclusion, with protests achieving little for teachers. In Mexico, the dissident teacher movement pressured SNTE to democratize in the late 1980s, but then was coopted; despite the influence that the dissident teachers had on the 2019 changes to teacher evaluations by President Andrés Manuel López Obrador, the legacy of dissident teacher mobilization remains unclear. Protests are blunt instruments for getting attention, and there are limits (i.e., budget constraints) that prevent policymakers from responding to teacher demands.

This book then is a cautionary tale in the effectiveness of mobilization from below. Teacher movements sometimes succeed, and bottom-up mobilization can draw attention to teacher issues that have been ignored. However, protests can also create a repertoire that is routinized and routinely ignored. Some union leaders in Argentina voiced concern about teacher protests not achieving the desired results and their negative effects on students. Ongoing protests have a downside, in terms of stigmatizing teachers who are blamed for school closures and students falling behind. In studying other forms of popular sector representation, scholars should keep in mind the broader social costs and negative externalities of ongoing protests. Rather than doubling down on protest repertoires, teacher movements may need to innovate and develop new strategies, reframe their demands, and seek new allies to gain the attention of policymakers.

New Patterns of Labor Politics

Research on teachers suggests more attention to new patterns of labor politics is needed. The old pattern was defined by corporatism, a closed economic model, and strong worker cohesion to (or dependence on) certain political parties. The focus was on peak-level associations (i.e., national labor centrals), which brought together workers across diverse economic sectors. Teacher politics point toward a new pattern that is defined differently. Corporatist structures have eroded and unraveled, albeit unevenly. The economic model is open, and there is greater market competition among workers. Worker ties to parties are weaker, both in terms of parties being less responsive to unions and workers being less beholden to parties (Collier and Chambers-Ju 2012). The dominant narrative on contemporary labor politics is one of union decline (Posner et al. 2018) and party system dealignment or collapse (Roberts 2014).

This book suggests that unions can also be studied in a more granular, disaggregated way to reveal new patterns. We know little about the subset of unions, with teachers at the forefront, that have proven resilient in the new economic and political environment. Indeed, by shifting the focus to the level of a specific sector of labor (i.e., teachers), a different kind of labor politics has been identified. More work should be done to uncover the changing structure of the labor movement, and specifically the public sector in which workers are making militant demands. Aside from teachers, there is little scholarly work on other public sector unions in Latin America, such as health workers, childcare workers, and public employees.

The analytical approach that I have developed should be applied to a wider swath of public sector unions. Public sector unions, like those for teachers, are a relatively new phenomenon; they are late bloomers in the labor movement. Like teachers' unions, forming unions of public employees is uneven across countries and these workers have achieved different levels of organization. Future research should analyze the development of other public sector unions, especially the parallels and divergences between teachers versus other public employees. One approach to studying public sector mobilization, advocated by Etchemendy and Lódola (2023), is to analyze the legality of collective bargaining, exchanges between labor and the government, and government spending priorities. Complementing this work, scholars should also consider the organizational characteristics of these unions, namely whether they have more of a top-down or bottom-up structure, the character of factional competition, and how union leaders direct these organizations. To uncover these organizational dynamics, it is important to study the relationships between public sector workers and the state, namely how labor unions evolved vis-à-vis the state provision of their specific service (i.e., public health or public administration), what labor laws were adopted to protect them, and how these sectors were reorganized by certain policy and institutional reforms.

Such an approach would reveal the organizational characteristics of public sector unions and the political repertoires they rely on. It could also yield other features of contemporary labor politics. A focused analysis of public sector unions could help to uncover the relationships between the emerging labor organizations and the more established industrial unions. As the balance of power has shifted among unionized workers from industrial to public sector workers, in many countries public sector workers (often teachers) now lead labor centrals and speak on behalf of all workers. This raises the question of how the demands and strategies of public sector workers spill over and serve to represent or not represent other workers.

Union strategies and demands may be narrow, parochial, and self-serving or they may be broad-based and solidaristic. Public sector unions may respond more to their own members, and thereby make narrow demands for salaries and benefits that exacerbate labor market segmentation. Indeed, the Mexican teachers' union and its use of instrumentalism seems to be narrow in its focus; SNTE operated separately from other workers. There may be a go-it-alone approach, in line with the idea of rent-seeking, in which each union negotiates separately to maximize benefits for their specific group. But the rise of social movement unions in some countries suggests that organized labor can show solidarity with informal sector workers (Garay 2023). Teachers could be a lynchpin of broad-based progressive coalitions and they could advocate on behalf of lower- and middle-class interests; for instance, they could advocate for a broader conception of social citizenship. Based on this analysis, movementism and leftism have some potential, at least in theory, to benefit nonteacher groups.

Research should explore how teacher demands and strategies have affected other sectors of labor, and the extent to which they helped other workers, or not. There are many questions to explore: how teachers are situated in the labor movement, the relations of teachers to other public sector workers, and the ways in which public sector workers shape the accessibility and quality of public services. A focused analysis of teachers therefore raises many important questions for further comparative inquiry.

References

Abal Medina, Juan. 2009. "The Rise and Fall of the Argentine Centre – Left: The Crisis of Frente Grande." *Party Politics* 15(3): 357–75.
Abers, Rebecca N, and Luciana Tatagiba. 2016. "Institutional Activism: Mobilizing for Women's Health from Inside the Brazilian Bureaucracy." In Federico M. Rossi and Marisa von Bülow, eds., *Social Movement Dynamics*. London: Routledge, 72–101.
Aisenstein, Ángela, Jennifer Luciana Guevara, and Macarena Feijoó. 2017. "Estado de la cuestión acerca de las investigaciones históricas sobre la formación inicial docente de maestros y profesores en Argentina en el período 1860–1990." *Anuario de la Sociedad Argentina de Historia de la Educación* 18(1), 133–55.
Andelique, Carlos Marcelo, and María Cecilia Tonon. 2014. "La conflictividad docente en la década del ochenta en Argentina: el caso de los docentes santafesinos y la huelga de 1988." *Naveg@mérica* 12, 1–24.
Angell, Alan. 1982. "Classroom Maoists: The Polities of Peruvian School Teachers under Military Government." *Bulletin of Latin American Research* 1(2), 1–20.
Anria, Santiago. 2018. *When Movements Become Parties: The Bolivian MAS in Comparative Perspective*. New York: Cambridge University Press.
Anzia, Sarah F. 2014. *Timing and Turnout: How Off-Cycle Elections Favor Organized Groups*. Chicago: University of Chicago Press.
Anzia, Sarah F. 2022. "Pensions in the Trenches: How Pension Spending Is Affecting US Local Government." *Urban Affairs Review* 58(1): 3–32.
Arce, Moisés. 2008. "The Repoliticization of Collective Action after Neoliberalism in Peru." *Latin American Politics & Society* 50(3): 37–62.
Arza, Camila, Rossana Castiglioni, Juliana Martínez Franzoni, Sara Niedzwiecki, Jennifer Pribble, and Diego Sánchez-Ancochea. 2022. *The Political Economy of Segmented Expansion: Latin American Social Policy in the 2000s*. New York: Cambridge University Press.
Asciutto, Alejandro Ernesto. 2013. "Prácticas gremiales, funcionamiento interno e identidad del sindicato de trabajadores de OSPLAD." Sociology Master's Thesis, Universidad Nacional de San Martín.

Ascolani, Adrián. 2019. "La huelga de profesores en las escuelas normales: los directores, entre la adhesión y la denuncia." *Revista Educação e Emancipação, São Luís* 12(3).

Arnaut, Alberto. 1996. *Historia de una profesión. Los maestros de educación primaria en México, 1887–1994*. Mexico, DF: Centro de *investigación* y Docencia Economicas.

Arnaut, Alberto. 1998. *La federalización educativa en Mexico: Historia del debate sobre la centralización y la descentralización educativa (1889–1994)*. Mexico, DF: El Colegio de Mexico y Centro de *investigación* y Docencia Economicas.

Baker, Andy, and Kenneth F. Greene. 2011. "The Latin American Left's Mandate: Free-Market Policies and Issue Voting in New Democracies." *World Politics* 63(1): 43–77.

Balarin, María. 2021. "The Political Economy of Education Reforms in Peru." GRADE Final Report. https://riseprogramme.org/sites/default/files/inline-files/The%20Political%20Economy%20of%20Education%20Reforms%20in%20Peru%201995-2020.pdf.

Baldez, Lisa. 2002. *Why Women Protest: Women's Movements in Chile*. New York: Cambridge University Press.

Barnes, Tiffany D., Yann P. Kerevel, and Greg Saxton. 2023. *Working Class Inclusion: Evaluations of Democratic Institutions in Latin America*. New York: Cambridge University Press.

Bascia, Nina, ed., 2016. *Teacher Unions in Public Education: Politics, History, and the Future*. New York: Springer.

Bellei, Cristian, and Xavier Vanni. 2015. "Chile: The Evolution of Educational Policy, 1980–2014." In Simon Schwartzman, ed., *Education in South America*. London, UK: Bloomsbury Academic, 179–200.

Bellin, Eva. 2000. "Contingent Democrats: Industrialists, Labor, and Democratization in Late-Developing Countries." *World Politics* 52(2): 175–205.

Benavides, Eduardo. 2002. "ADIDA, 50 años de lucha." Revista de Cedetrabajo, Antioquia.

Bensusán, Graciela, and Arturo Tapia. 2011. "El SNTE: una experiencia singular en el sindicalismo mexicano." *El Cotidiano* 168: 17–32.

Bensusán, Graciela, and Kevin J. Middlebrook. 2012. "Organized Labor and Politics in Mexico." In Roderic Ai Camp, ed., *The Oxford Handbook of Mexican Politics*. New York: Oxford University Press, 335–66.

Bishara, Dina. 2018. *Contesting Authoritarianism: Labor Challenges to the State in Egypt*. New York: Cambridge University Press.

Bishara, Dina. 2020. "Legacy Trade Unions as Brokers of Democratization? Lessons from Tunisia." *Comparative Politics* 52(2): 173–95.

Bocanegra Acosta, Henry. 2009 "Los maestros colombianos como grupo de presión 1958–1979." *Diálogos de saberes: investigaciones y ciencias sociales* 30: 61–88.

Bocanegra Acosta, Henry. 2010. "Las políticas educativas y el magisterio colombiano en la década de los 80." *Diálogos de saberes: investigaciones y ciencias sociales* 32: 29–44.

Bocanegra Acosta, Henry. 2013. "Sindicalismo docente y politicas educativas en Colombia." Sociology Ph.D. Dissertation, Universidad Externado de Colombia.

Bocking, Paul. 2019. "The Mexican Teachers' Movement in the Context of Neoliberal Education Policy and Strategies for Resistance." *Labor and Society* 22(1): 61–76.

Borjas, George, and Olga L. Acosta. 2000. "Education Reform in Colombia." In Alberto Alesina, ed., *Institutional Reforms: The Case of Colombia*. Cambridge: MIT Press. Fedesarrollo, 245–72.

Brown, David S., and Wendy Hunter. 2004. "Democracy and Human Capital Formation: Education Spending in Latin America, 1980 to 1997." *Comparative Political Studies* 37(7): 842–64.

Bruns, Barbara, and Javier Luque. 2014. *Great Teachers: How to Raise Student Learning in Latin America and the Caribbean*. Washington, DC: World Bank.

Buitrago, Francisco Leal, and Andrés Dávila. 1990. *Clientelismo: el sistema politico y su expresión regional*. Bogotá: Tercer Mundo.

Burgess, Katrina. 2004. *Parties and Unions in the New Global Economy*. Pittsburgh: University of Pittsburgh Press.

Burton, Guy. 2012. "Hegemony and Frustration: Education Policy Making in Chile under the Concertación, 1990–2010." *Latin American Perspectives* 39(4): 34–52.

Cabal, Manuel. 2021. "Elite Conflict and Developmental Public Goods in Revolutionary Mexico." Political Science Ph.D. Dissertation, The University of Chicago.

Calvo, Ernesto, and Juan Abal Medina. 2001. *El federalismo electoral argentino: sobrerrepresentación, reforma política y gobierno dividido en la Argentina*. Buenos Aires: Eudeba.

Calvo, Ernesto, and María Victoria Murillo. 2019. *Non-Policy Politics: Richer Voters, Poorer Voters, and the Diversification of Electoral Strategies*. New York: Cambridge University Press.

Campo, Daniel. 2020. "Historia reciente y educación. La Carpa Blanca en tiempos del neoliberalismo (1997–1999)." History Master's Thesis, Universidad Nacional de General Sarmiento.

Cano, Arturo, and Alberto Aguirre. 2013. *Doña Perpetua: el poder y la opulencia de Elba Esther Gordillo*. Mexico: Debolsillo.

Caraway, Teri L. 2012. "Pathways of Dominance and Displacement: The Varying Fates of Legacy Unions in New Democracies." *World Politics* 64(2): 278–305.

Caraway, Teri L., María Lorena Cook, and Stephen Crowley, eds., 2015. *Working Through the Past: Labor and Authoritarian Legacies in Comparative Perspective*. Ithaca: Cornell University Press.

Caraway, Teri L., and Michele Ford. 2020. *Labor and Politics in Indonesia*. New York: Cambridge University Press.

Cárdenas, Mauricio, Roberto Junguito, Mónica Pachón. 2006. *Political Institutions and Policy Outcomes in Colombia: The Effects of the 1991 Constitution*. Inter-American Development Bank.

Carnoy, Martín. 2007. "Improving Quality and Equity in Latin American Education: A Realistic Assessment." *Pensamiento Educativo* 40(1): 103–30.

Carroll, Leah A. 2011. *Violent Democratization: Social Movements, Elites, and Politics in Colombia's Rural War Zones, 1984–2008*. Notre Dame: University of Notre Dame Press.

Castells, Manuel. 2012. *Networks of Outrage and Hope: Social Movements in the Internet Age*. Cambridge: John Wiley & Sons.
Castro de los Rios, Luz Ángela. 2015. "Asesinato de maestras y maestros en Colombia durante las últimas decadas." Cultural Studies Master's Thesis, Universidad Nacional de Colombia.
Chang, Mae Chu, Samer Al-Samarrai, Sheldon Shaeffer, Andrew B. Ragatz, Joppe De Ree, and Ritchie Stevenson. 2014. *Teacher Reform in Indonesia: The Role of Politics and Evidence in Policy Making*. Washington, DC: World Bank.
Chiappe, Mercedes. 2012. "Las relaciones entre Ctera y el gobierno nacional en el marco de la reinstitucionalización laboral. dinamica entre provincias y paritaria nacional docente. periodo 2006–2012." Working Paper.
Chiroque Chunga, Sigfredo. 2005. "Estudio de los conflictos en los sistemas educativos de la región: agendas, actores, evolución, manejo y desenlaces. Estudio de caso: el conflicto educativo en Perú (1998–2003)." *Observatorio Latinoamericano de Políticas Educativas (OLPEd)*, Serie Ensayos & Investigaciones No 7.
CINEP. 2010. Reconocer el pasado, construir el future: Informe sobre violencia contrasindicalistas y trabajadores sindicalizados 1984–2011. www.co.undp.org/content/colombia/es/home/library/democraticgovernance/-informe-sobre-violencia-contra-sindicalistas-y-trabajadores-sin.html.
Cobble, Dorothy Sue. 2003. *The Other Women's Movement. Workplace Justice and Social Rights in Modern America*. Princeton: Princeton University Press.
Collier, Ruth Berins, and Christopher Chambers-Ju. 2012. "Popular Representation in Contemporary Latin American Politics: An Agenda for Research." In Peter Kingstone and Deborah Yashar, eds., *Routledge Handbook of Latin American Politics*. New York: Routledge.
Collier, Ruth Berins, and David Collier. 1979. "Inducements versus Constraints: Disaggregating 'Corporatism'." *American Political Science Review* 73(4): 967–86.
Collier, Ruth Berins, and David Collier. 1991. *Shaping the Political Arena. Critical Junctures, the Labor Movement, and Regime Dynamics in Latin America*. Princeton: Princeton University Press.
Collier, Ruth Berins, and Samuel Handlin, eds., 2009. *Reorganizing Popular Politics: Participation and the New Interest Regime in Latin America*. University Park: Penn State University Press.
Cook, María Lorena. 1996. *Organizing Dissent: Unions, the State, and the Democratic Teachers' Movement in Mexico*. University Park: Penn State University Press.
Cook, María Lorena, and Joseph C. Bazler. 2013. "Bringing Unions Back in: Labour and Left Governments in Latin America." Cornell ILR Working Paper.
Corrales, Javier. 1999. The Politics of Education Reform: Bolstering the Supply and Demand; Overcoming Institutional Blocks. No. 22549. The World Bank.
Corrales, Javier. 2002. *Presidents Without Parties: The Politics of Economic Reform in Argentina and Venezuela in the 1990s*. University Park: Penn State University Press.
Corrales, Javier. 2004. "Multiple Preferences, Variable Strengths: The Politics of Education Reform in Argentina." In Robert Kaufman and Joan M. Nelson,

eds., *Crucial Needs, Weak Incentives: Social Sector Reform, Democratization, and Globalization in Latin America*. Woodrow Wilson Center Press with Johns Hopkins University Press, 315–49.
Corrales, Javier. 2021. *The Politics of LGBTQ Rights Expansion in Latin America and the Caribbean*. New York: Cambridge University Press.
Cortina, Regina. 1990. "Gender and Power in the Teacher's Union of Mexico." *Mexican Studies/Estudios Mexicanos* 6(2): 241–62.
Crisp, Brian, and Rachael E. Ingall. 2002. "Institutional Engineering and the Nature of Representation: Mapping the Effects of Electoral Reform in Colombia." *American Journal of Political Science*: 733–48.
Cruz Olmeda, Juan. 2003. "Estudio Comparado Sobre el Estado, el Poder y la Educación en las 24 Jurisdicciones Argentinas: Provincia De La Rioja." CIPPEC.
CTERA. 2003. Encuesta Nacional Docente.
Cuenca, Ricardo, and Julio César Vargas Castro. 2018. "Perú: el estado de políticas públicas docentes. Lima: IEP." *Documento de Trabajo* 242.
Daby, Mariela, and Mason W. Moseley. 2022. "Feminist Mobilization and the Abortion Debate in Latin America: Lessons from Argentina." *Politics & Gender* 18(2): 359–93.
Dargent, Eduardo, and Paula Muñoz. 2011. "Democracy Against Parties? Party System Deinstitutionalization in Colombia." *Journal of Politics in Latin America* 3(2): 43–71.
Dean, Adam. 2022. *Opening Up by Cracking Down: Labor Repression and Trade Liberalization in Democratic Developing Countries*. New York: Cambridge University Press.
Delgado, Marta. 2002. "El sindicalismo docente frente a la aplicación de las políticas neoliberales en educación: el caso de Ctera y las transferencias de servicios educativos a las jurisdicciones provincials." Social Science and Education Master's Thesis, Flacso-Argentina.
De Luca, Romina. 2018. "La izquierda en docentes: Entre el crecimiento de la multicolor y el seguimiento a la celeste." *Razón y Revolución* 30. https://razonyrevolucion.org/la-izquierda-en-docentes-entre-el-crecimiento-de-la-multicolor-y-el-seguimiento-a-la-celeste/.
De Ree, Joppe, Karthik Muralidharan, Menno Pradhan, and Halsey Rogers. 2018. "Double for Nothing? Experimental Evidence on an Unconditional Teacher Salary Increase in Indonesia." *The Quarterly Journal of Economics* 133(2): 993–1039.
Díaz Ríos, Claudia. 2016. "When Global Ideas Collide with Domestic Interests: The Politics of Secondary Education Governance in Argentina, Chile and Colombia." Political Science Ph.D. Dissertation, McMaster University.
Diaz de la Torre, Juan, José Guadalupe Montano Villalobos, Alfonso Cepeda Salas, and Victor Hugo Calvillo Mendoza. 2013. *Vision Colectiva de una profesion: SNTE*. Mexico DF, Editorial del Magisterio.
Donaire, Ricardo. 2009. "La clase social de los docentes." *Condiciones de vida y de trabajo*. https://agmer.org.ar/index/wp-content/uploads/2013/03/encuentro-I-la-clase-social-de-los-docentes-donaire.pdf.
Doner, Richard F., and Ben Ross Schneider. 2016. "The Middle-Income Trap: More Politics than Economics." *World Politics* 68(4): 608–44.

Donoso, Sofía. 2016. "When Social Movements Become a Democratizing Force: The Political Impact of the Student Movement in Chile." In Thomas Davis, ed., *Protest, Social Movements, and Global Democracy since 2011*. Emerald Publishing, 167–96.
Duarte, Jesús. 1998. "State Weakness and Clientelism in Colombian Education." In Eduardo Posada-Carbo, ed., *Colombia: The Politics of Reforming the State*. New York: St. Martin's Press.
Duarte, Jesús. 2003. *Educación pública y clientelismo en Colombia*. Medellin: Universidad de Antioquia.
Dugas, John. 2001. "The Origin, Impact, and Demise of the 1989–1990 Colombian Student Movement: Insights from Social Movement Theory." *Journal of Latin American Studies* 33(4).
Duverger, Maurice. 1954. *Political Parties: Their Organization and Activity in the Modern State*. New York: Methuen & Co.
Eaton, Kent. 2004. *Politics Beyond the Capital: The Design of Subnational Institutions in South America*. Stanford: Stanford University Press.
Eaton, Kent. 2010. "Subnational Economic Nationalism? The Contradictory Effects of Decentralization in Peru." *Third World Quarterly* 31(7): 1205–22.
Eaton, Kent. 2015. "Disciplining Regions: Subnational Contention in Neoliberal Peru." *Territory, Politics, Governance* 3(2): 124–46.
Eisenstadt, Todd. 2000. "Eddies in the Third Wave: Protracted Transitions and Theories of Democratization." *Democratization* 7(3): 3–24.
Eisenstadt, Todd A. 2004. *Courting Democracy in Mexico: Party Strategies and Electoral Institutions*. New York: Cambridge University Press.
Elacqua, Gregory, Diana Hincapie, Emiliana Vegas, and Mariana Alfonso. 2018. *Profesión: Profesor en América Latina, ¿Por qué se perdió el prestigio docente y cómo recuperarlo?* Washington, DC: Inter-American Development Bank.
Engerman, Stanley L., and Kenneth L. Sokoloff. 2002. "Factor Endowments, Inequality, and Paths of Development Among New World Economies." *Economía* 3(1): 41–110.
Engerman, Stanley L., Elisa Mariscal, and Kenneth L. Sokoloff. 2012. "The Evolution of Schooling: 1800–1925." In Stanley L. Engerman and Kenneth L. Sokoloff, eds., *Economic Development in the Americas since 1500: Endowments and Institutions*. New York: Cambridge University Press, 93–142.
Espinosa, José Antonio. 1982. "Los maestros de los maestros: las dirigencias sindicales en la historia del SNTE." Instituto Nacional de Antropologia e Historia, Revista Historias 1.
Etchemendy, Sebastián. 2011. *Models of Economic Liberalization: Business, Workers, and Compensation in Latin America, Spain, and Portugal*. New York: Cambridge University Press.
Etchemendy, Sebastián. 2013 "La 'doble alianza' gobierno-sindicatos en el kirchnerismo (2003–2012): Origenes, evidencia y perspectivas." In Carlos H. Acuña, ed., *¿Cuanto importan las instituciones? Gobierno, Estado y actores en la politica argentina*. Buenos Aires: Siglo Veintiuno Editores, 291–324.
Etchemendy, Sebastián, and Ruth Berins Collier. 2007. "Down but Not Out: Union Resurgence and Segmented Neocorporatism in Argentina (2003–2007)." *Politics & Society* 35(3): 363–401.

Etchemendy, Sebastián and Germán Lódola. 2023 "The Rise of Public-Sector Unions in the 21st Century: A Theoretical, Mixed-Methods Approach with Evidence from Argentina." *Politics & Society*.

Evans, Allison D. 2022. "Privatization and Judicialization in Resource Extraction: Comparing Labor Militancy in the Oil Fields of Russia and Kazakhstan." *Comparative Politics* 55(1): 71–93.

Falleti, Tulia G. 2010. *Decentralization and Subnational Politics in Latin America*. New York: Cambridge University Press.

Finger, Leslie K. 2018. "Vested Interests and the Diffusion of Education Reform across the States." *Policy Studies Journal* 46(2): 378–401.

Finger, Leslie, and Julián Gindin. 2015. "From Proposal to Policy: Social Movements and Teachers' Unions in Latin America." *Prospects* 45(3): 365–78.

Feldfeber, Myriam, Adriana Puiggros, Susan Robertson, and Miguel Duhalde. 2018. "La privatización educativa en Argentina." *Education International*.

Fernández Martínez, Marco Antonio. 2019. "Claroscuros de la centralización de la nómina magisterial en México."

Foweraker, Joe. 1993. *Popular Mobilization in Mexico: The Teachers' Movement 1977–87*. Cambridge: Cambridge University Press.

Galeano, Eduardo. 2004. *Las venas abiertas de América Latina*. México: Siglo XXI.

Garay, Candelaria. 2010. "Including Outsiders: Social Policy Expansion in Latin America." Ph.D. Dissertation, Department of Political Science, UC Berkeley.

Garay, Candelaria. 2017. *Social Policy Expansion in Latin America*. New York: Cambridge University Press.

Garay, Candelaria. 2023. "Redefining Labor Organizing: Coalitions between Labor Unions and Social Movements of Outsider Workers." In Miguel Centeno and Agustin Ferraro, eds., *State and Nation Making in Latin America and Spain: The Neoliberal State and Beyond*. New York: Cambridge University Press, 411–27.

Gervasoni, Carlos. 2018. *Hybrid Regimes within Democracies: Fiscal Federalism and Subnational Rentier States*. New York: Cambridge University Press.

Gibson, Edward L. 2005. "Boundary Control: Subnational Authoritarianism in Democratic Countries." *World Politics* 58(1): 101–32.

Gindin, Julián J. 2006. "Sobre las asociaciones docentes de comienzos del siglo XX."

Gindin, Julian J. 2011. "Por nos mesmos: As praticas sindicais dos professores publicos na Argentina, no Brasil e no Mexico." Sociology Ph.D. Dissertation, State University of Rio de Janeiro.

Ginsburg, Mark B., and Monte Tidwell. 1995. "Political Socialization of Prospective Educators in Mexico: The Case of the University of Veracruz." In Carlos Alberto Torres, ed., *Education and Social Change in Latin America*. Australia: James Nichols Publishers, 127–42.

Gomez Buendia, Hernando, and Rodrigo Losada Lora. 1984. *Organización y conflicto: la educación primaria oficial en Colombia*. Ottawa: CIID.

González, Lucas I. 2016. *Presidents, Governors, and the Politics of Distribution in Federal Democracies: Primus Contra Pares in Argentina and Brazil*. New York: Routledge.

Grindle, Merilee. 2004a. *Despite the Odds: The Contentious Politics of Education Reform*. Princeton: Princeton University Press.
Grindle, Merilee. 2004b. "Interests, Institutions, and Reformers: The Politics of Education Decentralization in Mexico." In Robert Kaufman and Joan M. Nelson, eds., *Crucial Needs, Weak Incentives: Social Sector Reform, Democratization, and Globalization in Latin America*. Baltimore: The Johns Hopkins University Press.
Hacker, Jacob S., and Paul Pierson. 2014. "After the 'Master Theory': Downs, Schattschneider, and the Rebirth of Policy-Focused Analysis." *Perspectives on Politics* 12(3): 643–62.
Handlin, Samuel. 2017. *State Crisis in Fragile Democracies: Polarization and Political Regimes in South America*. New York: Cambridge University Press.
Hanson, E. Mark. 1996. "Educational Change Under Autocratic and Democratic Governments: The Case of Argentina." *Comparative Education* 32(3): 303–18.
Hartlyn, Jonathan. 1984. "The Impact of Patterns of Industrialization and of Popular Sector Incorporation on Political Regime Type: A Case Study of Colombia." *Studies in Comparative International Development* 19(1): 29–60.
Hartlyn, Jonathan. 1988. *Politics of Coalition Rule in Colombia*. New York: Cambridge University Press.
Hartshorn, Ian M. 2019. *Labor Politics in North Africa: After the Uprisings in Egypt and Tunisia*. New York: Cambridge University Press.
Hecock, R. Douglas. 2014. "Democratization, Education Reform, and the Mexican Teachers' Union." *Latin American Research Review* 49(1): 62–82.
Hellman, Judith A. 1988. *Mexico in Crisis*. New York: Holmes and Meier.
Hertel-Fernandez, Alexander, Suresh Naidu, and Adam Reich. 2021. "Schooled by Strikes? The Effects of Large-Scale Labor Unrest on Mass Attitudes toward the Labor Movement." *Perspectives on Politics* 19(1): 73–91.
Hexter, James H. 1979. *On Historians*. Cambridge: Harvard University Press.
Hite, Katherine, and Paola Cesarini. 2004. *Authoritarian Legacies and Democracy in Latin America and Southern Europe*. Notre Dame: University of Notre Dame Press.
Hochstetler, Kathryn, and Margaret E. Keck. 2007. *Greening Brazil: Environmental Activism in State and Society*. Durham: Duke University Press.
Hunter, Wendy. 2010. *The Transformation of the Workers' Party in Brazil, 1989–2009*. New York: Cambridge University Press.
INEE [Instituto Nacional para la Evaluación de la Educación]. 2015. *Los docentes en México*. Informe.
Inter-American Development Bank. 2019. "Los sindicatos docentes como socios para mejorar la calidad docente."
Jaume, David. 2020. ¿*Los paros docentes afectan a todas las provincias por igual?* Argentinos por la Educación.
Kapiszewski, Diana, Steven Levitsky, and Deborah J. Yashar, eds., 2021. *The Inclusionary Turn in Latin American Democracies*. New York: Cambridge University Press.
Kitschelt, Herbert. 1994. *The Transformation of European Social Democracy*. New York: Cambridge University Press.

Kurtz, Marcus J. 2004. "The Dilemmas of Democracy in the Open Economy: Lessons from Latin America." *World Politics* 56(2): 262–302.
Langston, Joy K. 2017. *Democratization and Authoritarian Party Survival: Mexico's PRI*. Oxford: Oxford University Press.
Larreguy, Horacio, Cesar E. Montiel Olea, and Pablo Querubin. 2017. "Political Brokers: Partisans or Agents? Evidence from the Mexican Teachers' Union." *American Journal of Political Science* 61(4): 877–91.
Lavery, Lesley. 2020. *A Collective Pursuit: Teachers' Unions and Education Reform*. Philadelphia: Temple University Press.
LeBas, Adrienne. 2011. *From Protest to Parties: Party-Building and Democratization in Africa*. Oxford: Oxford University Press.
Lee, Yoonkyung. 2011. *Militants or Partisans: Labor Unions and Democratic Politics in Korea and Taiwan*. Stanford: Stanford University Press.
Lessing, Benjamin. 2015. "Logics of Violence in Criminal War." *Journal of Conflict Resolution* 59(8): 1486–516.
Levitsky, Steven. 2003. *Transforming Labor-Based Parties in Latin America: Argentine Peronism in Comparative Perspective*. New York: Cambridge University Press.
Levitsky, Steven, and Scott Mainwaring. 2006. "Organized Labor and Democracy in Latin America." *Comparative Politics* 39(1): 21–42.
Levitsky, Steven, and María Victoria Murillo. 2003. "Argentina Weathers the Storm." *Journal of Democracy* 14(4): 152–66.
Levitsky, Steven, and Kenneth M. Roberts, eds., 2011. *The Resurgence of the Latin American Left*. Baltimore, MD: Johns Hopkins University Press.
Levy, Jonah D. 2023. *Contested Liberalization: Historical Legacies and Contemporary Conflict in France*. New York: Cambridge University Press.
Lipset, Seymour Martin, Martin Trow and James S. Coleman. 1956. *Union Democracy: The Internal Politics of the International Typographical Union*. New York: The Free Press.
Locke, Richard M., and Kathleen Thelen. 1995. "Apples and Oranges Revisited: Contextualized Comparisons and the Study of Comparative Labor Politics." *Politics & Society* 23(3): 337–67.
López, Margarita. 2008. "El sindicalismo docente en Colombia." In *Sindicatos docentes y reformas educativas en América Latina*. Brasil: Fundación Konrad Adenauer.
Lowden, Pamela. 2004. "Education Reform in Colombia: The Elusive Quest for Effectiveness." In Robert Kaufman and Joan M. Nelson, eds., *Crucial Needs, Weak Incentives. Social Sector Reform, Democratization, and Globalization in Latin America*. Washington, DC: Woodrow Wilson Center Press.
Loyo, Engracia. 1998. "Los mecanismos de la 'federalización' educativa, 1921–1940." In Pilar Gonzalbo Aizpuru, ed., *Historia y nación. Historia de la educación y enseñanza de la historia*. México, El Colegio de México.
Loyo, Aurora. 2008. "El sindicalismo docente en Mexico." *In Sindicatos docentes y reformas educativas en América Latina*. Brasil: Fundación Konrad Adenauer.
Lupu, Noam. 2016. *Party Brands in Crisis: Partisanship, Brand Dilution, and the Breakdown of Political Parties in Latin America*. New York: Cambridge University Press.

Lyon, Melissa Arnold. 2023. "Current Perspectives on Teacher Unionization, and What They're Missing." *Educational Policy* 37(5): 1420–43.
Magaloni, Beatriz. 2006. *Voting for Autocracy: Hegemonic Party Survival and its Demise in Mexico*. New York: Cambridge University Press.
Mazzuca, Sebastián L. 2017. "Critical Juncture and Legacies: State Formation and Economic Performance in Latin America." *Qualitative & Multi-Method Research* 15(1): 29–35.
McAdam, Doug, John D. McCarthy, and Mayer N. Zald, eds., 1996. *Comparative Perspectives on Social Movements*. New York: Cambridge University Press.
McAdam, Doug, and Sidney Tarrow. 2010. "Ballots and Barricades: On the Reciprocal Relationship between Elections and Social Movements." *Perspectives on Politics* 8(2): 529–42.
McEwan, Patrick J., and Lucrecia Santibáñez. 2005. "Teacher and Principal Incentives in Mexico." In Emiliana Vegas, ed., *Incentives to Improve Teaching: Lessons from Latin America*. Washington, DC: World Bank, 213–54.
McGuire, James W. 1992. "Union Political Tactics and Democratic Consolidation in Alfonsin's Argentina, 1983–1989." *Latin American Research Review* 27(1): 37–74.
McGuire, James W. 1996. "Strikes in Argentina: Data Sources and Recent Trends." *Latin American Research Review* 31(3): 127–50.
Michels, Robert. 1962. *Political Parties: A Sociological Study of the Oligarchical Tendencies of Modern Democracy*. New York: the Free Press.
Middlebrook, Kevin J. 1995. *The Paradox of Revolution: Labor, the State, and Authoritarianism in Mexico*. Baltimore: Johns Hopkins University Press.
Migliavacca, Adriana G. 2009. "La huelga docente de 1988. Una aproximación desde la perspectiva de los docentes autoconvocados." EIXO Temático IV.
Migliavacca, Adriana G. 2011. *La protesta docente en la decada de 1990: Experiencias de organización sindical en la provincia de Buenos Aires*. Buenos Aires: Jorge Baudino Editores.
Migliavacca, Adriana G., and Andrea Blanco. 2011. "Organización sindical y movilización de los docentes de la provincia de Buenos Aires a partir de 2001. Entre las prácticas institucionalizadas y los nuevos espacios en construcción" In Julián Gindin ed., *Pensar las prácticas sindicales docentes*, Buenos Aires, Herramienta AMSAFE Rosario, AGMER, ADOSAC.
Migliavacca, Adriana G., Matías Remolgao, and Patricio Urricelqui. 2015. "Las políticas educativas en la Argentina de cambio de siglo."
Milkman, Ruth. 1987. *Gender at Work: The Dynamics of Job Segregation by Sex during World War II*. Champaign: University of Illinois Press.
Mizala, Alejandra, and Ben Ross Schneider. 2014. "Negotiating Education Reform: Teacher Evaluations and Incentives in Chile (1990–2010)." *Governance* 27(1): 87–109.
Moe, Terry M. 2011. *Special Interest: Teachers Unions and America's Public Schools*. Washington, DC: Brookings Institution Press.
Moe, Terry M. 2015. "Vested Interests and Political Institutions." *Political Science Quarterly* 130(2): 277–318.
Moe, Terry M., and Susanne Wiborg, eds., 2017. *The Comparative Politics of Education: Teachers Unions and Education Systems around the World*. New York: Cambridge University Press.

Montenegro, Armando. 1995. "An Incomplete Educational Reform: The Case of Colombia." *Human Capital Development and Operations Policy*. Washington, DC: World Bank.
Montero, Alfred P., and David J. Samuels, eds., 2004. *Decentralization and Democracy in Latin America*. Notre Dame: The University of Notre Dame Press.
Munck, Gerardo L. 1998. *Authoritarianism and Democratization: Soldiers and Workers in Argentina, 1976–1983*. University Park: Penn State University Press.
Muñoz Armenta, Aldo. 2008. "Escenarios e identidades del SNTE: entre el sistema educativo y el sistema político." *Revista mexicana de investigación educativa* 13(37): 377–417.
Muñoz Armenta, Aldo. 2011. "El SNTE y Nueva Alianza: del control político del magisterio a la cohabitación pragmática electoral." *El Cotidiano*, 168: 95–107.
Muñoz Armenta, Aldo. 2020. "Los efectos políticos de la reforma educativa en la campaña presidencial de Morena." In Aidé Hernández García, Aldo Muñoz Armenta, and Guillermo Rafael Gómez Romo de Vivar, eds., *El triunfo izquierda en las elecciones de 2018*. Mexico: Editorial Grupo Grañén Porrúa.
Muñoz Armenta, Aldo and Rosalinda Castro Maravilla. 2019. "La reforma educativa de los gobiernos sin mayoría en México." In Rosa María Mirón Lince and Luisa Béjar Algazi, eds., *Dos décadas sin mayoría. El impacto del pluralismo en el Congreso*. Mexico: Facultad de Ciencias Políticas y Sociales.
Murillo, María Victoria. 1999. "Recovering Political Dynamics: Teachers' Unions and the Decentralization of Education in Argentina and Mexico." *Latin American Politics & Society* 41(1): 31–57.
Murillo, María Victoria. 2001. *Labor Unions, Partisan Coalitions, and Market Reforms in Latin America*. New York: Cambridge University Press.
Murillo, María Victoria, and Lucas Ronconi. 2004. "Teachers' Strikes in Argentina: Partisan Alignments and Public-Sector Labor Relations." *Studies in Comparative International Development* 39(1): 77–98.
Murillo, Victoria, Mariano Tommasi, Lucas Ronconi, and Juan Sanguinetti. 2002. "The Economic Effects of Unions in Latin America: Teachers' Unions and Education in Argentina." In Peter Kuhn and Gustavo Marquez, eds., *What Difference Do Unions Make?* Washington DC: Inter-American Development Bank.
Nardacchione, Gabriel. 2012. "La disputa retórico-educativa en la Argentina de los años 1990: entre la modernización del sistema y la defensa de la escuela pública." *Revista Mexicana de Investigación Educativa* 17(53), 407–35.
Nardacchione, Gabriel. 2014. "Una rara avis en el sindicalismo argentino: los sindicatos docentes (1880–2001)." Working Paper. https://ridaa.unicen.edu.ar:8443/server/api/core/bitstreams/b154a664-0028-4528-ac9f-4c6a71448576/content.
Narodowski, Mariano, Mauro Carlos Moschetti, and Silvina Alegre. 2013. "Radiografía de las huelgas docentes en la Argentina: Conflicto laboral y privatización de la educación." Working Paper.
Navia, Patricio, and Andrés Velasco. 2003. "The Politics of Second-Generation Reforms." In Pedro Pablo Kuczynski and John Williamson, eds., *After the Washington Consensus*. Washington, DC: Institute for International Economics.

Nelson, Joan M. 2007. "Elections, Democracy, and Social Services." *Studies in Comparative International Development* 41(4): 79–97.
Nicolini, Juan Pablo, Josefina Posadas, Juan Sanguinetti, Pablo Sanguinetti, and Mariano Tommasi. 2002. *Decentralization, Fiscal Discipline in Sub-National Governments and the Bailout Problem: The Case of Argentina*. Washington, DC: Inter-American Development Bank.
Oliveros, Virginia. 2016. "Making it Personal: Clientelism, Favors, and the Personalization of Public Administration in Argentina." *Comparative Politics* 48(3): 373–91.
Ornelas, Carlos. 2008. "El Snte, Elba Esther Gordillo y el gobierno de Calderón." *Revista Mexicana de investigación Educativa* 13(37): 445–69.
Ornelas, Carlos. 2012. *Educación, colonización y rebeldia: la herencia del pacto Calderón-Gordillo*. Mexico: Siglo XXI.
Ornelas, Carlos. 2018. *La contienda por la educación: Globalización, neocorporativismo y democracia*. Mexico: Fondo De Cultura Economica.
Ortiz Jimenez, Maximo. 2003. *Carrera Magisterial: Un proyecto de desarrollo profesional*. Mexico City: Secretaria de Educación Pública.
Pachón, Mónica, and Matthew S. Shugart. 2010. "Electoral Reform and the Mirror Image of Inter-Party and Intra-Party Competition: The Adoption of Party Lists in Colombia." *Electoral Studies* 29(4): 648–60.
Paglayan, Agustina S. 2014. "Teacher Unions and Education Reform in Argentina." Stanford Working Paper.
Paglayan, Agustina S. 2019. "Public-Sector Unions and the Size of Government." *American Journal of Political Science* 63(1): 21–36.
Panebianco, Angelo. 1988. *Political Parties: Organization and Power*. Cambridge: New York: Cambridge University Press.
Paschel, Tianna S. 2010. "The Right to Difference: Explaining Colombia's Shift from Color Blindness to the Law of Black Communities." *American Journal of Sociology* 116(3): 729–69.
Paschel, Tianna S. 2018. *Becoming Black Political Subjects: Movements and Ethno-Racial Rights in Colombia and Brazil*. Princeton: Princeton University Press.
Peláez, Gerardo. 1984. *Historia del sindicato nacional de trabajadores de la educación*. Mexico: Ediciones de Cultura Popular.
Perazza, Roxana. 2016. "La normal aboral docente en Argentina: entre la historia y los retos futuros." Social Science Master's Thesis, FLACSO.
Perazza, Roxana and Martin Legarralde. 2008. "El sindicalismo docente en la Argentina." In *Sindicatos docentes y reformas educativas en América Latina*. Brasil: Fundación Konrad Adenauer.
Pereyra, Ana. 2008. "La fragmentación de la oferta educativa: la educación pública vs. la educación privada." SITEAL, UNESCO.
Pérez, Guillermo, and Guillermo Sandoval. 2008. "Sindicatos Docentes y Reformas Educativas en América Latina: Chile." In *Sindicatos docentes y reformas educativas en América Latina*. Brasil: Fundación Konrad Adenauer.
Pierskalla, Jan H., and Audrey Sacks. 2020. "Personnel Politics: Elections, Clientelistic Competition and Teacher Hiring in Indonesia." *British Journal of Political Science* 50(4): 1283–305.

Pinilla Diaz, Alexis Vladimir. 2012. "Entre 'solana y umbría': memorias de la movilización magisterial en Colombia." *Revista Historia de la Educación Colombiana*, 15(15), 259–78.
Pizarro, Eduardo. 2006. "Giants with Feet of Clay: Political Parties in Colombia." In Scott Mainwaring, Ana María Bejarano, and Eduardo Pizarro, eds., *The Crisis of Democratic Representation in the Andes*. Stanford: Stanford University Press, 78–99.
Posner, Paul W., Viviana Patroni, and Jean François Mayer. 2018. *Labor Politics in Latin America: Democracy and Worker Organization in the Neoliberal Era*. Gainesville: University Press of Florida.
PREAL [Program of Education Reform for Latin America]. 2006. *Quantity without Quality: A Report Card on Education in Latin America*. Washington, DC, and Santiago.
Przeworski, Adam, and John Sprague. 1986. *Paper Stones: A History of Electoral Socialism*. Chicago: University of Chicago Press.
Pulido Chaves, Orlando. 2007. "La federación colombiana de educadores (Fecode) y la lucha por el Derecho a la Educación. El Estatuto Docente." *Serie ensayos e investigaciones*, 31.
Quinto de la Cruz, Elmer F. 2007. "Conflicto y crisis de representación en el SUTEP de la Región Central." Sociology Master's Thesis, Pontificia Universidad Católica del Perú.
Ramírez, María Teresa, and Juana Patricia Téllez. 2006. *La educación primaria y secundaria en Colombia en el siglo XX*. Colombia: Banco de la República.
Raphael, Ricardo. 2007. *Los socios de Elba Esther*. Mexico: Editorial Planeta Mexicana.
Ravitch, Diane. 2013. *Reign of Error: The Hoax of the Privatization Movement and the Danger to America's Public Schools*. New York: Alfred A. Knopf.
Reyes Aliaga, Rodrigo. n.d. "Tácticas político-sindicales de la conducción demócrata cristiana en el Colegio de Profesores (1985-1995)." Working Paper Centro de Investigación Político Social del Trabajo.
Rich, Jessica. 2019. *State-Sponsored Activism: Bureaucrats and Social Movements in Democratic Brazil*. New York: Cambridge University Press.
Rivas, Axel. 2003. *Provincia de Corrientes: Estudio comparado sobre el estado, el poder y la educación en las 24 jurisdicciones argentinas*. CIPPEC.
Rivas, Axel, Alejandro Vera, and Pablo Bezem. 2010. *Radiografío de la educación argentina*. CIPPEC.
Roberts, Kenneth M. 2014. *Changing Course in Latin America*. New York: Cambridge University Press.
Rodríguez, Abel. 2002. *La educación después de la constitución del 91, de la reforma a la contrarreforma*. Bogotá: Magisterio y Tercer Milenio.
Rodríguez, Oscar. 2014. "La configuración de las relaciones de poder: Legitimidad y liderazgos en la Sección 20 del SNTE, Nayarit." Sociology MA Thesis, UNAM.
Rosaldo, Manuel. 2016. "Revolution in the Garbage Dump: The Political and Economic Foundations of the Colombian Recycler Movement, 1986–2011." *Social Problems* 63(3): 351–72.
Rosser, Andrew J., and Mohamad Fahmi. 2016. *The Political Economy of Teacher Management in Decentralized Indonesia*. Washington, DC: World Bank.

Rossi, Federico and Donatella Della Porta. 2015 "Mobilizing for Democracy: Social Movements in Democratization Processes." In Bert Klandermans and Cornelis Van Stralen, eds., *Movements in Times of Democratic Transition*. Philadelphia: Temple University Press.

Rossi, Federico M., and Marisa von Bülow, eds., 2016. *Social Movement Dynamics: New Perspectives on Theory and Research from Latin America*. London: Routledge.

Rueschemeyer, Dietrich, John D. Stephens, and Evelyne Huber Stephens. 1992. *Capitalist Development and Democracy*. Chicago: the University of Chicago Press.

Samstad, James G. 2002. "Corporatism and Democratic Transition: State and Labor during the Salinas and Zedillo Administrations." *Latin American Politics & Society* 44(4): 1–28.

Santamaria Fajardo, Mariela. 2017. "Presencia y aportes de los maestros al movimiento pedagógico nacional." Education Master's Thesis, Universidad Pedagogica Nacional.

Santiago, Paulo, Isobel McGregor, Deborah Nusche, Pedro Ravela and Diana Toledo. 2012. "OECD Reviews of Evaluation and Assessment in Education: Mexico." www.oecd.org/mexico/Mexico%20Review%20of%20Evaluation%20and%20Assessment%20in%20Education.pdf.

Sartori, Giovanni. 1970. "Concept Misformation in Comparative Politics." *American Political Science Review* 64(4): 1033–53.

Schipani, Andrés. 2021. "Awakening the Invertebrate Giant: The Labor Strategy of the Kirchners' Administrations (2003–2015)." *Revista SAAP* 15(2), 389–419.

Schipani, Andrés. 2022. "Left Behind: Labor Unions and Redistributive Policy under the Brazilian Workers' Party." *Comparative Politics* 54(3): 405–28.

Schmitter, Philippe C. 1974. "Still the Century of Corporatism?" *The Review of Politics* 36(1): 85–131.

Schneider, Ben Ross. 2022. "Teacher Unions, Political Machines, and the Thorny Politics of Education Reform in Latin America." *Politics & Society* 50(1): 84–116.

Scully, Timothy R. 2017. "A Fourth Critical Juncture? Chilean Politics after Military Rule." *Qualitative & Multi-Method Research* 15(1), 21–26.

Secretaria de Educación Pública Mexico. 2020. *Principales cifras del sistema educativo nacional 2019–2020*. Dirección General de Planeación, Programación y Estadística Educativa.

Shefter, Martin. 1977. "Party and Patronage: Germany, England, and Italy." *Politics & Society* 7(4): 403–51.

Silva, Eduardo. 2009. *Challenging Neoliberalism in Latin America*. New York: Cambridge University Press.

Simmons, Erica S. 2016. *Meaningful Resistance: Market Reforms and the Roots of Social Protest in Latin America*. New York: Cambridge University Press.

Skocpol, Theda, and Margaret Somers. 1980. "The Uses of Comparative History in Macrosocial Inquiry." *Comparative Studies in Society and History* 22(2): 174–97.

Slater, Dan, and Daniel Ziblatt. 2013. "The Enduring Indispensability of the Controlled Comparison." *Comparative Political Studies* 46(10): 1301–27.

Slater, Dan, and Erica Simmons. 2013. "Coping by Colluding: Political Uncertainty and Promiscuous Powersharing in Indonesia and Bolivia." *Comparative Political Studies* 46(11): 1366–93.

Snow, David A., and Sarah Anne Soule. 2010. *A Primer on Social Movements.* New York: W.W. Norton.

Solano, Laura Poy. 2009. "Misael Núñez Acosta, un símbolo de la lucha magisterial." *El Cotidiano* 154: 95–100.

Somma, Nicolás. 2012. "The Chilean Student Movement of 2011–2012: Challenging the Marketization of Education." *Interface* 4(2): 296–309.

Stokes, Susan C. 2001. *Mandates and Democracy: Neoliberalism by Surprise in Latin America.* New York: Cambridge University Press.

Suárez, Daniel. 2005. "Conflicto social y protesta docente en américa latina. estudio de caso: el conflicto docente de Argentina (1997–2003)." Serie Ensayos e Investigaciones num. 4, Buenos Aires: Observatorio Latinoamericano de Politicas Educativas.

Svampa, Maristella, and Sebastián Pereyra. 2003. *Entre la ruta y el barrio. La experiencia de las organizaciones piqueteras.* Buenos Aires: Biblos.

Szwarcberg, Mariela. 2013. "The Microfoundations of Political Clientelism: Lessons from the Argentine Case." *Latin American Research Review* 48(2): 32–54.

Tamayo Valencia, Alfonso. 2006. "El movimiento pedagógico en Colombia." *Revista Histedbr* 24: 102–13.

Tarlau, Rebecca. 2022. "Take or Reject State Power? The Dual Dilemma for Teachers' Unions in Brazil and Mexico." *Studies in Comparative International Development* 57(3): 1–24.

Tarrow, Sidney. 2011. *Power in Movement: Social Movements and Contentious Politics.* New York: Cambridge University Press.

Tedesco, Juan Carlos. 2003. *Educación y sociedad en la Argentina (1880–1955)* Buenos Aires: Editorial Universitaria.

Teitelbaum, Emmanuel. 2011. *Mobilizing Restraint: Democracy and Industrial Conflict in Post-Reform South Asia.* Ithaca: Cornell University Press.

Tiramonti, Guillermina. 2001. "Sindicalismo docente y reforma educativa en la América Latina de los 90." Working Paper # 19, Washington, D. C. PREAL.

Valdez Tappatá, María Jimena. 2015. "Sindicalismo de movimiento social bajo gobiernos de nueva izquierda latinoamericana: El caso de ATE y CTERA en el kirchnerismo." Political Science Master's Thesis, Universidad Torcuato Di Tella.

Van Cott, Donna Lee. 2002. "Constitutional Reform in the Andes: Redefining Indigenous-State Relations." In Rachel Sieder, ed., *Multiculturalism in Latin America.* London: Palgrave Macmillan, 45–73.

Van Cott, Donna Lee. 2005. *From Movements to Parties in Latin America: The Evolution of Ethnic Politics.* New York: Cambridge University Press.

Vargas, Thomas R. 2022. "Decentralization as a Political Weapon: Education Politics in El Salvador and Paraguay." *Comparative Politics* 55(1): 23–45.

Vargas Castro, Julio César. 2005. "Como la flor en la rama. Magisterio y política en el Perú (1972–2005)." Clacso working paper.

Vaughan, Mary Kay. 1982. *The State, Education and Social Class in Mexico, 1880–1928.* DeKalb: Northern Illinois University Press.

Vaughan, Mary K. 1997. *Cultural Politics in Revolution: Teachers, Peasants, and Schools in Mexico, 1930–1940*. Tucson: University of Arizona Press.

Vazquez, Silvia. 2005. *Luchas político educativas: El lugar de los sindicatos docentes*. CTERA.

Vazquez, Silvia and Juan Balduzzi. 2000. *De apóstoles a trabajadores*. Editorial CTERA, Buenos Aires.

Vazquez de Knaugh, Josefina. 1970. *Nacionalismo y educación en México*. El Colegio de Mexico.

Villalobos Dintrans, Cristobal. "Los conflictos sociales en el campo educativo en el Chile post-dictadura (1990–2014)." Social Science Ph.D. Dissertation, Universidad de Chile.

vom Hau, Matthias. 2009. "Unpacking the School: Textbooks, Teachers, and the Construction of Nationhood in Mexico, Argentina, and Peru." *Latin American Research Review* 44(3): 127–54.

Voss, Kim, and Rachel Sherman. 2000. "Breaking the Iron Law of Oligarchy: Union Revitalization in the American Labor Movement." *American Journal of Sociology* 106(2): 303–49.

Wampler, Brian, and Leonardo Avritzer. 2004. "Participatory Publics: Civil Society and New Institutions in Democratic Brazil." *Comparative Politics* 36(3): 291–312.

Weinstein, José. 2006. "La negociación MINEDUC-Colegio de Profesores: Chile 2000. Una visión personal." *Trabajo presentado en la IX Reunión del Diálogo Regional de Política. Red de Educación. BID.*

Weldon, Jeffrey. 1997. "The Political Sources of Presidencialismo in Mexico." In Scott Mainwaring and Matthew Shugart, eds., *Presidentialism and Democracy in Latin America*. Cambridge: Cambridge University Press.

Williams, Mark E. 2001. "Learning the Limits of Power: Privatization and State-Labor Interactions in Mexico." *Latin American Politics & Society* 43(4): 91–126.

Wilson, Suzanne, and Leah A. Carroll. 2007. "The Colombian Contradiction: Lessons Drawn From Guerrilla Experiments in Demobilization and Electoralism." In Kalowatie Deonandan, David Close, and Gary Prevost, eds., *From Revolutionary Movements to Political Parties*. New York: Palgrave Macmillan.

Index

analysis of opportunity structures, 20
Anzia, Sarah
  influence of teacher unions on policy process, 210
  on off-cycle school board elections, 211
Argentina. *See also* Maffei, Marta; Sánchez, Mary
  Alfonsín, Raúl (1983–1989) of the Radical Party (UCR) enacted policies to democratize the education system, 113
  Argentine Workers' Central Union (CTA), 138
  Big March for Work led by Argentine Workers' Central Union (CTA), 138
  Buenos Aires recruitment of non-Argentine teachers, 127
  class differences among teachers, 43
  consequences of decentralization of CTERA, 123
  CTERA aided creation of the Argentine Workers' Central Union in 1991, 128
  CTERA avoided electoral politics, 112
  CTERA leaders who became national deputies, 141
  CTERA reflects a stronger propensity to express opposition and protests state actions, 111
  CTERA resembles a social movement union, 111
  CTERA suffered severe repression in the 1970s, 62
  decentralization and labor grievances, 125–8
  decentralization and political de-alignment, 128–9
  decentralization and weakening organizational hierarchies, 123–5
  decentralization led to convergence of different teacher organizations, 129
  deteriorating political and economic context from 1999 to 2002, 137
  difficulties in creating a unified union, 43
  education spending rose steadily from 1983 to 1986, 113
  efforts by political elites to build a centralized organization to control teachers failed, 53
  end of national collective bargaining did not put an end to movementism, 151
  formation of stark urban–rural divide in education (segmented school system), 42
  founding of CTERA (1973), 61
  Granja Educativa (Education Farm), 139
  had robust labor unions that were incorporated into the Peronist party, 36
  institution of collective bargaining became the primary axis of conflict over education policy, 148
  La Celeste became a multi-party vehicle for power-sharing, 128
  Láinez rural schools, 43
  Law of Education Finance (2005) increased funding for education, 145
  Law of Education Financing created the Paritaria Nacional Docente, 145

Argentina (cont.)
  Lista Celeste, 116, 119, 125, 128, 130, 131, 135
  Lista Celeste came to dominate CTERA, 118
  Lista Celeste sought to Peronize the union, 117
  Lista Celeste took control of CTERA's executive committee, 118
  Menem's decentralization undermined national union leaders and empowered militant groups, 112
  movementism became CTERA's political strategy, 113
  movementism led to national collective bargaining, 143–9
  National Fund for Teacher Incentive (FONID), 137
  national union leaders had a limited capacity to constrain local protests, 112
  paired with Peru, 192
  Paritaria Nacional Docente (national collective bargaining), 144
  Peron/Peronism division between industrial workers and urban teachers, 45
  Peronist General Confederation of Labor (CGT) organized thirteen general strikes during the Alfonsín presidency, 114
  Peronists coopted the traditional leaders, 44
  piqueteros (defined), 135
  President Kirchner takes action to resolve teacher protest in Entre Ríos, 144
  President Macri dismantled collective bargaining with teachers, 150
  protest and political autonomy, 61–2
  protest by self-mobilized teachers (*autoconvocados*), 138
  protests led to impeachment of Braillard Poccard, Pedro (Governor of Corrientes), 137
  Radical Civic Union (UCR), 53
  recurrent protests, 193
  resistance to corporatism, 53–5
  rival teachers' unions to CTERA, 116
  Roca, Julio Argentino (President) enacted compulsory secular education, 42
  Sánchez, Mary led the White March, 119
  Sarmiento, Domingo (President) promoted and supported public education, 42
  segmented teacher movement, 41
  self-mobilized teachers and *piqueteros* blocked roads, 139
  teacher mobilization in response to austerity measures in, 138
  teacher opposition to Peron's policies, 19
  teachers had a more heterogenous set of partisan identities than other unions, 36
  teachers thought of themselves as middle-class professionals, 43
  transitioned to democracy (1982), 1
  union leaders avoided politicizing the union, 143
  urban guerrilla warfare in Entre Ríos, 138
  White March (1988), 117, 126, 135, 136
  White March (1988) fostered a network of activists, 115
  White March (1988) lasted 42 days, 115
  White March stimulated grassroots activism, 116
authoritarian legacies
  are fixed and rooted firmly in the past, 19

Caraway, Teri. *See also* historical legacies of labor incorporation
  authoritarian regimes and links to democratization, 35
  historical legacies and union trajectories, 18
  historical legacies of corporatism, 28
  Indonesia unfavorable electoral rules, 19
  legacies of corporatism, 18
  union democracy and mechanisms of control, 24
  union militancy and restraint, 21
Chile, 196–202
  Colegio de Profesores (CUT), 5, 196, 197
  CUT supported military rule, 198
  Figueroa, Barbara (CUT), 196
  leftism political strategy, 12
  paired with Colombia, 6, 192
  as a shadow case, 192
  union enacted protests, 6
clientelism
  abusive forms of, 64
  based on regional union party bosses, 69
  Colombia's Teacher Statute protected teachers from, 65
  means to control dissident teachers in Mexico, 68
  provincial-level, 68

Index 237

teachers' unions fostering of, 9
unions as the vehicles of, 69
Collier, David
  contrast of teacher and worker incorporation, 67
  cooptation and labor peace, 18
  corporatist labor unions loyal to the regime, 40
  labor as a macropolitical actor, 13
  los tres ochos, 47
  state subsidies and constraint on union demand making, 182
  teacher influence over education policy may be contingent, 213
  teacher mobilization as project from above, 28
  teacher mobilization as project from below, 28
Collier, Ruth Berins, 3, See also corporatism
  contrast of teacher and worker incorporation, 67
  cooptation and labor peace, 18
  corporatist labor unions loyal to the regime, 40
  labor as macropolitical actor, 13
  los tres ochos, 47
  segmented neocorporatism, 144
  state subsidies and constraint on union demand making, 182
  teacher influence over education policy may be contingent, 213
  teacher mobilization as project from above, 28
  teacher mobilization as project from below, 28
Colombia. *See also* Ramírez, Gloria Ines
  Carvajal, Adalberto, and Movement of Education Action (MODAE), 57
  Colombian Federation of Educators (FECODE) supported left-of-center parties, 153
  Conservative Hegemony (1884–1930) and shaping of education, 45
  discovery of corrupt practices by Dussan, 175
  Dusan's Education, Work, and Social Change faction, 173
  Dussan, Jaime (President of FECODE) included in negotiations with President Gaviria, 162

factional importance of competitive union elections for the national executive committee of FECODE, 175
factionalism generated leftism, 171
factions limited influence on policy, 183
FECODE created Center of Study and Research on Teaching (CEID), 158
FECODE formed teachers into a national political voting bloc, 153
FECODE launched the journal *Education and Culture*, 158
FECODE launches Pedagogical Movement (MP) in 1982, 157
FECODE made relations in the union hierarchical, 153
FECODE's control of protests, 179–82
FECODE's electoral mobilization, 178
FECODE's Hunger March, 56
Federation of Colombian Educators (FECODE), 2
Federation of Colombian Educators (FECODE) created in 1959, 56
ideological factions within FECODE, 154
interest of Afro-Colombians and Indigenous communities were integrated, 162
intermittent protests, 193
La Violencia, 56
Labor Code of 1939 denied teachers the right to strike, 48
leftism encompassed elements of electoral mobilization of instrumentalism and the oppositional behavior of movementism, 171
leftist parties brought the teachers' movement together, 55
Maoist party (MOIR) a central protagonist, 63
MP focused on professional expertise and the practice of teaching, 158
MP marked a generational and ideological shift that divided the radical and center left, 157
MP opposed the technology of education and goals of efficiency, 157
MP pushed for popular education, curricular changes, and pedagogical innovations, 155
MP's separation from FECODE, 166
the National Front, powersharing pact, 56
oppositional corporatism, 55–8
paired with Chile, 192

Colombia (cont.)
  Pedagogical Movement (MP), 154
  period known as the political genocide, 155
  Petro, Gustavo, first leftist President of, 2
  President Barco enacted Fondo de Prestaciones del Magisterio (1990), 160
  President Lleras Restrepo and creation of regional funds, 56
  President López Pumarejo's expansion of public education, 47
  President Samper and Dussan, Jaime, negotiated the 'three eights', 163
  President Samper named Rodríguez, Abel as vice minister of education, 163
  primary education became compulsory (1927), 46
  primary education made free but not compulsory (1903), 46
  protest and oppositional politics, 55–8
  refusal to pay teachers led to early episodes of labor conflict, 49
  regional governments controlled education, 47
  Robledo, Jorge, elected to the Senate with Maoist support, 176
  Rodríguez, Abel elected to the Constitutional Assembly, 160
  Rodríguez, Abel, president of FECODE (1982), 157
  state pact with the church restricted the scope of public schools, 46
  subsidized parochial schools, 46
  teachers among the victims of the violence during the political genocide, 155
  Thousand Day War (1899–1902), 46
  Toro, German elected to the Constitutional Assembly, 160
  Turbay, Julio César (President) enacted the pro-teacher statute (1979), 65
  unions were weak and coopted by the traditional political parties, 35
Confederation of Education Workers of the Republic of Argentina (CTERA), grassroots activism. *See* Argentina
controlled comparison, 31
Cook, María Lorena, 50, 78
  assassination of Núñez Acosta, Misael, dissident leader, 74
  cohort of union leaders and creation of a national faction, 52
  dissident teacher movement in Mexico, 29
  dissident teachers victories, 74
  emergence of teacher movements, 21
  fragmentation of teachers' movement in Mexico, 38
  Gordillo's strategy to control dissidents, 81
  Gordillo's use of dissident groups, 84
  Jonguitud, Carlos, as cacique of SNTE, 60
  leftist governments response to unions, 3
  opening for teachers to challenge union leadership at SNTE, 72
  opposition to Gordillo from union bosses in several states, 75
  President Cárdenas consolidation failed, 41
  pushed for central control within SNTE, 52
  Robles Martínez, Jesús, continued power in SNTE after stepping down as Secretary-General, 52
  shift from ideological differences to personal loyalties within SNTE, 60
  state-brokered consolidation of teacher unions, 51
  teacher protest reached a peak in 1989 in Mexico, 74
  teachers and democratic reforms, 5
  union democracy and mechanisms of control, 24
corporatism
  association with authoritarian rule, 18
  beyond, 216–18
  defined, 18
  diverse forms in Argentina, Colombia, and Mexico, 49
  exclusionary, in Indonesia, 209
  importance of segmentation of teachers, 19
  incorporation and control of workers, 18
  legacies of, explain union politics, 18
  legacies of, shape union trajectories, 11
  and political elites, 18
  societal, in Colombia, 55
  state, in Latin America, 152
  state-determined, 50
Cristero Wars (1926–29), 39

decentralization, either strengthened or undermined teacher organizations, 30
divergent paths of labor unions and social movements, 3

Index 239

Etchemendy, Sebastián
  cooptation of labor unions during neoliberal restructuring, 30
  data on teacher protests (2006–2019), 180
  Menem's simultaneous rewarding some unions, while repressing others, 119
  and neocorporatism, 144
  Paritaria Nacional Docente (PND) and the enablement of national collective bargaining, 145
  state funds and demobilization of protests, 144
  state neo-corporatism and alliance with CTERA union leaders, 145
  suggestion on studying public sector mobilization, 217

factionalism, 11, 25, 26
  competition, 25
  leftism, 25
  movementism, 25
Falleti, Tulia, 77, 121, 163, *See also* Argentina
  Argentina's fortification of education, 42
  Argentina's subsidization of rural education (Láinez schools), 43
  on decentralization, 30
  decentralization of education in Argentina, 114
  education and political realignment, 119
  effects of decentralization, 30
  on elections of governors, 159
  on federalization, 77
  neoliberalism and decentralization of education, 62
  President Menem's agreement with governors, 122
  waterdowned decentralization and concessions to SNTE, 77
Federation of Colombian Educators (FECODE). *See* Colombia
Fox, Vicente (President). *See* National Action Party (PAN)

Gindin, Julián
  Argentina's church sponsored anticommunist federation of teachers, 44
  cooptation of teachers, 44
  CTERA granted *personeria gremial* (1985), 114
  law made union leaders buyers and sellers of teaching positions, 60
  military rule and restrictions on unions, 62
  opposition to Peronism, 142
  parallel school systems with different labor codes, 43
  Peron's civic, moral, and religious curriculum, 45
  Peronist Party endorsed the United Teachers of Argentina (UDA), 44
  PRI granted resources to SNTE to purge rivals, 52
  on professionalization and training, 5
  SNTE as a singular labor organization in Mexico, 72
Gomez Buendia, Hernando, 63
  98 teacher strikes in Colombia, 64
  regional funds to cover teachers' wages, 56
  unions and powersharing in Colombia, 57
Gordillo, Elba Esther. *See also* Mexico
  accused of corruption and clientelism, 214
  accused of diverting funds from ISSTE to her New Alliance party, 97
  arrested and indicted on charges of money laundering, 106
  build a vast network of political brokers, 90
  challenges faced by, 75
  and clientelism based on promises of teaching positions, salary bonuses, and other union advocacy services, 93
  criticized for advancing her personal interests, 214
  deployed her dominant faction to control state resources and capacity to advance political careers to maintain loyalty within SNTE, 86
  eclipsed the power of Jonguitud's Revolutionary Vanguard in SNTE, 83
  foreclosed the possibility for union democracy, 71
  freedom of partisanship, 80
  head of National Union of Education Workers (SNTE), 1
  held high-ranking positions in the PRI, 1
  her political endorsement became coveted by political candidates, 95

Gordillo, Elba Esther (cont.)
  hired political consultants and operatives with advanced training in computer science, communication, and polling, 91
  instrumental negotiations hinged on the consolidation of power under, 95
  led the National Organization of Popular Organizations of the PRI from 1995 to 2001, 95
  negotiated a salary increase for teachers, 1, 78
  negotiated directly with President Fox (PAN), 1
  new faction referred to as the hegemonic or institutional group, 71
  Salinas, Carlos (President) replaced Jonguitud, Carlos as head of SNTE with, 74
  selected as the secretary general of the PRI, 96
  served as senator from 1997 to 2000, 95
  sought to suppress the vote tally of both López Obrador and Madrazo, 100
  steps taken to consolidate control of SNTE, 80–3

historical legacies of labor incorporation
  need to examine diverse pathways and time periods, 19
  shape contemporary union strategies, 18

Indonesia, 6, 206–9
  democratization and union decentralization, 208
  enactment of Teacher Law (2005), 208
  instrumentalism political strategy, 12
  paired with Mexico, 192
  Persatuan Guru Republik Indonesia (PGRI, Teachers Association of the Republic of Indonesia), 206
  PGRI a weaker organization after democratization, 209
  PGRI and promiscuous powersharing, 207
  PGRI contrast to leftist and movementist unions, 207
  as a shadow case, 192
  similarities with Mexico, 207, 210
  unfavorable electoral rules, 19
  union and government strategic partnership, 207
  union avoids protests, 207
  union ruled by dominant faction, 209
  union support for Suharto dictatorship, 208
Institutional Revolutionary Parti (PRI), 1
instrumentalism, 11, 12, 15–16, See Indonesia; Mexico
  described, 14
  determined by mode of mobilization and partisan alliances, 14
  downside to, 110
  electoral as the primary mode of mobilization in Mexico, 14
  shifting party alliances in Mexico, 14
interviews conducted
  Argentina (26), Colombia (57), and Mexico (46), 33

Jonguitud, Carlos. See also Robles Martínez, Jesús
  as cacique of SNTE, 60
  controlled SNTE from 1972 to 1989, 60
  made a large contribution from the salaries of ordinary teachers to the presidential campaign of Salinas, Carlos, 73
  male-dominated Revolutionary Vanguard faction in SNTE, 73
  predatory clientelistic practices of, 68
  Revolutionary Vanguard. See also Robles Martínez, Jesús
  Revolutionary Vanguard faction in SNTE, 71, 72
  teachers as electoral plumbers, 90
  use of clientelism to control dissident teachers, 68

labor politics, 18–21
labor unions
  marked by decline, 3
leftism, 17–18, See Chile; Colombia
  described, 14
  electoral as primary mode of mobilization in Colombia, 14
  stable alliance with left parties in Colombia, 14
Losada Lora, Rodrigo, 63, 64
  banding of teacher' unions, 63
  political diversity within FECODE, 57
  radicalization of FECODE, 57

Index

Maffei, Marta. *See also* Argentina
CTERA, 1, 128, 136, 140, 141, 145
elected to Chamber of Deputies (2003), 1
national protest movement, 136
Secretary General of CTERA, 1, 128
supported by Affirmation for an Egalitarian Republic (ARI), 1
Mexico. *See also* Gordillo, Elba Esther
1934 law made public education compulsory and free, 39
assassination of Núñez Acosta, Maisel, 74
authoritarian regimes shaped labor politics, 35
Ávila Camacho (President) institutionalized the PRI, 50
Calles, Plutarco Elías (President) fostered an anti-clerical education, 39
Cárdenas, Lazaro (President) sought to consolidate teachers into a single union, 41
Civic Association of the Teaching Profession (ACM), 98
Confederation of Mexican Workers (CTM, 1936), 50
Coordinadora Nacional de Trabajadores de la Educación (CNTE), 72
decentralizatio fostered by technocrats at SEP, 75
dirty war within SNTE, 74
discontinuity across SNTE caciques, 88
dissident challenge to SNTE, 71–5
dissident protests also called for union democracy, 73
dissident teachers faction, National Coordinator of Education Workers (CNTE), 2
early labor laws for teachers, 40
Eleven Year Plan to Expand and Improve Education, 59
federal government's expansion of public education challenged regional elites, 39
Federal Law of Service Workers of the State, 59
Fox (President) signed the Social Compromise for Education Quality (2002), 97
General Law of Professional Teacher Service enacted major changes in education, 105
guaranteed source of income for teacher, 60
informal linkage between teachers and the PRI, 51
intermittent protests, 193
National Agreement for the Modernization of Basic Education (1992), 77
National Confederation of Popular Organizations (CNOP), 50
National Labor Congress ensured Díaz de la Torre's, Juan, as president of SNTE, 107
National Union of Education Workers (SNTE) and clientelism, 67
New Alliance (PANAL), teacher-based party, 90, 92
New Alliance Party won seats in proportional representation districts, 94
Obregon, Álvaro (President) created the Secretariat of Public Education (SEP), 38
over 700 teachers' unions by the 1930s, 38
paired with Indonesia, 192
partisan subordination, 58–61
Peña Nieto reforms, 105–6
Peña Nieto supported by Mexicanos Primero, 105
salary increases under Carrera Magisterial, 79
Salinas (President) enacted Vivienda Magisterial (VIMA), 79
Salinas (President) removed Bartlett as Secretary of Education and appointed Zedillo, Ernesto, in his place, 77
Sindicato de Trabajadores de la Enseñanza de la República Mexicana (STERM), 41
SNTE as an instrument of political control, 58
SNTE received legal recognition as *personalidad juridica*, 1944), 51
SNTE responsible for disciplining teachers and managing labor conflict, 58
SNTE shifted alliance from PRI to PAN, 70
state corporatism, 50–3
state transfer of one-percent of teachers' salaries into SNTE, 78
state-sponsored union consolidation, 51

Mexico (cont.)
    teachers affiliated with CNOP, and not with CTM, 50
    teachers' union as extensions of the party-state apparatus, 49
    teachers' union had close ties to the PRI party, 36
    VIMA used to funnel money to union leaders and their families, 79
Michels, Robert
    iron law of oligarchy, 118
Migliavacca, Adriana G., 138
    Argentina's austerity measures, 137
    autoconvocados (self-mobilized), 135
    broad teacher protests in Argentina, 138
    dramatic decline in teachers' salaries, 127
    drastic decline in teachers' salaries, 115
    factions within CTERA, 117
    patacones (IOUs) for teachers, 137
    union leaders resisted consolidation, 118
    White March and emergence of *autoconvocados* (self-mobilized), 116
    White March as challenge to political leadership, 116
Moe, Terry M., 192
    challenge of vested interest in educational reform, 211
    influence of teacher unions on policy process, 210
    teachers' unions as labor organizations with economic interests, 9
    on teachers' unions as vested interests, 8
movementism, 16–17, See also Argentina; Peru
    contentious mobilization in Argentina, 14
    CTERA as a paradigmatic case of, 16
    described, 14
    no party alliance in Argentina, 14
    pattern in Argentina, 111
    state response to, 16
    SUTEP actions resemble, 202
    teachers at forefront of labor conflict, 6
    and teacher militancy, 16
    unions as independent of political parties, 16
    and weak organizational hierarchy in Argentina, 12
Muñoz Armenta, Aldo, 15, 51, 105
    discontent with teacher evaluations and renewed protests, 106
    Fox alliance with Gordillo, Elba Esther, 2
    lower transparency and corruption, 106
    Mexican presidents without a legislative majority, 95
    on Peña Nieto reforms, 105
    sizeable network of SNTE political operators paid as teachers, though did not teach, 93
    SNTE clientelist operation, 93
    on the success of the Civic Association of the Teaching Profession (ACM), 98
Murillo, María Victoria, 21, 122, 123
    Argentina's political instability, 137
    complex interactions between workers, union leaders, and political parties, 21
    on conflict between Arizcuren and Garcetti, 117
    economic restructuring and union dilemmas, 13
    factionalism can lead to greater union militancy, 179
    labor politics as cooperative or adversarial, 3
    Menem pegged the Argentine peso to the US dollar, 119
    militancy among rival unions, 133
    new cycle of teacher protests (1996–2000), 134
    political causes for decentralization, 30
    President Menem did not negotiate with CTERA, 122

Nardacchione, Gabriel, 54
    advantages of national Láinez rural schools, 43
    contrast between *cuadros* and *operadores*, 142
    creation of commission to promote union unity, 55
    efforts to assert political autonomy in Argentina, 45
    Menem placed UDA in charge of administering social funds, 123
    politics of regional elites, 44
    union principles emphasized secular, state-provided public education, 61
National Action Party (PAN), 1–2
National Union of Education Workers (SNTE). See Mexico
Nelson, Joan
    political parties sought to capitalize on teachers' organizational clout, 6
neocorporatism. See also corporatism

Index

neoliberalism
  impact on labor unions, 3
  and labor repression, 3
new social movements
  organized protests, and formed new alliances with political parties, 4

Peron/Peronism
  coopted some unions and marginalized opposing unions, 44
  curriculum emphasizing moral, religious, and civic education, 45
  distinction between *personeria gremial* and *personeria profesional*, 44
  divided manual from intellectual laborers, 44
  divided teachers, 44
  a group of teachers resisted, 111
  presidency (1945–55), 44
  some teachers supported, 44
  UDA failed to integrate most teachers, 44
Peru, 202–6
  Castillo, Pedro, elected President, 206
  early affiliation with Popular Revolutionary Alliance (APRA), 203
  efforts under the Teacher Committee for Unification and Struggle (COMUL), 203
  enactment of General Law of Education (2003), 204
  enactment of teacher law (1984), 203
  movementism political strategy, 12
  paired with Argentina, 192
  pauperization of teachers, 127
  as a shadow case, 192
  SUTEP composed of various local factions, 205
  SUTEP leadership part of Peruvian Communist Party, 202
  SUTEP opposed García's educational reforms and organized strikes, 205
  SUTEP's limited role in electoral politics, 202
  SUTEP's driven by local unions, 202
  Teacher Law, 204
  teacher reform law (2012), 205
  teachers articulate interests through bottom-up protests, 206
  teachers as classroom Maoists, 203
  teachers mobilized against neoliberal policies, 202
  Unitary Union of Education Workers (SUTEP), 202
  Zevallos, Horacio, led SUTEP, 203
policy-focused political science, 28
political strategies, 14–18, See also movementism; leftism; instrumentalism
  actions by social movements and labor unions to make claims on the state, 14
  defined, 3
  and factional competition, 6
  and hierarchical relations, 6, 25
  and how teachers mobilize, 3
  importance of organizational decisions, 6
  inadvertent outcomes of state support, 7
  prioritize protest or electoral mobilization, 3
  rooted in the internal organization of the unions, 24
programmatic dealignment
  described, 128

Ramírez, Gloria Ines, 2. See also Colombia
  criticized neoliberalism and Pastrana, Andres (President), 2
  elected to the Senate with support from the Communist Party, 176
  head of Federation of Colombian Educators (FECODE), 2
  member of the Communist Party, 2
  mobilized teachers to support the left-coalition, Democratic Alternative Pole, 2
  Petro, Gustavo (President) appointed her as Minister of Labor, 2
Raphael, Ricardo, 79, 82, 91, 96
  Calderón support for SNTE, 15
  creation of National Organization of Electoral Observation of the Teaching Profession (ONOEM), 92
  decline of teacher salaries in Mexico under de la Madrid, Miguel (President), 73
  Gordillo negotiated her exit with Madrazo, 97
  on Gordillo's, Elba Esther, political control, 84
  Gordillo's last minute support for Calderón, 100
  on Gordillo's loyalty of candidates for leadership positions, 85

Raphael, Ricardo (cont.)
  Mexican state subsidization of SNTE.
    See also National Union of Education
    Workers (SNTE)
  Mexican state subsidization of teacher
    unions, 80
  mobilization of electoral brokers, 96
  New Alliance party, 23
  re-emergence of clientelism, 93
  support for Zedillo, Ernesto
    (President), 92
  teacher unions as neutral election
    observers, 92
  on teachers voting for the left, 100
  VIMA as symbol of corruption, 79
Robles Martínez, Jesús. See also Jonguitud,
    Carlos
  blamed poor condition for teachers
    on ideological divisions within
    SNTE, 52
  creation of the Revolutionary Vanguard
    faction in SNTE, 60
  Secretary General of SNTE and
    personalistic following, 52

Sánchez, Mary
  elected as a National Deputy, 140
  helped to negotiate the National Fund
    for Teacher Incentive (FONID), 140
  played a role in the creation of the
    Frente Grande, 128, 140
  Secretary General of CTERA. See also
    Argentina
  withdrew from the Peronist party
    and joined the Broad Front (Frente
    Grande), 128
Schneider, Ben Ross, 199
  and defense of status quo by teachers, 9
  influence of teacher union on policy
    process, 210
  significant increase in wages for Chilean
    teachers, 200
  support of leftist government in
    Chile, 201
  teacher opposition to reforms, 211
  teachers, 9
  union democracy and mechanisms of
    control, 24
self-mobilized teachers
  (autoconvocados), 137
  some controlled local unions, 138

shadow cases
  Chile, 196
  focus on organizational mechanisms, 196
  Indonesia, 196
  Peru, 196
social movements and political parties, 21–4
Stokes, Susan C.
  Menem's neoliberalism by surprise, 119

teachers (public school)
  asserted pressures to democratize union
    leadership, 29
  contested austerity measures in
    Argentina, Colombia, and Mexico in
    the 1980s, 29
  as contingent democrats, 10
  demands for higher pay may exacerbate
    the segmentation between the formal
    and informal sectors, 8
  emergence as the largest and most
    politically active group of workers, 4
  first-generation reforms, macro-
    economic stabilization reforms, 4
  have advantages that other workers
    do not, 8
  head national labor federations, 5
  protest movements emerged in parallel
    with other protest movements, 5
  referred to as political apostles, 49
  second-generation reforms sought to
    improve efficiency and service in the
    public sector, 4
  and "thick" strategies, 13
teachers' unions
  autoconvocados (self-mobilized), 135
  confront political environment, 192
  criticized for focusing narrowly on labor
    issues and establishing standards, 8
  decline in industrial workers and rise in, 4
  defended for playing a vital role in
    democratic engagement and education
    policy making, 8
  early teacher movements fragmented and
    weak, 37
  exhibited relative autonomy from the
    state, contentious mobilization and
    protest, and novel partisan alliances, 4
  historical structures shape political
    strategies of, 192
  a leading role in shaping landmark
    education legislation, 8

legacies of union founding, 66
may be an impediment to better public schools, 8
and mobilization against policies that harm children, 9
and new forms of labor politics, 192
prominent role in the policy process, 192
rarely organize workers in private schools and universities, 5
resemble new social movements, but important differences remain, 21
strategies located between those of labor unions and social movements, 4
uneven gains across nations, 193
traits of teachers' unions
forms of collective action, 24
and strong hierarchical relations, 24
and weak hierarchical relations, 26

Vélez, Cecilia Maria
"the iron lady," 181
vom Hau, Matthias
and military regime, 203

Peron sought to integrate unions in his populism, 112
Peronist personality cult, 45
teachers as modernizers of Indigenous communities, 40

White Tent protest, 1
described, 136
fostered the enactment of pro-teacher law (1999), 1
a national spectacle. *See also* Argentina; Mafffei, Marta
organized by CTERA, 135
preceded by repression of teachers, 136
within-case analysis, 32
women
emergence as national leaders in education. *See* Gordillo, Elba Esther; Maffei, Marta; Ramírez, Gloria Ines; Sánchez, Mary
a majority in the teaching profession, 2
union leaders stressed gender equity, 3

For EU product safety concerns, contact us at Calle de José Abascal, 56–1°, 28003 Madrid, Spain or eugpsr@cambridge.org.

www.ingramcontent.com/pod-product-compliance
Ingram Content Group UK Ltd.
Pitfield, Milton Keynes, MK11 3LW, UK
UKHW031928260325
456741UK00012B/181